FROM A COTSWOLD HEIGHT

BISHOP'S CLEEVE CHURCH.

FROM A COTSWOLD HEIGHT

JOHN HENRY GARRETT

With a New Introduction by
David Aldred

ALAN SUTTON
1988

ALAN SUTTON PUBLISHING
BRUNSWICK ROAD · GLOUCESTER

First published 1919 by
J.J. Banks & Son, Cheltenham
First published in this edition 1988

British Library Cataloguing in Publication Data

Garrett, John Henry
From a Cotswold height.
1. England. Northern Cotswolds
I. Title
942.4′17

ISBN 0-86299-556-6

Printed in Great Britain

A NEW INTRODUCTION

David Aldred

"The greater part of the book will be found to consist of a record of rural excursions to which it has been sought to give a practical turn, that may be of use to any prospective visitor, by exact descriptions of place, scenes, roads or object. Though unexaggerated and purposely kept free from poetical licence and remote allusion, it is hoped that these simple descriptions of actual things will prove interesting for themselves both to the visitor from afar and to the local inhabitant."

Here, in the Preface, lies the secret behind the continuing interest in Dr Garrett's book. In its detailed descriptions of country rambles it remains an immensely practical book, to be followed with ease and pleasure on foot or from the armchair, whilst providing just enough period reference for the reader to be transported back to an earlier age of trams and teagardens, railway trains and roads before tarmac. Readers who seek a polished insight into a traditional world in its decline will be disappointed. There are none of the literary references of J. A. Gibbs' *A Cotswold Village* of 1898, nor the introspection or opinionation of H. J. Massingham whose writings on the Cotswolds appeared in the 1930s. Despite a verbosity which today serves to increase its period charm, *From A Cotswold Height* still comes across as a guidebook, or more precisely, as a series of short guides, in which flowers and trees, birds and animals fill the pages rather than eulogies to the picturesque, be they the permanent architectural features of church and manor, or detailed portraits of more transient humanity.

If you wish to find the best example of Dr Garrett's approach, turn to Chapter XVIII and read how, on a rare ramble by motor, he treats Broadway at a time when it was already gaining its modern reputation as a picture-postcard Cotswold village. His opinion of the village is terse but unambiguous, "This is what I have heard called 'Old World'." He continues, "To be appreciated it requires the artistic perception and the imagination that recalls the life that has been associated with such appearances." This brief description of the village is treated as but a prelude to the task at which he excels – a detailed panorama of the countryside seen from Broadway Tower.

Another strength of Dr Garrett's writing lies in his fascination with natural history. His acute eye for seeking out the minutiae in the landscape adds extra dimensions to his rambles; sheep eat the milk vetch on the common (Chapter IV); the red leaves of the creeper on Dumbleton church tower give it the appearance of being built from brick (Chapter XVII). He also introduces us to dun-coloured spiders, chirping grasshoppers and inebriated humble bees on Nottingham Hill (Chapter X) and a nightjar, rattling over Padcombe Bottom, delays the evening's return from Belas Knap in Chapter VII.

If the feeling for the natural world forms the strength of the book, some would see a weakness in the lack of comparable interest in the human world. People are usually unnamed passing actors, not essential to the purpose of creating a guidebook intended for use by others on other days. Cleeve Common is frequented by horses, cattle, sheep, and golfers with whom he occasionally converses; a shepherd shelters from the rain with him in a Dutch barn at Charlton Abbots (only readers who have been caught on the hill in the rain will really appreciate this episode in Chapter VI); and the little girl gathering wild strawberries above Corndean appears in Chapter VII fitted in between larches and woodpigeons on the one side and brambles, briars and furze on the other.

Yet if the chapters are largely devoid of humanity, the photographs abound with it. From Eastleach in the south to Winchcombe in the north, people here take their place as essential features in the landscape. They help to give immediacy to the writing. We are shown "the wheelmarks of His Majesty's mail van" and that "a group of soldiers and some men with horses were loitering in the space of ground that lies in front of the inn" on the occasion when Dr Garrett took his winter walk to Prestbury in Chapter XII.

My favourite photograph is "Woodmancote Green: Age in a smockfrock admonishing the youthful crowd" in Chapter IX. Fittingly it accompanies some of the best passages in the whole book; passages which show clearly that Dr Garrett could be a perceptive social observer and that his desire to compile *From A Cotswold Height* as a record of excursions stemmed from no real lack of ability to discern and communicate a feeling for the current age. In this chapter we learn of the gradual spread of "a great modernity" from Cheltenham into Bishop's Cleeve and Woodmancote showing "its influence in sons and daughters who have lived there and have returned, or who go to and fro daily by bicycle or train, bringing back with them innovations of dress and ideas, manners and speech". Dr Garrett felt life in the shadow of Cleeve Hill remained essentially "rustic", and yet change was apparent. Both these observations lie reflected in his photograph. Modernity, in the form of universal elementary education had led to literacy which had led to "the postman, in blue uniform with brass buttons and peaked cap, on his rounds, carrying a great brown letter-bag of Government provision slung over his shoulder". We can identify the postman as Harry Allen who made his rounds of Cleeve Hill and Woodmancote for over thirty years. Tradition, "the grandfather peasant proprietor, wearing a smock-frock . . . now gone out of rustic fashion so completely as to be obsolete in this locality, saving for this wearer and one other" has also been identified from elsewhere as Farmer Potter of King's Farm, adjacent to the green. We gain here the merest hints of regret at the passing of an age.

Such passages are, however, extremely rare, so that we have to turn to the book's period style as the best indicator of its origins in the first two decades of this century. Actual detailed references to these years have to be keenly sought out, lying as they do hidden in the unfolding narratives and descriptions of the succeeding rambles. Chapter XIX transports us to well-known Cotswold beauty spots – Lower Slaughter and Bourton on the Water – before they were taken over by today's more mobile tourists. The ensuing description of Stow's famous Horse Fair provides a rare example of Dr Garrett moulding one description out of several visits. Early in the book he provides us with a photograph of one of the very last ox-teams to work on the Cotswolds. Coming nearer to Cleeve, we read in Chapter XII of the new Prestbury Park Estate built "to provide rural residences outlying the village, for any immigrant who might fancy the situation". On the hill itself we learn from Chapter V how the Washpool was used for dipping sheep in May of each year. In Chapter VI we read an interesting description of the now deserted farmstead at Wontley, whilst in Chapter XI we find a valuable reference to the vanished upper corn mill in Stockwell Lane, Woodmancote.

However, the timelessness of many of the scenes masks the fact that much of the book was compiled and written during World War I as we learn from the few surviving notebooks to which Dr Garrett's son refers in the accompanying biographical note. There are only three clues to this in the whole book, Reference has already been made to the three soldiers in the photograph taken of the Rising Sun Hotel; in addition Dr Garrett passed "four mounted officers of the troops at the time stationed in Cheltenham" – a possible reference to the 9th Gloucesters who were training on Cleeve Common early in 1915. The third reference occurs towards the end of the book.

Having treated us to an interesting and sympathetic description of Cheltenham in these years, he notes that the racecourse buildings have been converted to form "The Racecourse Hospital" for wounded soldiers. Thus World War I is kept in the background and not allowed to intrude into the description of the rural rambles.

Without other knowledge we would never know that the visit of the Cotteswold Naturalist Field Club to Cleeve Common took place during the war years – on 10 July 1917. We can check Dr Garrett's own account of the meeting in Chapter VI with that in the club's Proceedings, Volume XIX Part 3. We find him, as we might expect, to be an accurate observer, but we can also use the club's account to fill in some missing details.

Seventy years ago the Cotteswold Naturalist Field Club served as the focus of interest in local archaeology, natural history, and the countryside more generally, for a select band of gentry and nobility, clergy, manufacturers and would-be gentlemen of leisure. The party took their picnic luncheon by the hillfort on the common. Dr Garrett continues that the party did "sit down upon the green turf to eat lunch, whilst one member delivers himself of a broad descriptive address upon Cleeve Common and its surroundings". That member was, as we might guess, Dr Garrett. He was followed by the President "tall, bearded, very learned in archaeological studies pursued at home and abroad". This was W. St. Clair Baddeley, the well-known county archaeologist and antiquarian. We can also identify from the Proceedings the other members who spoke. Charles Upton gave the talk on geology, and "the member who had studied the site of most ancient human occupation on Cleeve Common" can be identified as J. W. Gray whose report on his excavations had earlier appeared in Volume XV of the Proceedings. At the end of the day tea was taken lower down the hill at Haymesgarth, the home of Charles Bailey from Manchester. As if to emphasise the general anonymity of his figures in the landscape, here Dr Garrett, for the only time, identifies one of them.

Charles Bailey was one of a growing number of prosperous traders, manufacturers and people of independent means who had been attracted to live on Cleeve Hill in the years since the turn of the century. Dr Garrett himself, as Medical Officer of Health for Cheltenham, could be counted one of them for he was lodging in one of the recently built houses in Post Office Lane during the time he was writing the book. This was "Glendale", the home of Arthur Yiend, the person most responsible for the pre-war exploitation of the hill as a desirable distant suburb of Cheltenham. Many of the houses on this part of the hill were built by him, including Post Office Lane itself, together with its small extension along Besford Road.

The natural attraction of Cleeve Hill and its common had been the subject of a powerful publicity campaign, led by the Cheltenham-based publisher of guidebooks and postcards, Edward J. Burrow. Since the opening of the Cotswold Convalescent Home in a disused quarry in 1893, the area had been promoted as the "Cotswold Health Resort" to attract daytrippers, visitors and residents who provided a ready market for Dr Garrett's book. The arrival of the trams in 1901 facilitated such developments, as Cheltenham moved out-of-town to enjoy the recreational benefits of the common, tolerated by the commoners on annual payment of £50 from Cheltenham Borough Council.

Among the many prominent Cheltenham businessmen resident on the hill during the war years, was J. J. Banks, the Promenade bookseller who was responsible for publishing *From A Cotswold Height* in 1919. Cleeve Hill therefore not only provided the subject and market for the book, but also the link between author and publisher.

That the book is new being reprinted almost seventy years after its first appearance is evidence of a continuing local interest, not only in the book itself, but in the appeal of Cleeve Hill and its common as a place of recreation and an Area of Outstanding Natural Beauty. If this reprinting spreads further enjoyment of the hill to local inhabitants as well as visitors from afar, Dr Garrett would have been well pleased.

David H. Aldred
Summer 1988

Note to the reprint

Readers wishing to follow the notes described in the text or on the maps, must ascertain the continued existence of public rights of way.

BIOGRAPHICAL NOTE

John Henry Garrett M.D. D.P.H. F.L.S.
1858–1946

I am glad that through David Aldred's enthusiasm the re-issuing of my father's book, *From a Cotswold Height*, enables me to write a short biographical note about the author providing a link with a Cheltenham very different from today's and which may be of interest to the modern reader.

John Henry Garrett was born in 1858 in the small country town of Kineton, Warwickshire, the second son of a small yeoman farmer. No doubt his youthful experience of country life gave him his life-long interest in it.

He studied medicine in Newcastle-upon-Tyne and London and qualified in 1886, taking a gold medal in part of the course. His interest in science led him to specialise in the then comparatively new subject of Public Health and he took the Diploma in this in 1889. Later, seeking a further challenge, he studied law and qualified as a barrister in 1902.

His first post in Public Health work was in the rural district of Ampthill, Bedfordshire. He reported the extremely unsatisfactory conditions in which he found the rural poor there were living, in an article in the *Lancet* in 1892. Written in unusually strong terms for an article in a scientific journal, it condemned the apathetic local administration which allowed the conditions to continue and showed he was well aware of what at that time lay behind the rural scenes he was later to describe.

In June 1892 he was the successful one out of fifty-eight applicants for the post of Medical Officer of Health for Cheltenham Borough. At that time one-third of the houses in Cheltenham, mostly in the poorer districts, did not have a piped water supply and depended on easily contaminated shallow wells. To supply these houses it was necessary to extend the public water supply and this could only be done by drawing on the supply

J.H. GARRETT

from the river Severn at Tewkesbury. It was the work of the M.O.H. in diffusing knowledge about the satisfactory nature of this source, partly based on his own analyses, that resulted in its becoming Cheltenham's, and much later Gloucester's, main supply. In the five years after 1892 many wells were closed with benefit to the health of the inhabitants.

In the spring and early summer of 1896 a severe smallpox epidemic occurred in Gloucester and the danger of its spread to the nearby health and educational centre of Cheltenham, with lasting damage to the town's reputation, was considered very great. The M.O.H. and the public health committee initiated special emergency measures to prevent the spread of the epidemic. In the end Cheltenham escaped with twenty-three cases compared with Gloucester's two thousand. The Borough Council in gratitude for the work done by my father in the emergency, voted him an honorarium of fifty guineas. This he spent on a trip to Palestine and the other countries of the eastern Mediterranean. Accounts of this journey, entitled 'An Educational Tour to the Eastern Mediterranean', were sent back for publication in the Cheltenham *Examiner* and were his first published topographical writings.

Apart from scientific and technical papers, my father's publications include the 1903 and some later editions of the Cheltenham guide book, *A Garden Town* which contained a section on Cotswold villages illustrated with his own photographs. His next publication was *The Idyllic Avon* in 1906, an account of a trip up the Avon from Tewkesbury to Stratford by boat and again illustrated by his photographs. *From A Cotswold Height* followed in 1919 and his final book *Mass Education in England*, a personal and rather pessimistic account of state education, in 1929. His literary interests were also shown by his becoming the founder-president of the Dickens Fellowship in Cheltenham and he made short contributions to local papers, under his initials, mainly on travel and country topics. His practical hobby, besides botany, was photography, at first with a brass and mahogany quarter or half-plate camera, later with a roll film folding Kodak.

He lived on Cleeve Hill from about 1910 to 1923 and some of the note-books from which *From a Cotswold Height* were written have survived, showing his interest in scenery and plants of the region. From these it is possible to date some of the visits described in the book. A visit to Hailes Abbey, for instance, is dated '28/7/16' and the night time walk to Postlip Hall took place in August 1911. Botanical findings are also given and this interest enabled him to be elected a Fellow of the Linnean Society of London (F.L.S.).

In 1919, at the age of sixty-one, he married Victoria Parkinson, a lady from an old Cheltenham military family.

Events so unusual as those of the early years of his time in office were not to be repeated but he was able to see the beginning of slum clearance in Cheltenham before his retirement in 1929.

He was a Victorian of strong character whose opinions were often in advance of his time and who, although he sometimes did not agree with the Borough Council, always acted with the best interests of the town's inhabitants in mind. The title of his obituary notice in the *Gloucestershire Echo* of May 1946, 'His Zeal as MOH did much for Town' therefore seemed an appropriate epitaph.

John V. Garrett
Cleeve Hill, 1988

PREFACE.

INTEREST in rural objects varies with experience and knowledge. To persons bred and reared in cities the country is commonly like a book in an unknown tongue that may be indiscreetly mentioned but is never understood, and is apt to be the cause of pronounced boredom when chance has temporarily removed such persons from the surroundings to which they are accustomed, and placed them upon "A Cotswold Height," or in some such environment. But when those have been ruled out, there is still a remainder, and possibly a growing one, to whom rural nature has a larger meaning. These were born in the country, where they became acquainted with rural objects at first hand from their earliest years; or, being endowed with the required natural taste, were drawn into the interest in aftertime to find their pleasure in life immensely enhanced thereby. The object of this book is chiefly to assist such as these latter to an appreciation of a district which in respect of rural sights and scenes is unexcelled throughout the length and breadth of England. There may further be said of Cleeve Hill that no centre is more worthy of the title of "health resort" and none better suited for that sort of holiday whose activities are of the nature of those mentioned and described in the following pages, and whose result may be expected to manifest itself in a pronounced recuperation of worn down energies. The greater part of the book will be found to consist of a record of rural excursions to which it has been sought to give a practical turn, that may be of use to any prospective visitor, by exact descriptions of place, scene, road or object. Though unexaggerated and purposely kept free from poetical licence and remote allusion, it is hoped that these simple descriptions of actual things will prove interesting for themselves both to the visitor from afar and to the local inhabitant, and that the new map of Cleeve Common that is included, upon which the several parts and objects of the Common and neighbouring roads and footpaths are clearly delineated, will assist to bring this fine piece of public property within the acquaintance of more persons than at present have knowledge of it, for it is indeed a pity that such a delectable corner of the country should be subject to any neglect. As to the illustrations, the author is well aware, by prolonged personal experience, of the limitations of photography to represent the beauty of the open country, and especially those tremendous landscapes that are to be viewed from Cleeve Hill and other of the Cotswolds, and which are described in the text. It is not possible to reproduce by this or any other pictorial means the effect upon the senses of these magnificent views. Nevertheless, the pictures herein contained, being of the actual places and things described in the respective chapters to which they pertain, should not be found out of place, but may serve to recall to local readers who know them, the scenes and objects represented, and afford to strangers some idea of the actual realities, and so add, it is hoped, to the value of the book.

J. H. G.

CHELTENHAM, 1919.

CONTENTS.

LIST OF ILLUSTRATIONS.

MAPS.

FROM A COTSWOLD HEIGHT.

PART I.—General Description of the Cotswold Country and the Immediate Neighbourhood of Cleeve Hill.

CHAPTER I.

THE COTSWOLDS.

You can spell it "Cotswold" or "Cotteswold"; some prefer it with the one spelling and some with the other, and either may have good reasons for a preference this way or that. But the respective claims must be of about equal merit since both modes of spelling continue, and you are at liberty to adopt that one which, for any reason, you may find most appealing. The signification of the word, however spelt, may be taken to be "wooded height." The first part of the word is perhaps derived from the Celtic *coed*, a wood, which is still in use with that meaning in the Welsh language. It is also sometimes derived from *cote*, meaning a sheep-fold. "Wold" is related to "*Weald*," and "*Wald*," and appears to mean "forest" in the broader sense; but it has also come to have much the same meaning as "down," that is, a low hill with a broadly curved top. Hence, if you speak of the Cotswolds it is enough, and the "Hills" in "Cotswold Hills" is but a repetition.

Whether the Cotswolds were at any time covered with real tree forests is a doubtful matter. Patches of woodland of considerable extent there have doubtless always been. In some places on the higher tops, and particularly in the combes, and upon the escarpment slopes it is in the nature of things, even to this day, for trees of native species to propagate themselves thickly. But, as regards the broad, higher and more exposed parts, such as Cleeve Common, these have probably always been as bare of trees as we now see them.

The Cotswolds cover a considerable area of country, which lies chiefly in East Gloucestershire, but extends over the borders of Wiltshire and Oxfordshire, and touches outlying portions of Worcestershire. The surface of the land to a measurement of, say, fifty miles in length and from ten to twenty miles in width, or so, is tossed into ups and downs, the general altitude tending to rise from East to West, to a maximum of about a thousand feet. On its Western side the hilly country ends abruptly in an irregular range that drops, by a steep and sudden slope, to the much lower altitude of a broad vale. Through this vale country flow the River Severn and its tributary, the Upper Avon. To speak with particularity, the general direction of this ranging line of hill front, or escarpment of the Cotswolds, is North-East to South-West.

The Cotswolds, therefore, consist of this long front of steeps, and an up and down country that lies behind it to somewhere about the extent above indicated.

The highest part being on the Western side; and the general fall of the high ground being towards the East, it follows that its main water-shed is more or less Eastward. In fact, a number of streams flowing in that direction arise in the hills, which are presently destined to unite into one considerable river, namely, the Thames, which thus derives the main part of its head-waters from the Cotswolds.

A few other streams, however, finding origin in springs situated near the escarpment, slip out Westward, or towards the North-West, and join the Severn or the Avon after a short course.

The surface of the hills within the bordering escarpment exhibits broad, rolling outlines, which are broken here and there by narrow, steep valleys cut out by the streams that occupy them, which usually begin each in one or more combes or blind heads in the hillsides. In the North Cotswolds there is a tendency for the hills to form two or three high ridges, one beyond the other, from the West to the East.

The escarpment, or steep edge facing the vale, is also indented with combes and valleys, occupied by the little rivers that run westward, and the line of steeps is further broken and diversified by promontory hills that jut forward from the line, and by outliers that are situated a little way out in the vale, quite free from the range, like islands off a coast. Perhaps, at one time, in the far past, the escarpment line of the Cotswolds did form the cliffs of a coast, and the outliers were, in fact, islands in an arm of the sea.

The composition of the outer crust of the earth which forms the Cotswolds, or the geological substance of these hills, is called Oolite, a great band of which passes up from Dorsetshire to Lincolnshire and Yorkshire, right through England, and includes this district.

The Oolite is characterised chiefly by limestone rocks consisting of agglomerated particles resembling the hard roe of a fish, and the name "Oolite," derived from the Greek, means literally "egg-stone," having reference to this circumstance. The stone of this neighbourhood, which is of most homogeneous character, is extensively quarried for building purposes, and is called Cotswold freestone, on account of the ease with which it can be sawn and worked. Various qualities of the stone are known under the generic term of "grit," and the "pea-grit," or "pisolite," which exists at Cleeve Hill and elsewhere, is a coarse-grained, but hard and durable variety used by the builders for basement walls and the more exposed portions of buildings. The Oolite is divided into two series of rocks called the *Superior* and the *Inferior* Oolite, the former overlying the latter in the Southern and South-Eastern part of the Cotswolds. It happens, however, to be the uncovered Inferior Oolite that touches to the greatest altitudes along the escarpment and amongst the interior hills. The numerous fossils found in the Oolite, being the undeniable remains of marine animals, plainly indicate that these now solid rocks were formed by deposition at the bottom of a sea, at a period of time remote almost beyond human conception.

The surface of the land of the Cotswold Hills bears signs of an ancient occupation by mankind in the later Stone Age, or Neolithic period. Numbers of chipped flints, some being shaped into arrow-heads and other instruments, have been picked up in the ploughed fields, to which they must have been brought by man's agency from the flint-bearing chalk districts, and the nearest of these lies distantly beyond the Vale of White Horse. The Oolitic Rocks themselves naturally contain no flint to speak of.

Upon every prominent point of the escarpment of the Cotswolds, and on the summits of the outlying hills, are found entrenched fortresses of prehistoric age. Some call them Roman camps, in supposition of their use by the Romans. Others call them ancient British camps, supposing them to have been constructed against the attacks of neighbouring tribes before the advent of the Romans in England, and this is most likely to be the true case. They consist generally of a space of ground of varying measurement enclosed by a circle, or part circle, of deep trenches. There are usually two such trenches, one circling beyond the other, with alternating mounds, though their formation varies considerably. There is every indication of their having been made and used for defensive purposes. In the Stone Age they were doubtless effective in repelling the advance of an enemy in superior numbers, and the camps situated upon the escarpment commanded a very extensive view of the country westward, which, presumably, was occupied by the enemy, and it would have been easy to signal from camp to camp.

The ancient Britons have left other evidences of their occupation of these hills in numerous barrows, both round and oblong, in which they buried their distinguished dead. Fragments of coarse sun-dried pottery and other remnants of domestic life have also been found in old refuse heaps and elsewhere, and placed stones, some of which seem to have had connection with religious observances, and others which may have been merely landmarks, are discovered here and there.

The Roman occupation of the locality is still marked by the existence of numerous roads that were originally made by the Romans and which may usually be recognised by their passing in straight lines from point to point with a fine disregard to opposing obstacles. The Cotswold Roman city of Corinium, now Cirencester, was a great centre through

SCENE ON THE COTSWOLDS—OXEN AT PLOUGH.

THE LEACH AT EASTLEACH.

THE DICKLER NEAR STOW-ON-THE-WOLD.

THE CHURN NEAR NORTH CERNEY.

COTSWOLD STREAMS—HEADWATERS OF THE THAMES

or towards which most of the more important local Roman roads passed, the Ermine Street and the Fosse Road being the two great main roads that intersect each other here. The more important Roman roads were originally paved with stone blocks, and some of these stones may still be found where originally laid at the surface, and more might be found by excavating their surface covering. The remains of quite a number of large Roman houses, or Roman villas, as they are usually called, have also been unearthed upon these hills, exhibiting the mode of domestic architecture of the age in hypocaust pillars and tessellæ, with remarkable designs in floors laid with the latter, that show great art in mosaic work, an art that has been retained ever since by those master-masons, the Italians, who, even to-day, have to be called upon in England and elsewhere to do such work.

The Cotswolds form an almost purely agricultural district. The steep slopes of the escarpment are permanently green, where they sweep down to the rich lands of the vale; but the surface of the country behind the hill-edge is in chief extent tilled. The main products of the land are grain and sheep, with the wool that the latter yield. Formerly it was the custom to manufacture the wool into cloth within the district. This native and normal industry has in great part decayed, though sheep are bred as numerously as before. There are still a few local woollen factories, but much of the wool produced is now exported from the immediate locality.

The land of the hills is, therefore, divided into farms and these into fields, mortarless stone-wall fences being much in use, on account of the near neighbourhood of stone suitable for their erection. In many places the soil is shallow and of a fine red-brown colour when ploughed up, and often intermingled with so many loose stones as to lead to a wonderment that the growth of the crops is not seriously interfered with by them. Yet the crops often excite a greater wonder by reason of their luxuriance.

On account of there being but little permanent pasturage on the hills, the sheep-rearing is conducted mainly within hurdle-folds upon crops specially grown for the purpose.

Swedes and turnips, cabbage, kale, mustard, clover and sainfoin being usually cultivated for feeding sheep, and upon these the sheep thrive, and, with a little trough-feeding in addition, fatten and this intensive use of the land by the stock enriches it for the grain crop which follows in rotation.

The important towns of Cheltenham and Gloucester, which lie near the base of the Cotswold escarpment at the edge of the broad Vale of Severn, together with Cirencester, that calls itself the capital of the Cotswolds, and Stroud, the seat of the cloth manufacture, afford the chief markets of the district and are reached by rail, or by horse or motor vehicle from the more nearly neighbouring parts of the Cotswolds. The cities of Bath and Oxford, and the market town of Stratford-on-Avon, also lie within reach of different parts of the hills.

Nearer at hand, for the supply of the simpler home and farm necessaries, are several small towns or large villages lying at intervals in and about the Cotswolds. At the North end are those that bear the euphonious appellations of Stow-on-the-Wold, Moreton-in-the-Marsh, Bourton-on-the-Water, Winchcomb, Chipping Campden, Broadway and Chipping Norton. In the central portion, besides Cirencester and Stroud, there are Northleach, Burford, Fairford, Painswick, Minchinhampton and Nailsworth; and in the Southern part are Dursley, Wotton-under-Edge, Tetbury and Marshfield; and situated near the base of the Edge might also be included Chipping Sodbury, Charfield and Wickwar.

Between these little towns the Cotswold villages are numerous but often very small and remotely situated. Approached up a bye-road, whose surface is not always in too good a condition, especially in winter time, and which, perhaps, passes up a very steep hill, or down a very steep one, to reach its bourne, the village is often found to be of mere hamlet size. The farm-buildings are of more portentous aspect than the houses, but the church is there to indicate that it really does give title to a parish and to a definite settlement of humanity. The first impression obtained on entering such a village, if to enter is a proper term to signify an approach to two or three farm-houses and a few scattered cottages, is its insignificance. But a short stay in the place generally suffices to bring into evidence a certain character which every such village possesses and which is all its own. The smaller it is the more rustic, and the more intimately related to the fields which closely surround it. It has some special interest which, very likely, lies in its church, but which may be in its trees ; its village green and what is upon and around that ; its post office, or its manor-house, or manor farm ; its smithy, or its inhabitants.

The buildings of the Cotswold villages are all substantial, being of stone. They are hard and stolid in appearance, whitish-grey or yellowish, according to the district and the nature of the stone yielded by the local quarries, the warmer yellow tint of stone pertaining to the North Cotswolds. With an occasional amendment of the stone-slab roofs, which, by the way, always weather to a darker colour than the walls, they may almost be warranted to last for ever. The grey and buff tones of roof and wall contrast agreeably with the surrounding green of trees, shrubs and fields, and with the sky. There is something of dignity in the church, whose tower, or spire, shows with such effect in the scene. This dignity may be partly due to superior age, and though, in size, the church is less imposing than the tithe barn, which is separated from it by the extent of the farmyard, and is of much less seeming importance than the neighbouring manor-house, it yet lends to the great house, or to the whole village, an air of virtue with which nothing competes and which appears to be recognised with pride and gloried in by squire, yeoman and peasant.

The people who live in the towns at the foot of the escarpment make excursions into the hills by some one or other of the roads that rise quickly and steeply to the upper region, or slope more gradually to the same altitude up the valley of the Chelt, the Frome, or other stream, and so pass into and among the rolling uplands. The large fields along the hill-sides show in various crops and various colours, according to the time of year. The grey farm-buildings lie among them and the grey village, with its church-tower is seen, or partly seen, in the distance, and the grey stone wall runs along the roadside and divides the fields. There are pleasant scenes of farming, and the brisk, bracing air scents of the earth and of the flowers. The sheep are seen folded on the roots or the clover, and the shepherd, with his dog, is in proximity. Possibly a team of oxen may be seen at plough or harrow, a rare thing in England that at present can only be seen here and in one other district ; there will be three couples of oxen in the team, harnessed with collars and traces like horses, and not yoked in the Eastern manner.

The road presently dips to the course of one of the Cotswold rivers, that takes a quick run down its combe or winds sluggishly along a flat bottom of damp, green meadow, going Thameswards. The water of the stream is very clear in quiet weather and of the sort that suits trout and cray-fish. An opposite hill leads quickly again to the higher ground where there are more hills in view, rolling away in various directions and showing copses here and there of dark larch and fir, and a long stretch of beechwood which belts the road, shading it for a distance and temporarily hiding the view. And at length you enter the Cotswold town, an eminently stony place, with a centre space wider than the rest of the street, or streets, if there be more than one, and an old building known as the market-hall, not unlikely, more peculiar in its structure than beautiful in its architectural appearance. Also old houses with plain walls and stone gables above elongated rectangular windows heavily mullioned and perhaps barred. Some of the houses will be altered by insertion of shop fronts of more or less modern shape. There will be two or three old inns whose plain fronts being flush with the rest of the house-walls of the street, are not easily distinguished except by their signs ; also some quaint corners and side streets and strange courts. The houses generally will be of such plain and inconspicuous design as to escape notice or comment unless you have come to hunt for oddities, or to be shown them by a resident who has studied and become enthusiastic about them. A fine church, generally with a tall, square tower, occasionally with a spire, does much to make the town less plain—for plain and formal the little town certainly is, notwithstanding all its gables and however grand its church. If it were different or more ornate it would not be of the Cotswolds. It must have its characteristic plain stoniness and its unremitting clean angles to be a proper Cotswold town.

In most of the parishes there is one large house and sometimes more than one—a country ancestral seat or residence. It takes its name after the village, or, in a good many instances, has given its name to the village, being the House, Park, Manor, Court, Hall, or Grange, of that name. Beautiful houses are some of these, especially those that are of ancient build. A considerable number are of Tudor design, having been built in that era of prosperity and good taste, or rebuilt upon older foundations. It is the Tudor mansion in stone. There are many examples, too, of good houses of later date—of Jacobean, Queen Anne and Georgian periods, and some more or less pleasing Victorian erections, imitative of foreign styles, some of them in many storeys that look like great public hotels.

Pertaining to the great houses are parks, some of large extent, much beautified by tree growth, and containing in several instances herds of deer. The Duke of Beaufort's great park at Badminton, has herds of both red and fallow deer, and Earl Bathurst's park at Cirencester, which has many fine features as a park and is available for public recreation, though a private property, has a good herd of fallow. There are deer also in the Sherborne Lodge Park, in Brockhampton Park and elsewhere on the hills.

Some of the valleys or combes of the Cotswolds, especially those whose streams flow towards the Severn Valley, are remarkable for their beauty. The Stroud valley, with its branches the Painswick and Nailsworth valleys, and the combes or bottoms that open to the Severn Vale near the small towns of Dursley and Wotton-under-Edge, are particularly noteworthy, and the landscapes from the hillsides in the neighbourhood of these combes, together with the near and distant views presented from many points of the escarpment, form some of the most striking scenery that England affords.

CHAPTER II.

CLEEVE HILL AND ITS APPROACHES.

EVERY portion of the Cotswolds that is separated into an appreciably distinct mass, and particularly, every hill that is ascended by a road and, consequently, requires to be talked about, must, of necessity, be named, and it would be hard to say how many named hills there are in the Cotswolds.

It is common for the hills to be named after some place that is upon, near to, or opposite the hill, and the village of Bishop's Cleeve lies below this hill, in the vale. The origin of the name, however, is, perhaps, " cleve," an old form of " cliff," seeing that there is a cliff here, and in this case the village may rather have taken its name from the hill.

Cleeve Hill forms a part of the escarpment, or hill line, that faces the Severn and Avon valleys. If you divided the hills at the escarpment into North, Middle and South Cotswolds, it would be somewhere near the junction of the Middle and the North. The high road from Cheltenham to Winchcomb, Broadway and Stratford-on-Avon rises slantingly up its side. It is nearly three miles from Cheltenham to the foot of the hill and a mile and three-quarters thence to the highest part of the road, which reaches an altitude of about 800 feet, and two and a half miles of descent from the top into the small town of Winchcomb.

The ancient and very rustic village of Woodmancote, which lies on the lower part of the hill-flank, with some of its cottages and farms extending upwards, has now been enlarged at its upper end by a number of new houses occupied by the people who live at " Cleeve Hill." But Woodmancote itself is only a sub-parish of Bishop's Cleeve, the grey tower of whose mother-church can be seen below. A couple of very steep lanes ascend directly from the foot of the hill up

LANDSCAPE WITH CLEEVE HILL
FROM SLOPE OF NOTTINGHAM HILL.

LANDSCAPE WITH MOWING MACHINE

LOOKING TOWARDS CLEEVE HILL.

through Woodmancote to join the higher part of the Winchcomb main road.

The top of Cleeve Hill, above the houses, is occupied by Cleeve Common—a great undivided stretch of greensward land that measures three miles across in one direction and two miles in another. It includes the highest ground of all the Cotswolds, some points rising to nearly 1,100 feet, whilst a large part of the area has a height of over 900 feet. These altitudes together with the porous subsoil create a comparatively dry and bracing climate, which has brought the district a reputation for its good effect upon convalescents, and as a health resort generally. The existence of this great open tract of hill ground with its facilities for golf, riding and walking, naturally adds much to the interest and attraction of the place.

At the point where the main road reaches its greatest height there occurs a marked irregularity of the hill line. A promontory is thrown out almost at right angles. This is joined to the main escarpment by a narrow neck, and it is over this neck the road passes towards Winchcomb. This promontory hill has a length along its top of over a mile, and beyond its neck it rises gently to a hundred feet of greater altitude and widens out towards its end, also curving slightly round so as to present to the road and houses of Cleeve Hill a broad opposite hillside of great verdure and beauty. For dwellers and visitors upon Cleeve Hill that hillside is a source of everlasting delight to the eyes. "Nottingham Hill" they call it.

From the side or top of Nottingham Hill you get, in turn, a fine view of the higher part of Cleeve Hill where most of the houses are aggregated, and the houses look best at that distance. The appearance is as if the village were hanging precariously on the steep hillside, whilst, above the houses, rests the great, sage-green surface of Cleeve Common, which is elevated to the sky-line in further steep slopes, the grassy surface being a good deal broken by quarries, or rendered irregular by tumbled ground.

When viewing Cleeve Hill from the Nottingham Hill side, looking along under the edge of the common, you see the

Cotswold Convalescent Home occupying a good place above the high road, and about and beyond this building is a small copse of firs and larches. Further along, beyond Mile-stone Quarry, which is situated close to this road, some buildings are seen that stand right on the common, consisting of a dwelling-house and a low adjoining erection: these are Cleeve Hill racing stables—a training establishment for race-horses, for which purpose the common and its neighbourhood afford good exercising ground. Further beyond, where Post-Office Lane rises steeply to the main road in front of "Malvern View" Hotel, a plain building on the edge of the Common is the Golf Club-House and the second Golf Club-House, built in red brick, stands in a similar position in relation to the Common, just beyond where the road turns to pass out of sight towards "The Rising Sun" Hotel. The rest of the buildings in view are residential houses.

The junction of Nottingham Hill with Cleeve Hill, by reason of the former curving round in the manner described, makes a combe where springs issuing from the hillside begin a stream that flows down the bottom of the combe and, being presently joined by the waters from two or three further springs that tumble down from Cleeve Hill by steeper courses, becomes a brook at Lower Woodmancote. This goes by Bishop's Cleeve to augment other small streams derived from the hills, which unite to form the River Swilgate, that flows by Stoke Orchard and Tredington to form one of a quartette of rivers by which the town of Tewkesbury is encompassed, causing it to be likened by an old writer to the garden of Eden.

Cleeve Hill is reached from Cheltenham by the high-road, which, after leaving the town, first approaches the ancient village of Prestbury. From the open road between the town and Prestbury a view is obtained of the Cotswold edge in this neighbourhood. The escarpment is seen ranging up from beyond Leckhampton, whose hill, quarried to its summit, shows the bare rock below a fringe of trees. The hills then pass back by Charlton Common to edge the beautiful valley of the River Chelt above Charlton Kings. Across that valley the line is renewed at Ham Hill and Hewlett's Hill, which lie behind the lower rounded fore-hill called Battledown. So, on to the steep slope behind Prestbury, which is, naturally, Prestbury Hill, and thus to Cleeve Hill, evident by its bare, pale summit, beneath which in several places the naked rock is again exposed in patches of cream-white cliff.

The hill-top at the position of these exposed rocks is called Cleeve Cloud. The broken ground below, where several houses are seen to have a high location, is called Nutter's Wood. At the present time Nutter's Wood is destitute of trees, though there is a wood, as can be seen, on each side of it.

The road turns sharply three times in passing through Prestbury village, making as many dangerous corners ; then enters upon the straight mile to the hamlet of Southam. This mile of road is very near the base of the escarpment and affords a good and near view of the hillsides in clear weather, especially of the hanging patch of woodland known as " Queen's Wood," which is a fine adornment of that part of the hill, changing in appearance and hue with the seasons. By several paths and old, rugged wheel-tracks from this mile of road the hill can be ascended.

Passing the arched entrance of the Southam de la Bere demesne, where, hidden behind the tall trees, is an old Tudor mansion, one arrives at the picturesque entrance of Southam Lane, with its horse-trough, trees and cottages, and the interesting and sunny corner where the tram-car stops before beginning the ascent of the hill.

The largest houses of Cleeve Hill are on this first part, to left and right of the road. As you rise the great views across and up and down the Severn Vale come into sight, and the air grows lighter and fresher with every step, though, if you are walking upon a warm day, the steepness of the hill in some parts will require the pace to be slow in order to avoid too tiring a labour.

Considerably more than half-way up, by a couple of cottages of bungalow build, a path to the right leads, by a short but very steep course, on to the common. You are soon now within sight of " The Rising Sun " and, on reaching it, may again approach the common up the horse road that passes in front of the inn.

The rest of the road, where you pass the two little churches and the golf houses, Malvern View, the Racing Stables and the Convalescent Home, is less arduous, the only stiff gradient being the last hundred yards before the hill top is reached on the neck of Nottingham Hill, where the descent begins for Winchcomb.

An ancient road crossing at this point leads by the right on to the common where it is called Wickfield Lane, and to the left along the top of Nottingham Hill, where it bears the name of Greenway (Grinnell) Lane. The great common has been very near the highway through the three-quarters of a mile from the " Rising Sun," and can be entered directly at several points from the road.

A little way past the " Malvern View " Hotel there is a piece of broken ground covered with grass on the left, and open to the road. It is called Stockwell Common and, although separated now from Cleeve Common by the wall fence, it is evidently a piece cut off from the latter at some time, perhaps when the road was made—for this well-made highway is not the original road. That passes, as a mere rutty track, along the edge of the great common and within its fences, and still offers an alternative route to Winchcomb for foot or bridle passengers.

Ascending Cleeve Hill from Winchcomb, the gradient is a little longer and less steep. The views are confined but pretty. Opposite to the side of the hill upon which the road is constructed, at only a short distance away, is an outlier known as Langley Hill and a combe, or bottom, with its spring and brooklet, separates it from this main road.

Another alternative road between Winchcomb and Cleeve Hill passes on the other side of the bottom, along the flank of Langley Hill, near the farm-house of the same name that can be plainly seen from the main road.

On leaving Winchcomb for Cleeve Hill, when at a comparatively low altitude, not only is a part of Cleeve Common seen above to the left, but, to one side of it, another great, grassy, round-headed mass of hill, quite bare of trees, named

Postlip Warren, which pertains to the fine old Postlip Hall. This ancient house lies in the mouth of a double-headed combe that runs right up into the side of Cleeve Common, past the Warren Hill. The Warren has, no doubt, borne its name from remote time, being a very ancient rabbitry. It rises to nearly the same height as adjacent high parts of the common, its altitude being 937 feet.

Roads off the main highway on that side lead to Postlip Hall, and also to Postlip Paper Mills and to Postlip House, the latter being the residence of the leading partner in the firm of paper-makers, whose mill occupies an unexpected position. Nobody who uses its blotting-paper, which has a very wide distribution, would picture the factory in such surroundings as these. The stream on which the mill stands, however, and which is derived from springs whose water is mainly collected upon the surface of the great common above, supplied the originator of the mill both with motor-power and an extremely pure water in abundance—factors of prime importance in the manufacture which, very rightly, no doubt, determined the choice by the paper-maker of this site for his mill.

On reaching the hill-top from the Winchcomb side, the great scene of the Severn Valley, bursts suddenly upon the view. The sight is unexpected and rather bewildering. Looking across to the far horizon is something like looking out to sea, and it seems that water, with the usual accompaniment of sails and smoke trails from steamers, should be where there are endless fields. If there be a smoke trail in reality, it will be that of a passing train upon the distant railway, and this may help to dispel the false expectancy.

The road in the vale, called the Evesham road, that runs from Cheltenham through Bishop's Cleeve village, passes along at a distance of about a mile and a half from the foot of Cleeve Hill. From this road the hill may be ascended by several lanes. One goes off to the foot of the hill at Southam and two others, as mentioned before, pass from the neighbourhood of Bishop's Cleeve to the higher houses on Cleeve Hill through parts of Woodmancote. Their steepness is such as to have often proved too much for weak-engined motor vehicles.

Cleeve Hill can be approached directly from the hill country behind only by a bad road that passes over the common as a rough cart-track, and vehicles do best by making the detour through Winchcomb or Cheltenham. The pedestrian and horse passenger can, however, take the more direct route. Towards the interior hills, beyond the common, but accessible by a good walk from Cleeve Hill, run two roads parallel with each other. They ascend from Winchcomb, the one beginning at the entrance of that town on the Cleeve Hill side, where the hand-post points to Corndean, and the other is the Sudeley Castle road, which passes from nearly opposite Winchcomb Church over the bridge of the Isborne, by the entrance to the Castle, and up the Winchcomb Valley. These two roads intercommunicate beyond Corndean Hall. The smaller road of the two, separated from the other by the distance of a few fields, goes along close behind the Hall and, entering the fields at a high altitude, presently arrives at the buildings of Wontley Farm and, passing forward beyond this point, it crosses obliquely the narrow strip of Cleeve Common that is called the West Down. It is then continued past a couple of cottages and along the top of a commanding height that lies above Puckham Wood, and ultimately descends to Whittington village and the Oxford and Cheltenham main road. In parts this road is in a rough state with considerable ruts.

The other of these two roads, passing up the beautiful Winchcomb Valley above Sudeley Castle, gives excellent views of the valley and the country of Avon Vale into which it debouches, as well as the line of hills that lie opposite the road and that rise to Roel Gate and Hawling village. This road, which is of better construction than the other, passes the small villages of Charlton Abbots, Brockhampton and Sevenhampton, the last two lying less than a mile apart. Like the first described, this road has gates upon it where it passes unfenced from Sudeley towards Charlton Abbots, through the fields. It ends by junction with the Cheltenham to Stow-on-the-Wold main road, very near its fork with the

Oxford-Cheltenham road within half a mile of the village of Andoversford. It communicates with the first road described by two or three lanes, one of which passes as a rough track up through Westwood to Wontley Farm, and with a branch to the end of Cleeve Common. On the other side the same road sends off bye-roads up steep hills to Hawling and Guiting and, past these villages, to the Stow road, at various points in the heart of the North Cotswolds. The description of these roads requires for complete understanding a visit to make their acquaintance, but a study of the map contained in this book of "Cleeve Common and its Neighbouring Lands" will assist the reader.

A branch of the Great Western Railway runs from its junction with the main line at Honeybourne, by Broadway and Winchcomb, to Cheltenham, a little way from the foot of the Cotswold escarpment. It has a station at Bishop's Cleeve, situated a mile and a half from the high-road at Cleeve Hill, by one or other of the two steep lanes already mentioned. From the hill, also, the trains upon the Western main line of the Midland Railway that passes from Bristol through Cheltenham to Birmingham, and those upon its branches that leave the main line at Ashchurch for Evesham and Malvern, can be seen as they go up and down and across the Severn Valley. The usual way of approaching Cleeve Hill by rail is *viâ* Cheltenham, thence by the tram-line.

CHAPTER III.

HILLS AND LANDSCAPES NEAR AND FAR.

FROM every prominent height of the Cotswold escarpment a fine view is obtained into and over the vale country below, but nowhere are the views so extensive as at Cleeve Hill and in its neighbourhood. Because, at this point, the line of hills is beginning to pass away from Severn Vale, and the aspect is up the Severn as well as down and over it, and also up and across the Vale of Avon, which comes down from the North-East to join the wider Vale of Severn opposite Cleeve Hill, and the latter, together with the out-jutting Nottingham Hill, forms a high, prominent corner that commands a series of most extensive landscapes. Due North from the top of Cleeve Hill, however, the long view is obstructed and partly hidden by a number of those outlying island-hills before mentioned, which, nevertheless, in that quarter diversify and add greatly to the scenery. These outlying hills are best and most nearly viewed from the end of Nottingham Hill.

Every landscape must be limited by an horizon, near or far. When the country in front is flat the ultimate horizon is limited by the fact that the surface sinks out of vision at a certain distance on account of the rotundity of the earth. When beyond that vanishing point there are hills, however, the horizon is prolonged according to their height, and the very longest view will always be from mountain-top to mountain-top. This condition holds in certain directions at Cleeve Hill, the views extending to mountains situated very far away. Thus, in some of the views to be mentioned, the visible horizon is situated at considerably over fifty miles from the view point. Another important factor in the ability to see so far is the varying transparency of the atmosphere, and although the conditions in this regard are commonly

SUMMER EVE

LANDSCAPE OF SEVERN VALE FROM CLEEVE HILL.

SUNSET OVER THE MALVERNS FROM CLEEVE HILL.

preventive of the longest possible views being obtained, clear days arrive with sufficient frequency to enable the distant Welsh Hills and the Clee Hills of Shropshire, if not the Wrekin, to be seen by every one who stays a short time in the neighbourhood, and the great extent of the available landscapes to be thus duly appreciated. Apart from that fullest view, the changing atmosphere itself, which may be observed with great facility and effect from this locality, lends a variety to the general outlook that is very pleasing.

From the position of the Roman Camp and that corner of the common, the adjacent ranging sides of Prestbury Hill and Hewlett's Hill are the first objects to be viewed, with their rough slopes and hill farms and patches of enclosed larch and beechwood and banky fields, scattered trees and thick hedges sinking down towards Prestbury village, whose church and houses lie amidst much verdure. Then the lower hill, known as Battledown, will be noticed, which has some reservoirs of water upon it. In the hollow beyond lies the large village of Charlton Kings, backed by the hills that range from the ridge of Pegglesworth and Chatcomb to Charlton Common and Leckhampton Hill, the high location of Cowley Wood lying in a gap between, and the ridge of Birdlip showing here and there beyond Leckhampton and Crickley Hills. So round, in a gently curving line, by the Crippetts and Shurdington Hill to Cooper's Hill, beyond which Painswick and Haresfield Beacons are also showing.

In the bay thus formed by this curving line of the Cotswold edge lies Cheltenham, that beautiful town, with its spires and towers, varying in appearance at this distance so much according to light and atmosphere. The town is seen to extend backwards towards the white-faced cliff of Leckhampton Hill.

Extended out into the great vale beyond Cheltenham, two outlying hills are seen, one standing beyond the other, well away from the hill-line; these are Churchdown and Robinswood Hill. In front of Robinswood Hill, in the vale a dozen miles away, lies the city of Gloucester, the tower of whose cathedral stands up tall and distinct, an easily-found object when the air is clear, as we are here supposing it.

Down there, quite near to the cathedral tower, the River Severn flows, though we cannot see it unless the river be in flood, excepting where, lower down the vale, some parts of its widening estuary gleam white upon the horizon. All down that way, into the far South-West, the country is confined within a definite valley, a line of dark, tree-covered hills facing the Cotswold line, they being the hills of Dean Forest, which rise from near the Severn bank to an altitude of over 800 feet. The first part of that valley is the Vale of Gloucester, and the part beyond, by the gleaming water, is the Vale of Berkeley, these being portions of the one Vale of Severn.

Let us now walk along the top of the cliff of the common until we are at the high part above the "Rising Sun," and follow the horizon from the end of the Forest Hills as we go. At the Northern end of that long, dark, equal line of the Forest is the large, separate rounded hill, with trees upon the middle of its summit, called May Hill, and North of this the Western horizon recedes until it is formed by the Welsh Mountains, which look low and small at a distance of forty to sixty miles. First, over the top of the Forest Hills, to the left of May Hill, shows the rounded top of a mountain mass of short length called The Blorenge. Then, jutting from behind May Hill, is a slightly elongated angular mass of hill, to the right of which is a hill-top of conical shape. The former is Skirrid Fawr and the latter the Sugar-Loaf. These mountains are situated near the town of Abergavenny in further Monmouthshire, near the border of Brecknockshire. A mountain mass to the right of the Sugar-Loaf and further away is a portion of the Brecon Beacons. It requires a clear atmosphere for this part to be identified. The continuous hill-line to the right of the Sugar-Loaf passes within the border of the Welsh County of Brecknock and forms part of the Black Mountains of Brecknockshire. A mass of hill which ordinarily appears to form a part of the line of the Black Mountains, immediately to the right of the Sugar-Loaf as viewed from Cleeve Common, really stands a few miles nearer to us in Monmouthshire, and is locally known as the Graig, or in full Graig Serrerthin. The whole width of Herefordshire with all its minor hills, and considerable portions of Gloucestershire and Monmouthshire lie between Cleeve Hill and the mountains mentioned which form that most distant horizon.

Beyond the sudden drop that takes place in the line of the Black Mountains at Hay Bluff, there is but a comparatively short space, occupied by hills of lower altitude and nearer distance as ordinarily viewed, of which the Woolhope Hills are the chief, and then the Malvern Hills run out into the broadened Severn Vale, which here is the Vale of Worcester. But in that space between the Malverns and Black Mountains in the clearest of weather, a portion of the Cambrian Hills, beginning about the sources of the rivers Wye and Severn at Plinlimmon and stretching South-Westward behind Rhayader, Llandrindod and Builth, comes into view in the extreme distance, being only visible from the highest parts of Cleeve Common and not often seen.

The Malverns are much nearer at hand than the Welsh Mountains, being only eighteen or twenty miles distant in a line to their tops from Cleeve Common. They consequently present a bolder aspect than those mountains and are much more often in view. Their sinuous line passes from the West into the North-West, forming the horizon for the sun's setting in summer-time and remaining in the memory of those familiar with their aspect from this part in connection with many a fine sunset scene.

Over the tail of the Malvern Range, in clear times, a more remote hill-mass appears which is in the Welsh County of Radnor, being, in fact, the high moorland known as Radnor Forest. The distance to this is about fifty-five miles, and this hill-mass appears continuous with those distant Cambrian Hills above mentioned, when they also are visible, which is only rarely because their nearer distance must be about seventy miles, and Plinlimmon nearly ninety. It is in the evening that they are occasionally seen, when they lie for a short time gleaming in the rays of the setting sun.

At some short distance from the last rounded eminence of the Malvern ridge of hills, in a direction almost due North of it, are two oval-backed hills, one lying beyond the other up the country. These are in Shropshire and are the Clee

Hills, the nearest being the Titterstone and the furthest the Brown Clee Hill. Their distance is forty to fifty miles, and to see them it is necessary to look completely over Worcestershire. A little to the left of the Titterstone lies the ancient town of Ludlow, as will be seen by reference to a map. The Clee Hills, being in front and higher, hide the Wenlock Edge and the Caraocc Hills near Church Stretton.

Immediately to the right of the Clee Hills, at a nearer distance of about thirty to thirty-five miles, another short line of hills is seen to block the valley up in North Worcestershire. These are of less altitude than the Clee Hills, but of interesting and distinctive appearance, consisting of two rounded portions united by a centre and lower part. They are the Abberley Hills, named after the village that lies towards their right or upper end, the rounded hill at the opposite or lower end of the line being Woodbury Hill. On the centre, lower portion, which is called Witley Hill, there is a tower locally known as "Jones' Folly," which can be distinctly seen at this far distance by ordinary unassisted vision, when the weather is clear enough—which is not infrequently the case.

Beyond and to the right of the Abberley Hills, straight up in the North-North-West, past Worcester and Kidderminster, the Wrekin shows, but requires clear weather to be seen. This hill exhibits a low, rounded back, as viewed at this distance of about sixty miles. The town of Shrewsbury lies out in the vale, almost on a line with the Wrekin, to the left and a few miles from it. It is not unusual, throughout the year, for a couple of months to elapse without a sufficiently clear day to show the Wrekin from Cleeve Hill. As it lies very low on the horizon it is best seen from the top of the cliff, or, at least, from some distance up the steep slope of the common behind the "Rising Sun." The broad upland that lies to the right of the Wrekin and nearly due North represents the Lickey and Clent Hills.

The view Northward is now obstructed by Nottingham Hill, as well as by several outlying hills. The slope of Nottingham Hill, in fact, entered into the landscape that ended in the horizon where lies the Wrekin, and, when we are not too far along the hill Eastward, whether from the cliff or from the road, we see, pushing forward from immediately behind Nottingham Hill, the end of the local Woolstone Hill, with the village of that name upon it, the little church and rectory showing quite clearly, about five miles away.

But if we move further along the cliff top Eastwards, to a position above and beyond the racing stables, the view to the back of Nottingham Hill is obtained. The first thing noticed is the group of outlying hills, the largest and furthest away of these outliers from the Cotswold escarpment which, geologically, pertains to it, being Bredon Hill. A portion of the broad back of this hill will be seen and, some distance further to the right, another hill of symmetrical shape, highest in the centre part and lower at either side, which is Dumbleton Hill, named after the village that lies at its further side. The nearest hill, namely that lying immediately on the other side of the Winchcomb high-road, is Langley Hill, called Stanley Hill on its further slope and Stanley Mount at its more abrupt end. Glimpses of part of Woolstone and Dixton Hills are also in sight, the latter-named being a curious, low hill with bare, grave-like summit.

To the north-eastward the escarpment of the North Cotswolds is continued, after the break occasioned by the Winchcomb Valley, from Sudeley Hill by Hailes, Stanway and Broadway to Meon Hill, which is the furthest outlier of the Cotswolds. The Winchcomb Valley is really a long, broad combe pushed into the hills two or three miles behind Cleeve Common. In this valley, on a slight eminence, less than one mile behind the town of Winchcomb, stands Sudeley Castle, flanked on the further side by the steep hill edge over which you pass into the North Cotswold country.

The town of Winchcomb itself can be seen from various parts of the common, lying in the mouth of its vale where it opens out into the greater valley of the Avon, for it is the Avon Vale, otherwise the Vale of Evesham, which fronts the escarpment in this direction beyond Cleeve Hill and in which portions of the counties of Gloucester, Worcester and Warwick take part.

Though not so extensive as the Severn Vale, this other

great valley affords a very long view. The low hills upon its further side are those beyond Pershore and Evesham, upon which lie Craycombe, Wood-Norton, Church Lench and Rous Lench, whilst, beyond these, the country still rises towards the confines of Worcestershire and Warwickshire about the towns of Alcester and Redditch and towards Birmingham. Straight up the Vale of Avon the view passes over Warwickshire to end in Charnwood Forest in Leicestershire and in the neighbourhood of Naseby in Northamptonshire, where the Avon has its origin in the high plain. Within the country in sight are situated Warwick, Leamington, Coventry, Rugby and Stratford-on-Avon, the town of Shakespeare lying away in the vale six miles only off Meon Hill, which may be taken as a guide to its locality as looked at from here.

The view up Avon Vale is, however, better seen from the end of Nottingham Hill than from Cleeve Common, and from that nearer point it is also easier to identify the outlying hills of Dumbleton, Woolstone, Dixton, Bredon and Stanley Mount, as mentioned above, and to appreciate their beautifying effect on the landscape.

To the Eastward from Cleeve Common the views are into the nearer parts of the interior Cotswold country.

The extent of country visible from Cleeve Hill and its neighbourhood is, therefore, very great, including, as it does, so large a portion of the West-central parts of England, and its interest more than corresponds with its extent, on account of its unusually picturesque character. Perhaps what chiefly impresses the mind and memory is the extreme openness and almost limitless stretch of the landscapes. Here is a freedom of sight hardly equalled elsewhere, and one accustomed to such a wide outlook feels his view confined when he comes into a country of limited scenes, however pretty these may be. From the Forest-of-Dean Hills beyond Lydney to the Wrekin, South to North, it is nearly a hundred miles ; and from the furthest visible height of the Mountains and Beacons of Brecknockshire to the furthest horizon over Warwickshire a line of country lies exposed for an even greater distance.

In this vast area of country lie cities, towns and villages in considerable number, but very inconspicuously. It is, for the main part, a purely agricultural country; and, at a distance of many miles, there is practically nothing to distinguish the site of the aggregation of population represented by the town, much less by that of the village. England, amongst other countries, is understood to be comparatively thickly populated, but viewed in the broad way permitted by the position and elevation of Cleeve Hill, there is no sign of this—nothing more than an unstained rurality, the country appearing everywhere and the population almost nowhere. Even the positions of many of the towns and villages that might be seen are obscured by the numerous minor hills and hollows that really mark the surface of the country of Severn Vale and render it much less of a plain than it is judged to be in the long general view one may here take of it. It is also rather heavily wooded, and most of the villages and individual dwellings are lost to view in the verdure of trees and hedges. In the foreground of the view, certainly, the villages that lie near can be identified, their churches aiding greatly in their discovery; and houses, barns, hovels and hayricks can be traced when near at hand, and the fields be seen to be divided into a patchwork of variously tinted shapes by their hedge fences. But further away all the detail becomes confused, the lines being drawn together by the distance into one close general effect which even the telescope can but partially unravel. There is a certain amount of light and shade and colour in the further distances—green and yellow, and blue and purple—which vary with the time of year.

Amongst the towns of the Severn Vale, Cheltenham is the nearest and most plainly visible, its site and aspect being particularly charming. There is nothing in it that offends the eyes, but much that pleases them. Even its two tall chimneys, situated near together on the outskirts, which pertain to the municipal service, emit their smoke, when they do emit any that is visible, to the advantage of the scene judged as a picture. They suggest human life and activity more than the other buildings, especially to one

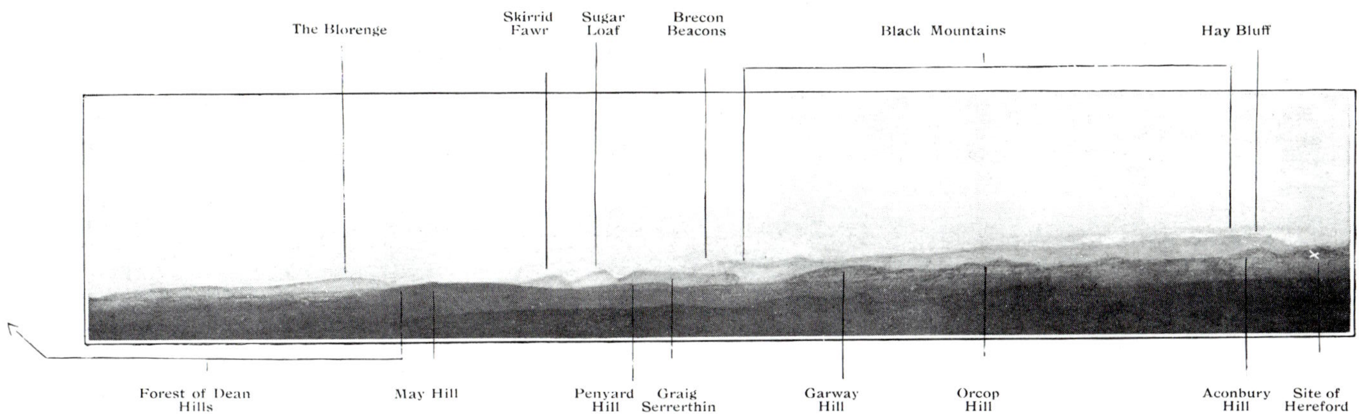

HORIZON HILLS TO SOUTH-WEST AND WEST.

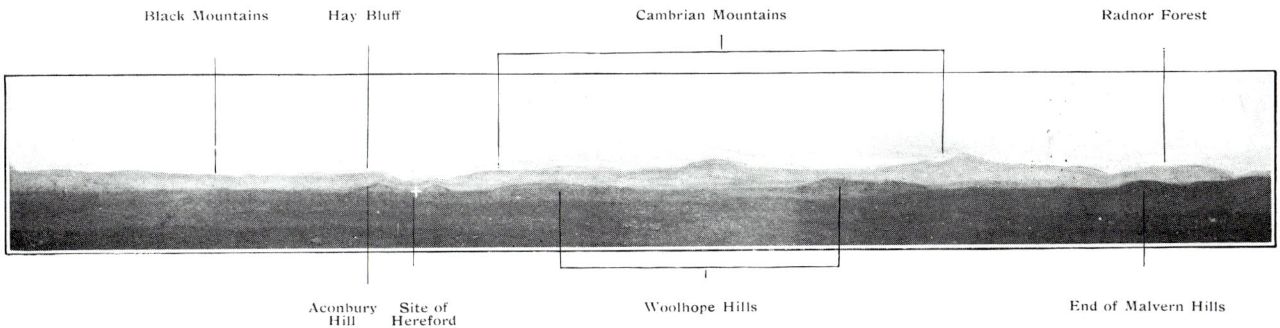

HORIZON HILLS WEST TO NORTH-WEST.

THE HORIZON HILLS AS VIEWED FROM CLEEVE CLOUD CLIFF, CLEEVE COMMON.

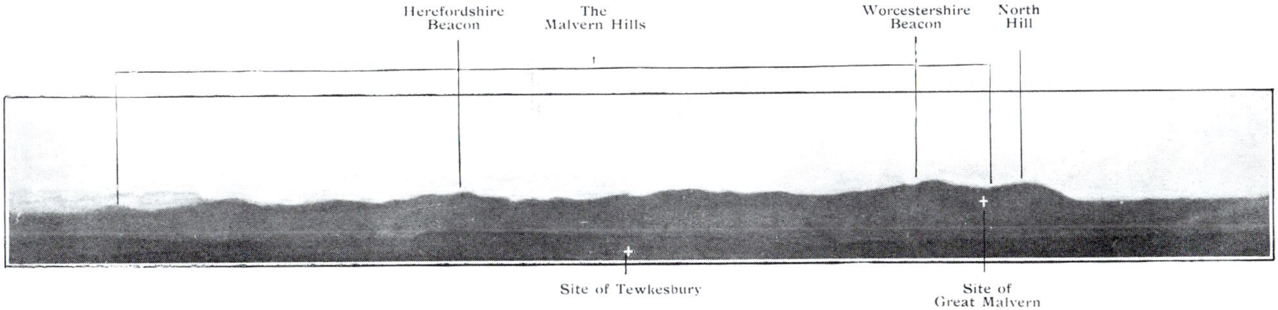

HORIZON HILLS TO NORTH-WEST.

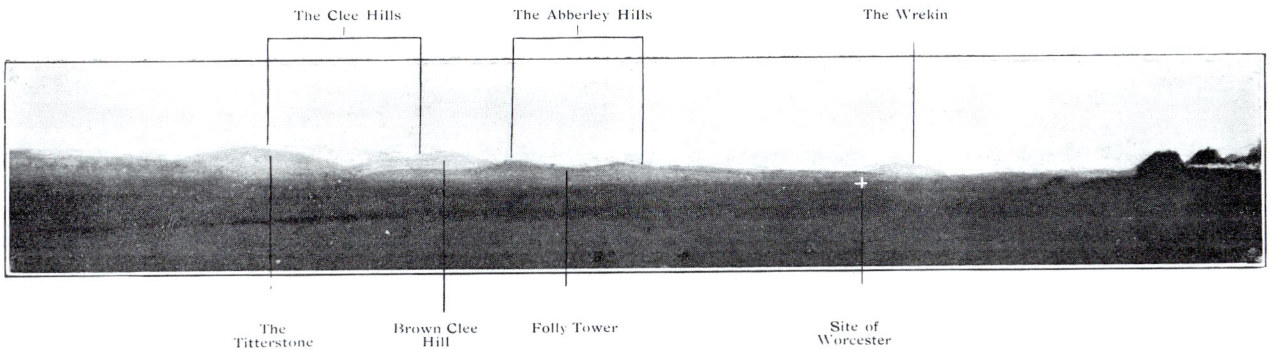

HORIZON HILLS NORTH-WEST TO DUE NORTH.

THE HORIZON HILLS AS VIEWED FROM CLEEVE CLOUD CLIFF, CLEEVE COMMON.

who is unfamiliar with those other buildings and the purposes they serve, such as the Queen's Hotel, the College Chapel and the great glass roof of the Winter Garden, not to mention numerous church towers and church spires, and churches without tower or spire. Cheltenham lies in a bay of the escarpment ; the hills circle half round it in a protecting way appropriate to its character, which is beautiful, gentle and somnolent.

Cheltenham may not call itself a city, as Gloucester does by virtue of that cathedral tower which we see standing up amidst other buildings. That city of Gloucester is seen to occupy a position in relation to the line of the Cotswolds almost as near as that of Cheltenham. But, its distance from Cleeve Hill being three times as far, its buildings cannot be seen as those of Cheltenham can. With the experience gained by a visit to these sister places, however, a mental comparison is possible between them, as we view them both from this height and at these distances.

The ancient town of Tewkesbury, which lies seven or eight miles up the vale towards the Malverns, can generally be discerned, and the village of Bishop's Cleeve, being near at hand, is always more or less prominent. But you must search for the positions of Upton-on-Severn, Twyning, Bredon, Ashchurch and other places, or wait until a gleam of sunlight falls upon them to illuminate brightly their locations and thus bring them temporarily into acute relief in the otherwise cloud-shaded vale. At times it is easy to overlook even Tewkesbury, and its ancient Abbey will sometimes pass alternately into and out of sight as you gaze, by reason of the changing light.

The town of Malvern, posed at the end of its line of hills and well up on the hillside, is clearly seen on bright mornings ; but it is only by an eye previously informed by aid of a telescope that the tower of Worcester Cathedral can be at once identified. The city, for the main part, lies by the Severn out of view, its place only indicated by the trail of light smoke that hangs over it, from which the upper half of the tower emerges. When once seen and its position in relation to other objects noted, it can be rediscovered, though it is but a small object as viewed from over twenty miles away.

Intervening hills hide the city of Hereford completely where it lies far Westward in the Wye Valley, and no one can have had more than an imaginary view of its cathedral from Cleeve Hill; the nearest parts towards it that can be identified in clear weather being Aconbury Hill and Dinedor Hill, five and three miles distant respectively.

Looking into the Vale of Avon, the little town of Winchcomb is seen near at hand, together with the grey stone walls of Sudeley Castle a mile to the right of it, and the hill of the same name rising behind the castle, with its very steep road. The spires or towers of the villages upon the slopes of the North Cotswold escarpment, or in the vale below, may also be sought from Cleeve Hill, or Nottingham Hill, and several of them be found, especially with the aid of a good glass. There will be no difficulty in seeing some of the houses of Broadway and its hill with the look-out tower upon it. But the several villages in the vale below, most of whose churches have steeples, will require search.

From the main road between Cheltenham and Bishop's Cleeve, and from the lanes between Southam and the latter village, the face of Cleeve Hill itself may be best seen. Thus viewed on a summer afternoon the hill, from the position of the Three Sisters and the Roman Camp, along to the part that is above the "Rising Sun" Hotel, is seen to have a summit of almost equal height. Being 1,000 feet at the camp, it may rise to about 1,050 at the two parts that swell a little upwards along this length of top. Woods and trees may be observed to cover a great part of the face of the slope. The enclosures known as the Thrift and Stutfield Wood, occupying a portion of the middle space of the slope, reach up to where the hill begins to rise to its top by an almost perpendicular cliff. Where the slope falls away to the right towards Southam a portion of the larger Queen's Wood is seen, and below the position of these woods are many trees, sometimes densely grouped, as immediately above Southam House and about the Haymes Farm. The bosky form of the tree-tops and their varied shadings of green are restful and pleasing to the eye. In the foreground are pale, grey-green, wind-blown willows, and above and about are the greens of elm, beech, oak, sycamore, horse-chestnut, poplar, thorn and orchard trees. Towards the North-Eastern end on the left the summit of Cleeve Common slopes down with a fine sweep to meet Nottingham Hill, and most of the houses of the hill are under that slope towards where the high-road goes slantingly up to pass over the neck of the promontory, afterwards to sink down by a long incline to Winchcomb.

CHAPTER IV.

CLEEVE COMMON AND ITS NEIGHBOURING LANDS.

GENERALLY speaking, commons constitute a remnant of an ancient social mode. They pertain to the Manor and its Lord and to the Commoners of that particular manor. Formerly the vulgar folk who lived within the manor had the use of the land in an agricultural sense, the lord retaining other rights, such as mineral rights. In the course of long years and during the uncertainty caused by a gradual change of ideas in freedom and proprietorship, many of the lands that had been held in common were enclosed by the more astute of the inhabitants, who, by an after occupation for a sufficiently long time, acquired an absolute and legal right of ownership over them. Thus, by a system of theft that was tolerably safe against punishment, when population was sparse and land of comparatively small value, and the feudal system broken up and the modern system in course of development, the commons were much reduced in size and, in many instances, were taken up entirely by those who could enclose and cultivate them as fenced fields. In other cases commons were enclosed and divided up by agreement between the parties who possessed a right in them, and the common ownership was so lost to posterity. The fact of common land in some cases remaining as such through all vicissitudes appears to have been due to some such simple fact as that the ground was of poor quality, or difficult to appropriate by reason of being very hilly, or, lying adjacent to a town, village or aggregation of population, its use was appreciated sufficiently to prevent encroachment upon the rights of all by any one.. At the present time the commons that continue are subject to a certain amount of rights by the Lord of the Manor in which the common lies, and to a certain amount of rights by the whole of the inhabitants of

MAP OF CLEEVE COMMON AND NEIGHBOURING LANDS

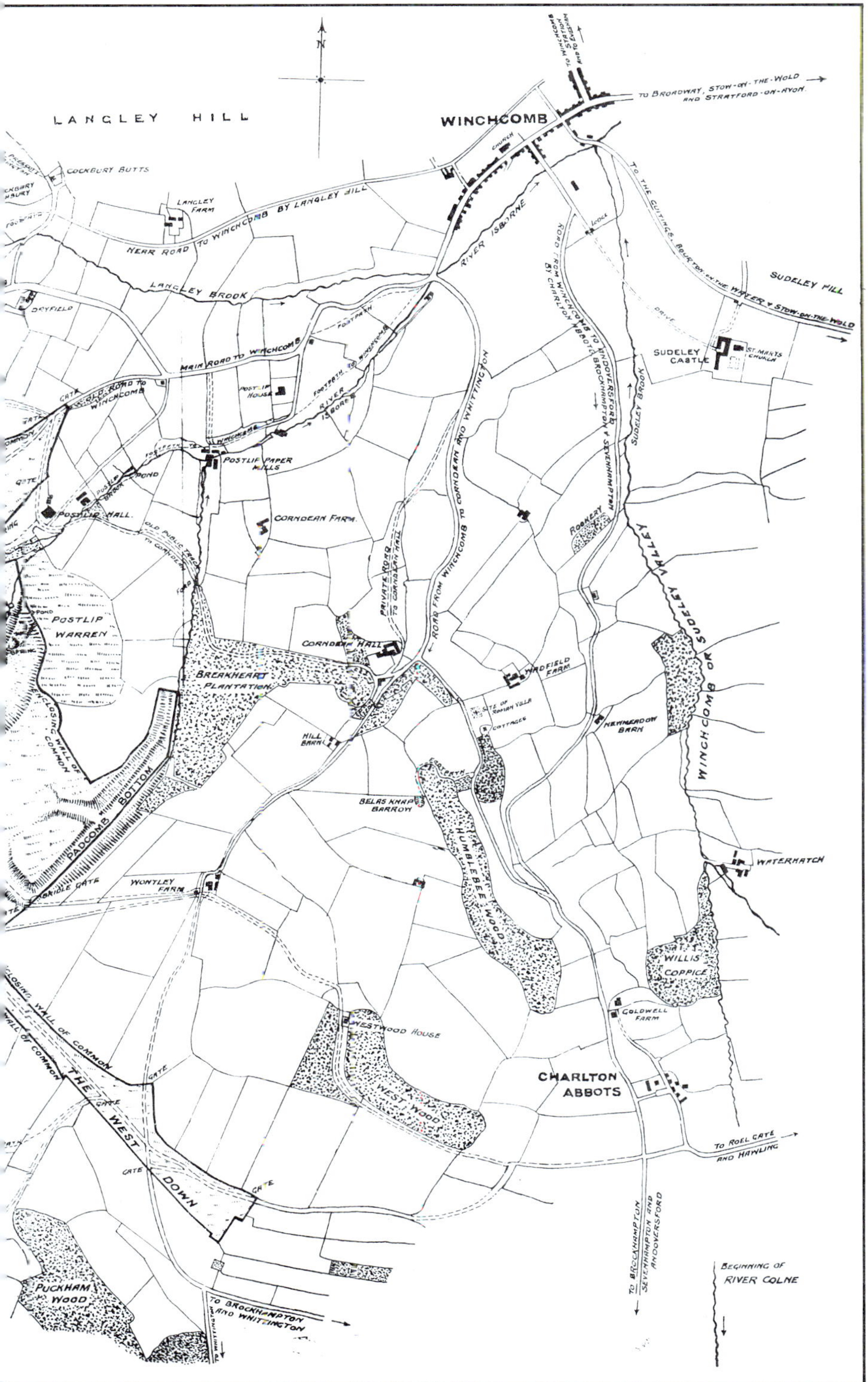
N
LANGLEY HILL
WINCHCOMB
TO WINCHCOMB STATION AND EVESHAM
TO BROADWAY, STOW-ON-THE-WOLD AND STRATFORD-ON-AVON
CHURCH
COCKBURY BUTTS
LANGLEY FARM
NEAR ROAD TO WINCHCOMB BY LANGLEY HILL
LANGLEY BROOK
RIVER ISBORNE
LODGE
TO THE GUITINGS, BOURTON-ON-THE-WATER & STOW-ON-THE-WOLD
SUDELEY HILL
DRIVE
SUDELEY CASTLE
ST. MARYS CHURCH
DRYFIELD
MAIN ROAD TO WINCHCOMB
FOOTPATH
FOOTPATH TO WINCHCOMB
POSTLIP HOUSE
RIVER ISBORNE
OLD ROAD TO WINCHCOMB
ROAD FROM WINCHCOMB TO CORNDEAN AND WHITTINGTON
ROAD FROM WINCHCOMB TO ANDOVERSFORD BY CHARLTON ABBOTS, BROCKHAMPTON & SEVENHAMPTON
SUDELEY BROOK
POSTLIP PAPER MILLS
POND
POSTLIP HALL
CORNDEAN FARM
OLD PUBLIC TRACK TO CORNDEAN
ROOKERY
WINCHCOMB OR SUDELEY VALLEY
PRIVATE ROAD TO CORNDEAN HALL
POSTLIP WARREN
BREAKHEART PLANTATION
CORNDEAN HALL
WADFIELD FARM
SITE OF ROMAN VILLA
COTTAGES
NEWMEADOW BARN
HILL BARN
ENCLOSING WALL OF COMMON
PADCOMB BOTTOM
FOOTPATH
BELAS KNAP BARROW
HUMBLEBEE WOOD
WATERHATCH
WONTLEY FARM
BRIDLE GATE
WILLIS COPPICE
COLDWELL FARM
WESTWOOD HOUSE
ENCLOSING WALL OF COMMON
THE WEST DOWN
WEST WOOD
CHARLTON ABBOTS
GATE
TO ROEL GATE AND HAWLING
TO BROCKHAMPTON SEVENHAMPTON AND ANDOVERSFORD
PUCKHAM WOOD
TO BROCKHAMPTON AND WHITTINGTON
BEGINNING OF RIVER COLNE

the manor. Those within the manor who are engaged in farming gain the greater advantage when the common is a large one by being able to turn out their animals to graze upon the surface during the summer months. In fact, apart from any claim by the over-lord upon the commoners, the ancient order remains to a large extent unaltered.

It has happened sometimes, however, that a large population has sprung up in the neighbourhood of the common, yet outside the particular manor to which the common pertains, and these, and other strangers, have trespassed upon the rights of the real commoners. In order to settle uncertainties of this sort, to make the best public use of the common and to ensure its retention for all time for common use, an Act of Parliament has, in such cases, been obtained which, overriding all former rights by custom, has defined the rights for the future, generally creating a public management by a commission, or committee of members elected from the neighbouring communities who exercise chief use of the common, the Lord of the Manor being also duly represented upon the managing board.

Cleeve Common is a common to which the above description applies and which is now managed by a Board of Conservators established some years since by Act of Parliament. Although theoretically, perhaps, its use is still for the residents of the original manors in which it lies, together with the inhabitants of the neighbouring town of Cheltenham, whose right depends upon the payment to the Conservators of an annual sum of money by the corporate government of that town as required in the Act, the freedom of the common for such recreative purposes as are allowed by the Conservators is for all who come without reserve. Only the rights over the yield of the common, such as grazing, quarrying and water, are reserved strictly to the lord and inhabitants of the manors within the bounds of which Cleeve Common lies.

The area of this common is unusually great, being 1,002 acres. In some parts of the country there are unfenced moors of much larger dimensions, and there are even some private parks as large or larger and several forest areas of greater magnitude, but few genuine commons. The thousand acres, to speak roundly, are surrounded by a single continuous fence which is a stone wall about five feet high. Such walls are expeditiously erected of loose unmortared stones superimposed, and wherever fences of this sort are in use suitable stone must be near at hand, and it is plentiful enough upon the common itself, where it is quarried in several localities.

The area is of fairly regular and compact shape, excepting for its extension on the South-East side by a long, narrow strip called the West Down. This narrow part has a general width of eighty or one hundred yards, contracted at one point to twenty yards and widened where the furze grows towards its end to two hundred yards and over.

At its North-West side the common presents a steep cliff which faces and commands the views over the great Severn Valley, and, turning a little more nearly due North, this cliff opposes the face of Nottingham Hill and, behind this, commands to some extent a view into the Vale of Avon. This cliff, varying in steepness from an actual precipice to a stiff grass slope, is about a mile and a half long. Throughout this length there is a stretch of ground that may be described as undercliff, which in many parts is very rugged and irregular by reason of the rock having fallen from the heights that rise a couple of hundred feet, more or less, above, but which affords a pleasant and protected walk by an irregular footpath, or rutty horse-road, all within the common. This undercliff ground is the part approached from the high-road, which it touches for some distance before the road arrives at its highest point at the neck of Nottingham Hill. It immediately overlooks the houses of Cleeve Hill; the two golf-club houses; the two churches, and the two inns. Several private houses, practically speaking, adjoin its wall fence. This fence afterwards passes some small woods, and the undercliff broadens towards its southern end and surrounds there the little island of stolen ground called Nutter's Wood, and, at its further, Western corner, sends down towards the high-road at Southam (here separated from the common near Nutter's Wood by the distance of half a mile) a woodland lane called Bentley Lane.

From the corner of the common where lies Queen's Wood we may follow the fence all round the great enclosure. Starting from this point the confining wall soon rises the cliff, and passes straight backwards for nearly three miles, the third mile measuring the distance of that narrow portion called the West Down. For the whole of this distance, on this side of the common, the ground is even of surface and high of elevation, the highest part of the common being reached three-quarters of a mile from the cliff, near the gate where the rough road passes off the common towards Hewlett's Hill, though here it cannot be more than a few feet higher than at some points near the cliff, or at the knoll that lies towards the Roman Camp and has some beech saplings planted upon it. Beyond the highest point the surface falls very gently down West Down to the furze that grows towards its extremity, where there are outlets towards the villages in the hills beyond the common. As far as the gate mentioned above rough grass-ground lies over the common wall, and, beyond that point and on both sides of the West Down, the common land is bordered by fields of Cotswold type in arable cultivation.

The North-Eastern side of the common is of much less regular aspect, the surface being here broadly scored by three deep combes or bottoms; namely, the two heads of the Postlip Combe, called respectively Dry Bottom and Watery Bottom, and the third combe situated on the further side of the common and called Padcomb Bottom. The returning wall, on leaving the West Down, passes down the middle of Padcomb Bottom, which, in places, is very narrow with steep sides. Beyond the wall of this deep combe is rough grass ground and the woodland known as Breakheart Plantation, which is continuous with the woods that lie behind Corndean Hall. Considerable springs issue in this bottom which supply water to the Postlip paper mills, and create a brook, which meets the Postlip brook and forms the head of the stream called the Isborne, that swirls down through Winchcomb and for a course of a dozen miles to the Avon near Evesham.

Rising out of Padcomb Bottom, the confining wall of

NOTTINGHAM HILL FROM CLEEVE COMMON.

THE POSTLIP COMBE

SHOWING PARTS OF POSTLIP HALL, CLEEVE COMMON, AND POSTLIP WARREN.

the common passes Northward and, for a time, the surface of the common in this part has a moderate upward or fairly flat slope and is also largely covered with furze. Adjoining the common at this part is the other hill of ground that is almost waste, known as Postlip Warren, and where the ground of the common begins to descend to Watery Bottom the wall turns back by the Warren at a sharp angle to enclose some quarries, the precipitous sides of which are so near as to make the passage by the wall difficult there. The ground has been much quarried hereabout, and there are large tips of waste material from the quarries, which give the two-headed Postlip Combe a broken and rugged appearance from wherever viewed.

Descending into Watery Bottom the strong spring giving rise to the Postlip Brook is soon discovered, and the stream is followed down to the pond and the sheep-wash, the former a reservoir for the latter, which is a circular, stone-built basin for washing the sheep before shearing, much used by the commoners and farmers of the neighbourhood in the sheep-washing season. Below the sheep-wash the wall comes down from behind the quarry and, presently, crosses the brook above a marshy place and fences a coppice, then leads up in front of the other part of the combe—Dry Bottom, in the close neighbourhood of the old mansion—Postlip Hall, and its grounds, which lie but just off the common. The wall, passing upwards out of the combe, comes very near this fine old house and close to its ancient chapel. It then edges an old cart-track, and soon after strikes the original old Winchcomb road, which breaks the continuity of the wall with a gate. Afterwards the wall borders an arable field that juts into the common and has been plainly stolen from it, and then separates the common from other ploughed fields, beyond which, and over the Winchcomb main-road, lies Langley Hill. Then the wall arrives at the gate of Wickfield Lane, which leads on to the common from the neck of Nottingham Hill, and so back to the cliff and the undercliff and again into view of the Severn Vale above the houses of Cleeve Hill, and so along above the Thrift Wood to the place whence we started. The length of the fence of the common which we have thus followed round is about ten miles.

Practically the whole of the large surface enclosed by this wall is covered with grass, and it is grass of a peculiar character, not the rich mixture of twenty or more species that luxuriate in the meadows, but a much simpler green-sward. It is cropped during the months when grass grows by the sheep, cattle and horses of the commoners, as well as by the rabbits ; but it does not lie in its nature to grow long and lush. When left during the summer it grows longer in places, but the blades are then harsh and dry and not of great pasturage value. This circumstance is favourable for walking upon the common, for, whilst the turf is springy, it is never wetting to the feet, even in damp, winter weather. There is a golf-course upon it whose single round measures over three miles, but in various directions the pedestrian may foot it for hours without leaving the common, and find it the most untiring of promenades, as well as the most bracing and recreative.

The grassy surface of the common varies much in regularity, and the golf links are said to be of a sporting sort, rather than cut out for the exhibition of prowess in making a short score, there being sundry hazards, such as drives up a precipitous pitch, across quarries and through furze, and approaches to putting greens down steep slopes, over the very deep fosses of a Roman camp, and so forth, in uncertain but happy variety.

On the one side of the common there is also the steep cliff, with much tumpy ground below, on another side those very sudden steep dips, one beyond the other, into the three combes, or bottoms, already mentioned. There is, consequently, much scope for scrambling for those who can scramble. Yet, although the quarries are not all fenced, and in parts the cliff is steep, the ground is not extraordinarily dangerous.

All down one side of the common it is plain walking when once the top is reached, and down there the walk can easily be extended to high country beyond the bounds of the common. Another good walk, at a high altitude all the way, is along the top of the neighbouring Nottingham Hill, which is very accessible and requires no climb to speak of from the road.

In varying directions across the common you may walk to arrive at places beyond ; or, by way of change, you can, as the hunting folk say, " sink the vale " to investigate the outlying hills and villages that lie there.

Perambulations off the common at the side furthest away from the inner Cotswold country must be to Nottingham Hill, or to Langley Hill, or down the escarpment into the Vale of Severn, or by the divers paths that lead towards Cheltenham and Charlton Kings on the one hand, and towards Winchcomb on the other.

The common is practically treeless throughout the whole of its thousand acres, for it has but three trees of note upon it. There may also be a few saplings planted more or less as an experiment by the Conservators, one of whose permissory powers, as definitely mentioned in the Act of Parliament, is to plant trees. On the principle that all their powers ought to be put into practice, the Conservators have sometimes planted trees, notwithstanding that the common is by nature an open, treeless tract, the better appreciated for its arboreal bareness in this country of trees. The three trees which adorn it only serve to accentuate the open-airiness of the whole. They are called the " Three Sisters," being three stunted, gnarled and wind-blown beeches, situated on the South-West corner of the common at the edge of the cliff near the Roman Camp. They maintain their existence by a desperate struggle against adverse circumstances, putting forth a thin crop of dry, hard leaves, which hardly seem to know the tenderness of Spring, so rapidly do they assume a stiff and glazed appearance, their thickened surface layer making an endeavour to suit itself to the strong winds and uncongenial soil. As to the saplings so assiduously planted and replanted, their existence, as a rule, is brief, the little flame of their life being soon blown out. Long before the time of natural leaf-fall their foliage has been thinned to ragged sparseness, the upper branches being raked ere summer is half out. If one has survived for any length of years it does not look as if it would ever reach the magnitude of a tree, being still of nursery size and like a badly-nourished and ricketty infant. Its leaves but barely function to maintain the next year's effort in a development of buds, slender and few and far apart. It is plainly against the order of Nature that trees should grow here. The Three Sisters have defied the order, but their persistence has been uniquely obstinate. There are some bushes, however, some of elder, for instance, situated on the sides of the older quarries, or on the slopes of the refuse tipped from them, and several examples of a species of pyrus that lean from soilless crevices at the cliff's face where they have found a casual origin from bird-dropped seeds. An occasional full green and deadly belladonna plant, which is almost a shrub, may be met with in secluded spots, producing its large, bell blossoms and shining black, button-like fruit. There are also furze bushes growing in patches here and there out on the open common, their presence marking a deposit of sand or siliceous soil in those places. Neither furze nor heather takes kindly to the Cotswold limestone, a few sprigs of ling, pale in colour and of short length, being the nearest approach to the purple covering of the northern moors.

The common has its smaller flora, but this amounts to nothing conspicuous apart from the thistles that exist in at least half a dozen species, one or other of which may be found in every part of the common, and the nettles that grow in the old quarries, the houndstongue by the wall and the hore-hound on dry banks below the cliff. For the main part the flora consists of very small plants indeed that go with the turf. There are specks of white when the purging-flax is in flower and the bits of gold of creeping potentillas and the paler yellow of rock-rose ; a pretty little nodding spurrey ; a tufted woodruff that blossoms close to the ground and whitens it in places when in full bloom, and a milk-vetch that rejoices in the full name of *Astragalus hypoglottis*, whose small stem and purple flowers, growing close to the earth, are never left by a sheep which passes that way. There also blossom, in due season, the frog orchis and the bee orchis, a mauve-flowered gentian, a cluster-headed campanula of deep purple and a yellow stonecrop, the last in some of the quarries, with a few other inconspicuous species.

Yet the surface is described as bare, which means that it is a great green, treeless, upland waste, characterised by a fine freedom of light and air. Where there is soil enough over the stone for the moles to bury in (and that is generally the case), there is a covering of the fine-leaved sort of grass already mentioned with its roots matted together to form a springy turf from which the water percolates rapidly, only leaving moisture enough for the growth of such things as above described.

Shade can well be dispensed with here, as the breezes are always moving over the common, and in the warmest weather the heat is never felt to be very great for that reason. But in winter, when the storms sweep over the hills, the weather is keenly felt, and there is no shelter against the rain when you are overtaken by a downpour on the common at any season. You must needs get wet.

Animal life is in perpetual evidence. The human species itself is of diurnal visitation. Men are very likely to be found at work in at least one of the quarries, probably in that yielding the freestone ; quarry-men and masons taking the produce of the common in building-stone by blasting-charge and wedge, and working it with stone-axe, mallet and chisel, or other tools of the craft. A visit to the quarries may be made in search of fossils, in which the Oolite is so rich, and though the Rolling Bank Quarry, that is so extraordinarily fossiliferous, is not now in work, plenty of fossils can be picked up there. Other members of humanity are sure to be met with in that part of the common where the golf links are laid out. Mankind is but rarely encountered in the more remote quarters and corners, the ground chiefly occupied being the limited round with its fixed object of golf. The magnificence of the views obtained from the high ground which are too wide and numerous to pall by frequent reviewing, and the freshness of the air that moves above the short, dry grass, add to the attractions of the golf-course for those who play here. Other folk come too, whose movements are even more limited than are those of the people whose interest centres in the little white ball which, with adroit stroke, is lifted up the bank or driven well over the quarry. Amongst those who come and do not play golf most are content with a small amount of exercise and with sitting in the sun upon the seats on the slope, or at the tables in the tea-gardens, whilst only a few are of such energetic turn as to venture away with vigorous stride to the further sides, dipping into Watery Bottom, or steering for the West Down, where solitude reigns so far as human beings are concerned, but where silence is broken by the language of wilder creatures, the song of many soaring larks, the scream of the peewit, the chat-chat of the wheat-ear and the stone-chat, the jew's-harp whistle of the flying linnets, or the startling swish of many wings where the flock of field-fares sweeps into the combe to settle for the night. Over there the rabbits scamper, suddenly showing their white tails as signs of alarm, amongst the furze. The occasional hare leaps up from her lair in the grass, and a brace of partridges are sometimes put up and go heavily whirring over the wall into the neighbouring field, and even a fox may, at long intervals, be seen galloping over a stretch of open common to leap the bordering wall or slink silently away through the furze bushes.

The sheep, cattle and horses enjoy a wide liberty over this great common, wandering to what parts they choose. The sheep, for the greater part, do not casually mix together, those seen in any particular neighbourhood belonging to the same owner, as evidenced by their bearing the same mark, though there be numerous differently owned flocks upon the common, marked in accordance with their ownership. The flock sometimes migrates from one part of the common to another in search of new feeding-grounds, the individual sheep following each other in single file by narrow tracks. The horses and cattle are more generally cosmopolitan and less inclined to adhere to original clanship.

Sometimes you meet the hayward who gives his attention to the general condition of the turf and the domestic animals turned out upon it, being employed by the Conservators for that purpose. The hayward not only sees to the safety and feeding of the sheep, cattle and horses, but takes care that the right of pasture is strictly reserved to the commoners. He also reports the infraction of any of the bye-laws, made for the management and regulation of the use of the common, to the Conservators, who may sue for the fine. The hayward guards the sward and, assisted by his collie, shepherds the flocks, the individual sheep of which bear the initials of their owners stamped in pitch upon their sides or quarters. He has but to utter his shrill whistle for the sheep to begin to run together to be driven, at sheep-washing time, to Watery Bottom, or home to the farm to which they belong to be shorn and re-marked ; or, at dipping-time, to acquire immunity from the terrible mutilating fly. He also gives an eye to the condition of the young cattle and to the ever hungry horses.

All these and other things may be discovered by the more intrepid and observant visitant. The earth and sky upon the common face each other openly, and the country lies broadly around. There is liberty here if anywhere. The width and height of view is entrancing during the daytime, grand and awe-inspiring when the stars are out. Here is turf and turf beyond, so untiring to foot that to walk upon it is a pleasure in itself, whether it be done in pursuit of golf or with no other object than healthful exercise with the passive expectancy of whatever hazard may bring to please the eye and ear, or move the mind to contemplation.

PART II.—A Round of Rambles over and about Cleeve Hill.

CHAPTER V.

RAMBLES OVER THE GREAT COMMON.

It is as glorious a May day as can well be with everything pertaining to the Maytide season showing. Along the undercliff the afternoon sun is shining with full power. House-martins are skimming the ground there, swifts are wheeling in the higher air and the cuckoo is heard down in the orchards of Woodmancote. A pair of wheat-ears, or horse-matchers, as they are locally called, fly along the banky ground beyond the golf-club house and settle to utter their cry of "Chat-chat, chat-chat-chat," before flying farther along to the next prominent mound. By the wall of the Thrift Wood is heard the soft coo of brooding doves, and it is possible to distinguish there the voice of the wood-pigeon from that of the turtle. A rocky knoll in the wood seen over the wall is covered with blossoming Solomon's Seal and the cool, green leaves of wild lily-of-the-valley, and blue-bells shine in purple glamour farther away beneath the trees.

I climb the cliff face by the wooden rail that comes down it to guard the quarried front of the cliff and there disturb a pair of blue rock-doves as well as a number of jackdaws that have their nests in the holes and crevices of the rocks. The jackdaws fly upward and circle round, uttering their "Jack-jack" in the various shades of tone which convey the meanings of their language, such as one may express in the simple ejaculation of "O!" according to its length and intonation.

Arrived at the breezy surface of the cliff-top the wonderful sight of the great vale in spring-time spreads its illimitable and enchanted scene before the eyes. The plum blossom has gone, but that of the apple and pear-trees dapples the orchards of Woodmancote and Bishop's Cleeve with pink and white. The bright green of the meadows is washed with the gilt of buttercups, and the budding foliage of the trees, not yet entirely out or covering the brown branches, is flushing the country with a tender new life. The brilliant green of the young corn now covers the fields where the brown ploughing had its place, and the bareness of the country's winter aspect is changed to these quickening delights of coming summer.

Away down the common under the bright sky the cool airs move over the high land above the springy turf, that is so pleasant and untiring to the tread, and the spirits rise to an equality with place and season and weather. In the grass are the white specks made by the small flowers of the purging-flax, and numerous other plants are again in flower and humble-bees abroad, buzzing in zigzag flight over the lengthy expanses of sun-warmed greensward. Again the ewes with their lambs dot the sides of Dry Bottom and Watery Bottom. Rooks and lapwings are on the common, walking or flying about; the lapwings running over the turf with nodding crests, or flying close around uttering their weird cry of "Pee-wheet, pee-wheet!" Pipits are running on the grass, and skylarks, and many of the latter are singing in the sky. Linnets also fly past, uttering their sweet little song as they go, full of the happiness of the moment.

Far down the common where grows the furze, between the bushes are interspaces of mossy grass, and some of the older and less densely-grown shrubs spread their twisted stumps to obstruct the passage and catch the toe of the unwary interloper. The yellow flowers are surrounded by spines sharp and long, providing the penalty for any attempt to gather them. A rabbit disturbed from his slumber in a clump of long grass leaps an obstructing portion of the furze as he makes for his sandy hole. A linnet leaves her nest, situated on a dense, high spray of one of the larger bushes, and her mate is warbling near by. A pair of stone-chats have also a nest in the furze. The male sits on a spray uttering his persistent "Chut-chut, psee chut-chut, psee-psee chut." He is a smart bird with black head, partially white collar, breast of orange-red and wings and back of red-brown with darker markings, varied with a few white feathers. He flies out to catch a fly and returns to the exact place of his former perch to wait the advent of another.

It is pleasant to lie down amongst the bushes where the golden blossoms are brightly glowing in the sunshine. The grass is dry and soft, and the little blue milkwort and yellow tormentil are in flower amongst it there. From the bushes is exhaled the faint, peculiar odour of the gorse blossom that you like and dislike by turn, as if it were compounded of the thorn as well as of the golden flower. Several larks are soaring near by, singing unceasingly, and as some come down others go up. The eye seeks them gazing upward into the blue and white sky, whilst the mind wonders how they are so sustained in the double effort of flight and song. Up, up they spring with bill directed heavenward, carolling aloud whilst still near to earth, but quickly mounting through the first part of their upward journey, then, when far and small, rising still by broad and easier spirals, increasing the altitude at each turn whilst never ceasing to sing. At last they rest on outspread wings and parachute back to earth, singing still a shrill, ecstatic crescendo, until within a few feet of the ground.

I rise and direct my steps down Watery Bottom. This combe divides towards its top into a main and a minor gulch and is broadly splayed upward towards the highest part of the common. These broad upward slopes, scantily set about with furze, form a semi-amphitheatre in which lie two golf-greens. I go down the deeper gulch whose sides are marked with successive sheep-tracks, one above another. The view to the outlet of the valley is at first cut off, and the steep grassy slopes that bound the bottom and lie in front are reminiscent of mountain moorland. The hollow gives a couple of turns, and after the second the larch plantations about the buildings of Postlip, and parts of those buildings, with more distant hills beyond, come into view in the mouth of the combe. The sides of this grow high and steep where tippings of the spoil of stone-quarries, situated above, have been cast down the sides, and numerous great stones lie about, requiring to be avoided in passing by. Presently the moist nature of the ground in the bottom indicates the near

CLEEVE COMMON—THE UNDERCLIFF.

THE THREE SISTERS.

THE ROMAN CAMP.

CLEEVE COMMON.

neighbourhood of clay, and, just below that, a strong spring of water bursts forth from under rocks and immediately forms a considerable stream which now streaks the bottom straight before me. The water in this brooklet is crystal clear and suitable to drink. There is evidence, near the spring, of a fire having been lighted to make tea by some party who has recently been there. The stream in the first part of its course runs over many loose stones, some of which are but half immersed, and upon these a pair of water-wagtails, smooth and dandily neat of limb and feather, are disporting themselves.

The brook formed at the spring, after flowing two hundred yards or less, fills a little pond whose purpose as a store of water is evident at this moment, for the sheep-pen, situated near the wall of the common just below, contains a flock of sheep that are being washed prior to their shearing. Against the sheep-pen is the stone-built, circular basin, or wash-pool, of Cleeve Common, which, for a period of two or three weeks at this season, is in constant use. The water from the pool above, that ordinarily flows past the wash-pool to continue the brook, is directed at such times into the basin, this being filled to the point of convenient overflow, whilst the stream continues to pour into it from a broad spout at one side. The sheep are thrown into the water, one at a time, by two men who, standing on either side of the animal, join their hands below its body and so lift and swing it over the brink of the washing-place. As the sheep swim they are caught by the neck by a long pole with some sort of crook at its end, and directed under the spout, their wool being also sometimes moved a little by a rake or other instrument. Within a minute or two they are allowed to swim off and scramble out up a built inclined gangway by which they reach dry ground again, dripping and baa-ing, but no worse for their involuntary immersion.

From watching the sheep-washing I return to Cleeve Hill along by the wall of Postlip Hall garden and up the trackway that joins the ancient road from Winchcomb to Cleeve Hill, and then by that old road. A little flowery meadow near Post-lip makes a brilliant yellow setting for several hawthorns that are white with may-bloom. The larches in the small copse that runs up from the brook to the stile where the footpath going towards the Hall crosses the meadow, and those in the spinney above the old chapel, are scenting the air and looking lovely with their slender branches tufted with new green needle-leaves, amongst which are young cones of a delicate pink shade. The enclosed ground that thrusts itself up the side of the common and through whose two gates I pass in returning is in sainfoin, now splendid with its pink and purple blossoms, and in a corner towards the gate a bunch of white lychnis and a big yellow hawkweed vary pleasantly the gorgeous and scented surface of the field.

It is again a day in summer with the season a little more fully advanced. The afternoon sun is shining full upon the undercliff, and making a sharp distinction between light and shadow in the gardens below, where visitors are regaling themselves at tables situated in the sunshine, or within the cooler recesses of open-fronted arbours near by sweet-smelling lilac bushes, and the laburnum's golden chains. The gay conversation and laughter and show of holiday apparel betoken the presence of youth that is potential for pleasure and enjoyment of living. This spreads itself from the tea-houses up the steep grassy slope of the common behind, where parties sit in couples and companies to sun themselves, or lean to the stiff climb that will bring them, after some rests for breath and gazing backward, to the more bracing summit.

Looking from the prominent knoll called Ben's Tump, which is towards the edge of the common, near the golf club, those tea-houses are within sight, as well as the happy humanity scattered along the side of the slope and about the quarries and broken ground by which its green surface is diversified. Along that way, towards the stone-built racing stables, goes the rutty old Winchcomb road, and outside the wall of the common stretches of the smooth white main road are seen, where it passes up to its highest point by some of the houses that count to Cleeve Hill.

From the same spot there is a fine prospect to the North-West where the broad Severn Valley extends with its numerous fields, and villages near and far. A light smoke hangs over the houses of Tewkesbury, and the Malvern Hills are just visible, showing through the hazy atmosphere in the same direction. Over in front is the beautiful side of Nottingham Hill. Round to the left lies Gloucester with its backing of the dark hills of Dean Forest, and Cheltenham with all its spires and towers in the nearer distance.

Climbing the hill slantingly, I strike the road that rises to the top of the Common from "Rising Sun" Lane, and by it pass up easily to the summit, and so along the top of the precipitous cliff that is called Cleeve Cloud. This cliff top is a pleasing airy place, with turf that is particularly nice to rest upon in dry weather, the grass being short and soft. Some bare rocks jut out from the cliff's face and cut the view of the vale towards where Cheltenham lies when you stand behind them. Below the cliff lies the Thrift Wood, occupying a part of the declivity, and showing its bushes and undergrowth in a bird's-eye view from above, as a sight of rich foliage, with shades of green varied by tinges of yellow and blue in ash and oak, hazel, beech and elder.

A little further along, the cliff immediately overlooks the very uneven tumbled ground that surrounds the small fenced-off patch called Nutter's Wood with its half-dozen small houses. The cliff being quarried is guarded by an iron railing. Just here one end of the trenches of the Roman Camp gives on to the precipitous cliff, and the arc of the trenches being followed round again comes back to the cliff near the wall of the common. In that prominent corner outside the camp grow the three beeches called the Three Sisters, and finding a wooden seat near them I sit for a time. Some few golfers come into distant sight, the golf hole being at the other end of the entrenchments. On my left the edge of the hills sweeps round to enclose Cheltenham in a wide semicircle where the town lies at the border of the vale. The woodlands by which the green hillsides are patched show in different shades of green as they consist of larch, beech or other trees. The upper border of the larger local holt called Queen's Wood shows a quarter of a mile away, below and to the left side of the camp.

On the common and within sight of the cliff, where the ground swells upward into a prominence, grows a little clump of sapling beeches within a guard of palings, and here I come and stand a moment to take note of the relations of the several parts of this great enclosure. A treeless tract of grass-covered land extends from the cliff behind me, where the Roman Camp is in sight, and sweeps far beyond this mound. A stretch of nearly level ground, limited and followed by a long stone wall, passes away on the right side, till grassy surface and wall sink together out of sight where the common goes down its narrow part more than a mile away. On the left the ground towards the cliff is uneven and presently broken by old stone quarries before it rises to the highest part of the cliff above the houses of Cleeve Hill. On this side further from the cliff are the marked variations of surface occasioned by those deep bottoms that run in from the North-Eastward and cut into the heart of the common.

I now walk over continuous turf along the tops of the first two of these combes—Dry Bottom and Watery Bottom—looking down them in succession to get different views of the coloured side of Langley Hill and the Vale of Winchcomb, with other hills of the Cotswold line that pass away behind that town to distance beyond distance.

Keeping on along the high ground to right of the furze, I gain a view into the interior part of the North Cotswolds, seeing fields and ridges of cultivated ground with lines of trees and more coppices, one ridge partly hiding another through a dozen miles of country. In view from here is that field at whose top corner is situated the ancient barrow called Belas Knap, which you shall visit with me upon another day, and with a glass may be seen a portion of that farthest ridge that comes within the title of the Cotswolds, and which overlooks the Evenlode River, and bears the look-out tower of Icomb, to which also I shall at last bring you.

Then I come to the head of the third combe of Cleeve Common—Padcomb Bottom, which rises to its highest part at the very point where the common becomes constricted into that narrow part called the West Down.

I turn down the side of this deep and narrow ravine whose

sides are roughened with furze and thorns, though bare and grassy at the very bottom where runs the wall. Over that wall on my right front is a very rough field, and beyond that is the wood of Corndean, called Breakheart Plantation, occupying the opposite slope. The steep surface of the wood is charmingly clothed with firs, and with bracken that grows between the trunks. As I rise out of the bottom to pass amongst the gorse on my left near where the enclosing walls of the common make a corner, I look over green banks to discover the chimney of the Postlip paper-mill sunk down among many trees where the valley is opening out to a larger landscape, in which, as I rise on to yet higher ground, I see Winchcomb showing very prettily. I go by the adjacent hill covered with long rough grass that bears the name of Postlip Warren, where, though not very distant, I am remote from the visitors to Cleeve Hill, because the other two deep bottoms of the common lie between me and them and the direct way across is laborious. To avoid that labour I now strike back through more furze that lies at the upper side of Watery Bottom and make the detour necessary to return without sinking deep into the combes ; for the further way, round their higher ends, is much less tiring to traverse.

Upon an autumn day I climb straight up to the top of the steep slope above "Malvern View" and the tramway terminus to find the whole grassy hillside flecked with thistle down. The stemless thistles have shed their winged fruits, and many of these are still sailing before the September breeze. They perceptibly thicken the air as with a fairy burden of softest and lightest gossamer, far less substantial than the finest snow flakes, or even the driving cloud, and more resemblant of smoke. Some float down the hill and fly about the gardens, and go astray through the windows into the rooms of the Cleeve Hill habitations, thus losing their purpose perhaps, though there is still a chance that they may be again brought forth in the dust and be thrown upon some place suitable for their development into new thistles.

Going over the top I find some golf players at the tee

whose drive is straight down to a green situated in the head of Dry Bottom. One stroke should put the ball on to the green, in fact the hole has occasionally been made in one stroke by lucky chance.

I pass down to the green with the players, and notice that it lies behind a mound of earth erected across the lowest part of the bottom to carry an old cart track that comes here down the side of the combe, having entered the common by the gate from the lane that crosses from Nottingham Hill at the highest part of the Cleeve Hill main-road. It is, in fact, the continuation of that very ancient road called Greenway or Grinnell Lane, which after passing over the whole length of Nottingham Hill, and through the portway of the entrenchments on that hill, goes by here over Cleeve Common. At this point it is joined by a second and similar track that comes up the bottom of the combe in continuation of an old road from Winchcomb, and the two roads pass over the longer side of the common together to gain the villages that lie beyond in the interior Cotswolds. A third similar track is the one that rises steeply from the " Rising Sun " to pass in the same direction as the others and ultimately become indistinguishable from them.

I walk down Dry Bottom by the side of one of these old tracks that represent the original roads which sufficed in ancient times when travelling was as slow, difficult and dangerous as their appearance to-day suggests. Probably they were here before the Romans came, passing up the hollow much as they do now, the couple of thousand years that have elapsed since then not being a long time as compared with the time Nature has required to make this combe, for it has doubtless resulted from a natural erosion caused by the running water of the rains, the solid material of the hill having been gradually washed away. But when I come to the tipping of the spoil of a stone quarry, that has its place above, the pale buff refuse stone and earth having been thrown down so as to lie across and partly hide the view down the bottom, I pick up a stone to contemplate the limey Oolitic particles of those layers that largely make the hill in which the combe has been eroded, and whose laying down from a supernatant ocean naturally preceded the emergence from the waters of this land, and was indefinitely anterior to the modification of the surface by the rainwater. Indeed the contemplation of the geological evidence supplied in this stone requires a length of time for the existence and continuance in unwritten history of this old earth such as confuses all thought.

Dry Bottom is so called because it has no spring or water observable in it, thus differing from its fellow combe Watery Bottom, already described. That there would be underground water flowing down its incline is, however, a natural expectation, and this must somewhere find an outbreak. So it does in fact, in the little coppice that faces the head of the bottom towards Postlip. Here amongst the trees just over the wall that separates the common from the copse there is a built cistern into which the spring at first discharges to make a water supply for the neighbouring Postlip Hall, and the copious overflow runs away down under the trees to form another little stream. I come to the wall, and, looking over it, I see amongst the undergrowth there several plants of belladonna. Their fine purple bell flowers have gone, leaving flat dark button-like fruit, which looks luscious but must not be tasted.

I climb the extremely steep side of Dry Bottom to directly gain the higher ground upon my return, glancing back but once over the mouth of the combe, its quarry tippings, rabbit holes and group of young cattle, to Postlip Warren beyond, and the rude wooden cross that stands on its crest. This might have denoted that a recent holder of the domain was of Roman Catholic faith and that the small, old chapel of the neighbouring hall, towards which I look as the thought strikes me, had gone back to the service of Mass and Vespers to which it was originally accustomed. However that might be and to whomsoever the property may at any time hereafter belong, the cross ought to be maintained on the hill, as it is an addition to the scene, as viewed from near or far away, that is not without its appeal.

Towards the top of the ridge I pass a company of young horses that are enjoying the great freedom of life and movement that the common affords, and down the opposite slope there is a considerable scattering of sheep. I notice the white side of the freestone quarry, and passing along its upper fenced border, I look down to the shedding and implements that show it to be in work equally with the clang of tools that ascends from where the men are handling the blocks of stone that have been won from the face of the rocks exposed above. Some steps further along I descend to approach the entrance to another quarry which presents a different appearance from the one just passed in that its sides and spoil heaps are of darker reddish hue. This is the "Rolling Bank Quarry," whose fossiliferous agglomerations have been taken from time to time for use in metalling the rougher roads of the neighbourhood.

This Rolling Bank Quarry stands pre-eminent amongst all quarries available, as a sort of geological El Dorado for collecting fossils pertaining to the Inferior Oolite. Although considerable intervals sometimes elapse between the times when quarrying leaves off and recommences, a sufficient number of fossils will be found in the neighbouring spoil at all times to provide an addition to the collection of the amateur geologist, who will no doubt study Mr. Richardson's book for a knowledge of the various strata exposed here and in other quarries on the common or in its neighbourhood, and of the fossils they respectively yield.

By an artless observation of the surface of the tipped refuse and of the crumbling pieces of rock that have fallen from the quarry face I am able to fill my pockets with specimens of a score of different fossils with intent to photograph them in their natural state. The fossils of this quarry include the great spiral Bourguetia and heavy Nautilus if these have not been all removed for garden decorations or similar purpose for which they are sometimes sought, and the mushroom-shaped Clypheus, derived from the top layer of the quarry, is lying about with various species of Terebratula, Rhynchonella, worm-bored rock and other remnants of ancient life pertaining to the sea and the seashore.

Present time passes quickly with one who searches for these things in such a place, turning over stones or trying to free a fossil from its hard matrix with hammer taps, or halting to rub with appreciation, a clear and well-formed specimen, and so it comes to evening and change of weather whilst I tarry in the quarry. A commencing rain awakes me to the hour, and I descend to the house which is not far off, for the quarry faces the Cleeve Hill high-road and the great vale. The latter presents as I descend a smeared and aqueous tableau beneath a leaden sky, though a line of livid light, extending from where the sun has set, defines the Malvern Hills, where they stretch across the vale, in dark metallic tone.

On the undercliff I meet a friend returning to the Golf Club, who asks me if I am interested to hear that there is a drove of golden plover on the common. He tells me they are over towards "The Cloud." Going that way I notice that the voices of the golf-players sound with extraordinary clearness. The prevailing atmospheric condition must be the cause of this.

The October evening is fine, but a clean fog lies thick in the valley and overspreads the hill-top with a thinner grey pall slightly tinged with pink in the clearer sky straight above—all soft and pearly. The thin crescent of the young moon is in the Western sky, her yellow colour deepened into dark orange by the mist which is condensing upon every suitable surface. A slight wind moves from the East, driving the mist at an almost imperceptible speed before it. It wets my garments and condenses upon my walking stick, making it very wet except the first few inches below the handle, where condensation is prevented by the warmth of the hand.

I hear some peewits utter their cry as I walk down the common from the Roman Camp towards West Down and see one plainly as it flaps a slow flight not far away, and I think my friend has mistaken the cry, heard at a distance, for that of the golden plover. I have been expecting to put up the drove, if there indeed be one settled upon the grass, and think to be made aware of the presence of the birds at least by the sound of their wings. When I turn for home, however, I hear an unaccustomed sound—a clear, short, metallic pipe—and, walking in the direction whence it comes, I draw near it when it is repeated and answered from afar. Then, when I have walked nearer, I hear the sound once more, this time surprisingly near. It is sharply doubled into a curious longer note and then ceases. I walk on in the direction but see no bird. It is now seven o'clock and too dark and misty to see him unless he rises quite near to me. He must have got up very silently or, perhaps, run away noiselessly over the grass. I walk further and hear the same thing repeated in several directions. I am evidently in the middle of the drove. The sound seeming very near me in one direction, I run suddenly and quickly towards it but see nothing and hear no wings, only the pipe is not repeated just there. The flight of golden plover must have settled here for the night whilst passing to more permanent quarters, and their sentinels have given warning of my presence.

It is a mid-winter day—January 6th. There has been some mild weather with rain, and the earth is moist. I walk up on to the common and make for the West Down. There is a breeze from the North-West, the grass is clean and soft to the foot as ever, and the usual exaltation is felt in breathing the keen, bracing air. As I come to the top strength and spirits seem to rise 100 per cent. I pass one party of golf-players and four mounted officers of the troops at this time stationed in Cheltenham, otherwise I am alone. The distant views are misty and yet visible. The Brecknockshire Mountains can just be seen, and the Forest Hills show their dark outline. Looking toward Gloucester a heavy cloud appears to be drifting over that city, shedding streamers of rain which temporarily hide the cathedral tower. When I am walking in the West Down the soldier horsemen ride past me and presently meet me on the return as they are galloping up the straight mile and a half of splendid turf that is there afforded. I walk to the very end of the common where the track passes through a gate to join, in a further mile, the made road near the village of Charlton Abbots. I see nothing alive in passing among the furze that grows towards the bottom of West Down, nor elsewhere. Yet there is something eloquent in the green turf and the hardy furze over which the weather seems to be brooding.

In returning it is harder walking against the slope, slight as it is, of West Down, and the wind is now in front. But the increased resistance and freshness of air are only the more invigorating, and some spots of rain carried wildly down the wind rather add to the enjoyment.

As I come along near the Roman Camp towards the cliff the sun is setting far back over the lower Severn Valley, well below Gloucester. He is splendid! His face before he sinks is the colour of flame when there is lime in the fuel. There are threatening masses of smoky cloud above, and those just over the sun are tinged with fire like the smoke of a great open furnace, whilst the face of the dun cloud-rolls above and along is all coppery in hue. In spaces where no cloud is beautiful pale blue streaks lie in the further depths of the sky. Below the glowing clouds is the sweep of circling hills behind Cheltenham and that town lying damp and darkling at their foot. Down there the smoke and fog and white steam from trains sluggishly cling about the houses, unable to rise or be quickly dispersed. On the other side of the heavens opposite to the sunset, and particularly in the North-East, the reddened clouds reflect a part of the glory, and elsewhere, towards the zenith, where the lower moving stratum remains of the colour of slate, higher and lighter clouds can be seen through interspaces that are all tinged to pale rose. The moon, that is close upon the full, also shows her polished brass disc, high in the East, where uncovered by the drifting wrack.

CHAPTER VI.

RAMBLES OVER THE GREAT COMMON—*continued.*

IT is July the ninth when I wander up on to the common in the afternoon without definite end. The thistles of various sorts in one part and another are all in bloom. In this locality and that I meet with several species. The grass of the common through large areas is marked with scattered purple splashes where grow the stemless sort, and in places there are handsome, nodding musk thistles and tall, ragged marsh thistles, some whitish and some purple, and the great cottony-headed eryophorus, with dullish claret-purple tops, and the thistle, pretty typical of the Scottish emblem, with its strong, lance-shaped, prickly leaves and its shapely flower-receptacles ; also pale mauve field thistles and the yellow carline thistle, the latter chiefly where the soil is thin and the stony undersoil very near the surface, and the former over the wall in the cultivated field. One would need to be an enthusiastic botanist who ventured to gather a bundle of all the sorts.

There are other flowers in the grass, including the close-growing Clustered Woodruff (*Asperula cynanchica*), that sprinkles the ground white in patches like salt. Purple sprigs of wild thyme grow along the edge of the ancient track-way, and the scattered yellows of rock-rose, bird's-foot trefoil, hop trefoil and horse-shoe vetch are in evidence. Towards the head of the freestone quarry are flowers of milk vetch and cross-leaved bedstraw and, under the edge of the quarry, a bunch of houndstongue whose flowers are past. On the further side of the common are pale mauve gentians, though they are not yet in full flower. There are euphrasias and bartsias and other small stuff on the rougher ground, where also the little frog-orchis may be found, as well as the bee-orchis.

A good-sized flock of starlings are on the grass along with the rooks and daws, most of them being young of this season in their first plumage. Very soon after the young starlings leave the nest they flock together with others of their kind. There are larks and tit-larks, or pipits, in numbers, and I see a young cuckoo, quite strong on the wing, but assiduously followed by a pair of small brown birds, his foster parents, which in the distance look like pipits. There are peewits, too; they are never absent from the common for any length of time.

I come along the top where some banks have been thrown up as bunkers for the golf-course and so round by the back of the Punch-bowl Quarries and down through the furze to the head of Padcomb Bottom. From the bit of copse by the bridle-gate down in the hollow there I disturb some turtle doves, which are plentiful birds enough in this region at this time of year. Through this gate I pass to go by the footpath on its other side, towards Wontley Farm. Just through the gate is much lady's-mantle, growing weed-like and flowering inconspicuously. In the field, before arriving at the farmstead, are two mares with their foals, one of the mares being an old grey, and her colt, though at present almost black with a few grey hairs, is destined, I know, to grow as white as his mother—if he lives long enough.

By this lone farmstead the land begins to form a shallow bottom, straight down which my road lies. Near the buildings are a good number of house-martins and a pair or two of swallows. I bethink me that had the house not been there the birds would never have halted in so out-of-the world a place, for the habitual association of martins and swallows with man and his habitations and buildings is one of the curiosities of Nature. The martins and swallows so confide in humankind.

At Wontley Farm, as I pass, I notice a cart-shed with a granary over it, a small house, a big barn, some cow-byres, a group of fine ash trees and a drinking pond at the corner of three enclosures, the fences going through its centre to render it available for the cattle in either of two fields and the farm-yard.

Lower down the shallow bottom I come to another house

at the corner of a wood; both house and wood are known as West Wood. Below the house the bottom forms a wide green drive between wooded banks on either side, but the greater part of the wood lies up the steep on my left. By the side of the rough track that runs down the glade, which is no doubt a trifle damp, I notice many leaves of colchicum surrounding the fruit developed from the purple crocus-like flowers of last October; also some flowering specimens of the not common plant *Geum rivale*. This is also a neighbourhood for wild lilies-of-the-valley whose season is now a good month past. Wild strawberries grow on the neighbouring banks in quantity.

Through a bridle gate on the left I enter West Wood by a steep path, with a surface of loose Oolitic stones, which passes up the wood. Here I find myself in intimate connection with what the wood contains. The larger growth chiefly consists of oak, but the underwood presents a great variety in hazel, maple, ash, buckthorn, spindle-tree, cornel, privet, elder, whitebeam, wayfaring-tree, holly and other species of small tree and shrub, with over-climbing clematis, woodbine, briony and the rest. There are pigeons in the wood, and a jay, and probably a fox has not long since passed across the path and is still in the wood, judging from the strong scent that assails the nostrils at the point where his trail lies. A woodpecker of some species is making the branch of an oak ring and reverberate sharply by the strokes he is delivering with his bill.

I come down again into the glade and follow the track that continues for yet half a mile along the border of West Wood, and by a high hedge where the blackbirds are uttering their note of alarm, and a nest of young bullfinches, with their parent birds, fly along in front of me for some distance until, growing tired of being so driven, they leave the hedge and take a circular flight back towards the wood.

I go past the junction of the track that comes to join the road here from the extreme end of the narrow part of Cleeve Common called the West Down, and, at length, I come to the main road that runs by Sevenhampton to Winchcomb and see opposite to me the bye-road that rises up a steep hill to

SPRING AND STREAM IN WATERY BOTTOM.

BRIDLE GATE IN PADCOMB BOTTOM LEADING TO WONTLEY FARM.

CLEEVE COMMON.

THE HIGH-ROAD AT TRAM TERMINUS.
(COMMON ENTERED HERE ON RIGHT.)

THE LOWER PART OF DRY BOTTOM WITH WINCHCOMB VALLEY.

CLEEVE COMMON.

Roel Gate. I stand a moment meditating whether or not to go up there, but a spot of rain striking my cheek determines me not to venture that way. I turn along the road towards Winchcomb and, at the end of half a mile, find myself at the small village of Charlton Abbots.

A change has come over the summer day; the sky is assuming a leaden hue, with darker clouds arising, and a fine rain begins to fall. Hoping it may cease, I enter a farm-yard and take refuge under a Dutch barn, or open-sided shed, where I meet a shepherd and get into conversation with him, staying on in the supposition that the rain is but a passing summer shower and that, presently, the clouds will lift. This, however, proves to be a forlorn hope, as the sky soon becomes covered with evenly-spread rain-cloud, and the chance of a wet night grows greater as darkness approaches. Thus it comes to pass that I overstay the daylight, for the walk this evening began late for so long a distance. It is nearer ten than nine o'clock by the sun's time and quite dark when I accept the shepherd's advice and start for home, taking the road he recommends that goes along the top of West Wood, as being nearest.

The unpleasant effect of the rain upon the cart-track is at once evident. It is now too dark to pick a path, and the conclusion is forced upon me that I am destined to get very wet. To take an unknown path in the dark is, moreover, a doubtful expedient, as is proved by the time I get to the end of the wood, when I lose the way in the darkness and have to fall back upon knowledge of general direction to get down into the bottom that leads up to Wontley Farm from the wood. I climb a wall to this end and leap down into a field of wet uncut mowing grass that reaches to the knees. I vainly seek a path in the long grass; I can, however, now see a light in the window of West Wood House, and I find the gate out of the mowing-grass that leads to the track in the bottom by which I had come. It is now quite night, and the continuous rain makes it a very dark one. I move up towards Wontley Farm and pass it without discerning the cottage, which is silent and dark, for the inhabitants have gone to bed. In the field beyond, of the two mares and their foals that I had seen on the outward walk, I have a dim glimpse of the white mare, and hear the others moving near me. Afterwards, as the path is near the edge of the field I find my way down to the gate in Padcomb Bottom without difficulty and have so reached the edge of Cleeve Common.

I have crossed the common to and from that point on several occasions and hope to do it now, but former experience in a fog has proved the ease of being temporarily lost on the open common. The rain has not abated, and the clouds and rain together make an Egyptian darkness.

Being now very wet, with shoe-leather sodden and feet a-slush, and my coat-sleeve heavy and cold with the absorbed rain, I prefer it to be a short rather than a long crossing. Rising up out of the bottom I endeavour to avoid the furze which grows so thickly on this part of the common above, but not with perfect success. At last I seem to have got clear of it and stride away over the grass in the apparently right direction. Soon, however, I find myself amongst the furze again, being suddenly tripped up by an old straggling stem. Afterwards I try to pick my way by means of my walking-stick held in front, striking forward to assure myself of the location of the furze bushes, and I seem to clear them and to be again upon the open ground beyond. I strike out quickly in what I hope to be the right direction ; though, by this time, having made many turns to avoid the furze, I am in extreme doubt of my bearings, and I am soon again amongst the bushes. I repeat the effort over and over again but am unable to get clear of the furze. I stop to think why that should be and take in this possibility : that, in walking in the dark, there might be a tendency to turn ever so little to one side, it being always the same side, and that would be sufficient to put me out of my course ; but, no doubt, the attempt to avoid the furze bushes has been the cause of greater divergence.

On a dark night with visible stars, the journey across Cleeve Common to the high-road could be made with ease and certainty. It would only require to walk continuously up a few points to the left of the North Star. Or a compass in such a situation, with a light from a few struck matches to look at it occasionally, would suffice. I have by this time had enough of the exposure to the wet and am desirous of getting home as quickly as possible. I turn over in my mind by what modes it is possible to ascertain direction and think first of these two and how I once found my way off Dartmoor when overtaken by night in the neighbourhood of Cranmere Pool by the star method, which is not now available ; and I have no compass. The rain, in heavier shower, striking my face viciously, gives the necessary fillip to my memory. I remember that when I took shelter in the shed at Charlton Abbots the rain had drifted in at one side and wetted the back of an iron water-cart that stood there, and I had stepped back further towards the other side of the shed to avoid it. The direction of the wind, judged from the position of that cart, must have been from the Northern side of the compass. There is still an emphatic slant in the rain which, at all events, gives a fixed point of direction. I stand straight and turn for the wind to blow on my right cheek and keep it there as I walk. This at once brings me out of the furze and, after some short time, to a place where the darkness seems suddenly to become more inky than before, which betokens some opaque object in front. Here my stick strikes the confining wall of the common, at the same time driving out some cattle that are harbouring there, for it is at a point where a little copse grows close to the wall in which there is a stile leading towards Prestbury Hill.

By following the wall along from this point I reach the Three Sisters and the Roman Camp at the edge of the cliff. Keeping away from the edge, I direct my steps along the top where I have been scores of times. I know I have to pass an old quarry, partly grass-grown, which is on the ground above the cliff and towards it. I pass part of it with care and, believing I have got beyond it, step boldly towards the whitish side at the further end, supposing that to be the beginning of the worn path that leads down the slope to the road. I leap at it eagerly. It is a mistake, and I fall some feet to the bottom of the pit and roll over among some weeds there which declare their nature in a positive way by stinging my face and hands. I recover myself, not much the worse, and soon afterwards reach home, when I find it is nearly two o'clock.

In the warm time of August I go forth at night, after all the house lights are extinguished. I walk up on to the top of the great common and, turning eastward, see the moon rising over Sudeley Hill. She comes up through a mist which glows about her in red layers, and, at first, I do not recognise that it is she, the appearance being as if some conflagration has broken out over there, and I stand still to wonder what it can be. This is soon made manifest. The moon rises an irregular, oval shape as she comes higher, leaving the dark-hued hill behind. Each minute she shows less red and more distinct as she clears the mist. Some thin clouds bar her path and are made beautiful by her light as they are blown slowly across her face. Ultimately, bright and perfect, she takes her place amongst the stars, partly eclipsing those in her neighbourhood by her greater light.

I walk down the opposite hillside to Postlip and see the moon shine through the tops of the larch trees there. Every branchlet is clearly outlined in a tender light. The tree-tops stand up pyramid-like, pointing to the stars in the zenith, and their shadows are cast distinctly on to the grass that is about the place where I stand.

Near Postlip Hall and outside its garden wall a spring empties itself into a grottoed stone receptacle, whose overflow sinks gurgling away to pass below the surface to the brook beyond the great house. A cup for the use of any passer-by stands upon the lip of the well. I take the cup and fill it and drink to the gibbous moon whose beams are glittering in the water.

Through the gate below I approach the front of the house and stand on the lawn before the five fine gables of its front, its several oriel windows and its beautiful arched doorway. My friends who live there are gone to bed, but a dull light burns behind a red blind in one of the front bed-chambers. The old hall stands silent and beautiful with the moonlight shining full upon it. Straight over its roof the seven chief stars of the Great Bear are standing in the sky.

Returning over the common I pass near a group of horses, and, about the old quarries that now form several pits covered with nice soft grass, I find a flock of sheep reclining in the moonlight in and about the pits, where they have settled down to pass the night. I enter one of the quarries and, approaching quietly, sit down among the sheep. Soon the ewe that is nearest me ceases to regard my presence with any curiosity, and another, that has got up, again lies down and continues quietly chewing her cud. I can see each "cud," or "quid," pass up and down her throat when she stays the movement of her jaws to swallow the portion chewed and to receive the next into her mouth from her many-valved first stomach. I count the bites she gives to each quid and find they average sixty-eight.

Some distance away down the misty slope I can hear some lapwings which are varying their usual cry of "pee-wheet" with a sort of mew, as they often do. A beetle or two buzz past; slight sounds come from the ruminating sheep, and I hear the dull, distant roar of a train. I can see on the sloping sides of the pit the shining points of light of several glow-worms. The moon and the stars are also still shining, and the sweet, dewy air of night is over all.

When presently I come back to the Cleeve Hill highway, the atmosphere being clear, the lights of the great Severn Vale show distinctly. There are those of the railway stations of Bishop's Cleeve and Ashchurch; a group of twinkling points denoting the position of Tewkesbury, and a fine long range of brilliantly gleaming lights where Malvern stands on its hill and altogether outshines Tewkesbury by reason of its elevated position permitting its many lamps being seen. Each lamp sends its rays with great power across the twenty miles of intervening space, and all the lamps together make such a brilliant illumination as to lead to doubts in the minds of new-comers to Cleeve Hill that the origin of the lights so plainly seen can be so far away.

It is a summer day when the members of the Cotteswold

Field Club come to Cleeve Hill. They have first listened to a lecture on " Pre-metallic Man " in the Cheltenham Museum and have then come by the tram-car, with their intelligences weighted with conjectures of antique humanity, based upon the testimony afforded by skulls reputed to be of prehistoric age and implements of flint and stone recovered from long hiding in cave or picked up upon the surface of the ploughed field. It is a preliminary well calculated to encourage the expression of any fancy or hypothesis, harboured in the ingenious minds of one or another of the members of the club, as to the origin of things to be met with on Cleeve Common.

The common is entered by the party at the " Rising Sun " lane, whence the cliff is ascended by the old road that passes to the summit at the Punch-bowl Quarries, and the route is then along the cliff called Cleeve Cloud to near the Roman Camp. Here the party sit down upon the green turf to eat lunch, whilst one member delivers himself of a broad, descriptive address upon Cleeve Common and its surroundings.

The beautiful summer day that favours the occasion, coming after a period of refreshing rain, is warm but not too hot by reason of the cooling effect of the breeze that moves, as usual, over the tops of the hills. A section of the party sit at the cliff-edge thirty yards away and gaze down into the misty vale whilst they converse together in disdain of the speaker whose back is towards them and whose harangue and gestures are directed to the group circled in front of him. The sun pours his rays upon the mist that fills the great Vale of Severn, but does not dissipate it. It is a July mist that lasts all day. It hides the distant scenes and horizons and shuts out the veritable objects described by the speaker as effectively as the mists of time, which are always present, hide the truths of antiquity that are presently to be guessed at by other talkers among the members of the Cotteswold Club. The speaker makes a call, therefore, upon their imaginations and asks them to take in faith what he says of the distant and the nearer landscapes, and in that way he also takes them round the whole ten-mile length of wall which encloses the great common, with the assistance of two small lengths of living hedge, and he speaks of the things and places it encloses and excludes, including the several old track-ways that cross its turf to find exit through gates in the wall at various points, leading to one place or another.

And then the President, tall, bearded, very learned in archæological studies pursued at home and abroad, distinguished among local authors, takes up the subject allotted to him and speaks of the camps, miscalled "Roman," which cap the prominent points of the Cotswold escarpment from end to end, as well as all the outliers. He enlarges upon their purpose and tells by whom they were most likely made; the state of this part of Britain at that era; the occurrence or non-occurrence of such camps elsewhere, and the names of the British tribes who lived in the neighbouring portions of hill and vale, and who were likely to have been at war with each other. The speaker also makes a score of little excursions into subjects that have little relation to the camps but which, out of his archæological erudition, very neatly and interestingly creep into his discourse.

After that there are quiet strolls across the common in company to other selected points, and it is the turn of the geologist, a very earnest specialist, who begins at a small quarry opposite the head of Dry Bottom where the "Harford Sands" form an outcrop. This layer of fine sand, agglomerated in part into boulder-like stone, has its occurrence as one of the several layers of rock that compose the Inferior Oolite, and why this sandy layer should be found interposed between limestone rocks in that situation wants explanation such as the most intelligent consideration can supply. Afterwards our geologist brings the party to the Rolling Bank Quarry, where there is much discussion as to the several zones exposed, each one yielding its own particular fossils,* and which now give opportunity for the study of the "Phillipsiana beds" and "the Bourguetia beds."

Coming back along the slope of the undercliff "The Ring" lies in the way and awakes speculative opinions as to

* For fuller description of the geology of Cleeve Hill see "Geology of Cheltenham and Neighbourhood," by L. Richardson.

its original object. Notwithstanding the circular fosse that gives the idea of its being a military work, the more likely view appears to be that it is an ancient arena for personal displays of skill and prowess, oratory and drama—the prototype of the modern stage, in fact. The sloping ground above lending itself so well to occupation by a crowd of onlookers, greatly assists this theory, the ditch being considered merely in the nature of a sunken fence between actors and audience.

Then comes the opportunity of the member who had studied the site of most ancient human occupation on Cleeve Common. That, too, is on the undercliff, above and South of the Golf Club Houses, where some sapling trees have been planted. Here is a considerable deposit of made ground, a hollow having been filled in with dark earth in which may be found numerous pieces of brick and pottery of the coarsest kind, some of it being merely sun-dried, with evidence of fire in burned stones as well as in burned clay—also numerous pieces of bone, more or less decayed. As to its representing dwellings—it hardly does that ; it only forms a small, flat surface on the slope of the common. Its contents are almost those of a refuse heap, though the refuse appears to be that of a long past era and is such as would be connected with a human settlement. It is consequently subject for both scepticism and enthusiasm, either of which states of mind is legitimate in the Cotteswold Field Club. Over bits of broken pottery and bone there is much scope for display of judgment and the argumentative faculty that is corrective as well as convincing. It all adds to the pleasurable intercourse of a body of men out for a holiday, who, combining the delights of country air and scene on Cleeve Common with gentle mental exercise over the objects above mentioned, enjoy themselves for two or three hours on this delectable hill and take away a happy memory of the meeting.

The meeting is, indeed, most pleasantly brought to an end by a refreshing tea at the house of a member * resident on Cleeve Hill, known to the University of Manchester, not only as a master of Science of that University, but as the donor of his monumental herbarium of dried plants, and

* Charles Bailey, M.Sc., F.L.S.

valuable library of books on Botany, Geography, Egyptology, etc., which at this time are on view to the members of the Cotteswold Field Club, as is also his beautiful garden that contains many living specimens of specially interesting plants.

CHAPTER VII.

TO BELAS KNAP AND BACK.

On the farther side of Cleeve Common, and a good mile beyond any part of its enclosing fence, in an elevated position near a wood, there is an elongated mound. From the highest ground of the common you can trace its position with the naked eye at a distance of two or three miles when, as the result of having been there, you have made the acquaintance of its exact locality. With a field-glass you can see, from this distance, that the mound is in the corner of a field, from which it is now separated by an enclosing dry-wall fence. The wood behind it is called Humblebee Wood, sometimes contracted to Hamley Wood, and the elevated corner where stands the mound is Humblebee Hough, or Hamley Hough (or How), so called by some of the natives of the town of Winchcomb, which lies below, almost within sight of the spot. Otherwise the mound itself is more widely known as Belas Knap. It is, in fact, one of those burial mounds, or barrows, that were raised by the ancient Britons—a long barrow, as distinguished from the other kind known as a round or short barrow.

The appellation "Belas Knap" is traditional. Some say it has been handed down from remote time when Bel, representing a materialistic deity, in which, perhaps, the sun and fire had a prominent part, was worshipped in this island. An idolatry of this sort was practised by the Phœnicians, who may have introduced it here when they were in trade communication with Britain, as we know they were. The word "Knap" means simply "knoll," "mound," or tumulus," and thus the barrow comes to be "Belas Knap." Other archæologists, however, scoff at this origin of the name and seek to derive it from some cognate British, or even Saxon, word.

When you come there you find the mound to be about sixty yards long and twenty-five yards wide, and standing ten feet or so above the level of the adjoining field, the direction in which it lies in its length being nearly North and South.

It is a burial place of an extraordinary sort, as are all barrows, connected with some great personage and some soul-stirring religious observance, or Druidical rite, that was considered of vast importance by the people who inhabited this region and which was part of a superstition by which those people were profoundly obsessed. The great dead were, at it seems, committed to the care of the god and sent along their eternal way with observances performed by aid of fire and, possibly, by human sacrifice.

The barrow, after remaining nearly intact through very many generations of men from whom it appears to have claimed a reverence that was continued from era to era, was opened to satisfy the cravings of archæological curiosity in the years 1863–4. It was found to consist of several cells, or chambers, rudely formed of great stones untouched by mason's tool, each chamber being the receptacle of a gruesome and suggestive content. There was a chamber at either end and one at either side of the barrow, as well as one towards the centre. The rest of the mound appears to have been made up of loose stones in a natural condition, thrown down to fill in the spaces between the chambers, and over them to create the whole knap, or barrow. A profusion of wood ashes in the surrounding soil showed that fire had been a part of the observance which had here taken place in honour of the fire god, the great dead, together with the victims, as they may have been, in part, at least, having been consigned in the midst of a funeral pyre of large dimensions. The red flames must have ascended high and, if the ceremony took place at night, must have been seen from afar and have shown the surrounding crowd of heathen, clothed, if at all, only partially, in untanned skins, and with their bodies stained with native dyes.

In the chambers were found more than thirty human skeletons, together with other human bones mixed with the bones and tusks of the wild boar; one of the skeletons presumably was that of a dead chief. In one cell were the skeletons of five children, varying from one to seven years of age, which were very suggestive of sacrifice. In another cell were the skeletons of twelve persons in a sitting posture. Some pieces of sun-dried pottery, a bone scoop and some flint arrow-heads were also found enclosed, which assisted in dating the barrow back to prehistoric time, being the remnant signs of the primitive age and state to which the human beings belonged who took part in the creation of Belas Knap, whether as principals, acting within and without the barrow, or as lookers-on.

From having been opened and plundered the great mound is now in a comparative state of ruin, but some of its openings, which are at the present time uncovered, remain in a fair state of preservation, so as to give a sufficiently good idea of the original construction. The entrance at the North end, for instance, is by an approach between stone-walling, widened, or splayed outwards, from where the opening to the cell is blocked by three great stones, two standing like posts and the third like a door between the others. The walling of the approach is without mortar, being simply built of superimposed stones; but these are much smaller than those used at the present for the dry-wall field fences of the Cotswolds and are very neatly and well laid, as may be judged from the fact of their having stood so long, the time being probably somewhere between 2,000 and 3,000 years. The stones used for filling in the interstices between the spaces and completing the mound are like those yielded by an old quarry immediately at hand, where any number of such flaky pieces are available. The larger stones, in a condition that required no touch of a tool, could also be obtained without difficulty from Cotswold quarries.

On a fine summer evening in the early part of July I started to walk from Cleeve Hill to Belas Knap. On entering the common I went to the left and upward by the freestone quarry that was in work, and over by the old grass-grown quarries that now make pleasant depressions in the surface of the common, with a delectable golf-hole in one of them

POSTLIP HALL

A RARE ARRAY OF GABLES AND ORIEL WINDOWS.

BELAS KNAP

THE MAIN ENTRANCE AT NORTH END OF THE BARROW.

and with furze growing near by, some of which was still in bloom. From here I descended the steep into the nearer part of Postlip Combe till I struck the old track-way that led me through a gate and down by the garden wall of Postlip Hall and, ultimately, round in front of this beautiful old Tudor house with all its great array of gables and oriel windows. Also by the fine barn hundreds of years old, that is built in great part of unmortared stones, but which is a very strong structure notwithstanding. The chirp of young birds came from the trees at Postlip, and the limes there, being in blossom, were alive with bees.

Having crossed the brook that rises at the spring in Watery Bottom, I went up under the branches of some chestnut-trees, by a triangular-shaped orchard, and passed along the lower edge of Postlip Warren, the wooden cross which stood upon its summit facing me immediately above.

The old road-track continued along the edge of some cultivated grounds that adjoin the warren, and along here was a view embracing Winchcomb and Sudeley. Fields where hay-making was in progress lay in the distance, and close to one side was a barley-crop with green, waving ears, covering the field with a silken surface of awns that rustled when rubbed together by the wind. Convolvulus was twining up the barley-stalks and, in places, thistles raised their mauve-coloured heads prettily above the pale green of the barley, and scarlet poppies made a brighter contrast with it. Down past where some mangold-wurzel showed their cool, richly-veined leaves, there was white cow-parsnip, and then, all down the descent into Padcomb Bottom, a tremendous display of violet-blue cranesbill now in fullest flower, with yellow vetchling in the hedge and much white clover blossoming in the grass, and big brambles overhanging the wall, whose pinkish-purple petals were beginning to show from woolly white calices, though their time to open was hardly yet.

The track comes into the bottom at a point so low down as to give the springs that rise out of its sides above a chance to form a considerable brook of clear, quick-running and noisy water that is here rudely forded by the old road. I crossed it, without difficulty or wetting of foot, at a spot some yards higher up than the ford, near where I observed dog-roses in blossom and vetch, myosotis, orchis and meadow-sweet, the latter in considerable store that scented the place.

Beyond the brook the track rose very steeply up a bank clothed with trees and shrubs, where the flowers of privet, woodbine and elder bloomed and mingled their scents. When I had attained some height I looked back over the deep bottom and along its steep side, where the first trees of Breakheart Plantation created an elegant patch of woodland, with firs and larches presenting in a minor way an almost alpine appearance on the slope, and with bare portions of Postlip Warren and Cleeve Common showing behind.

A little higher, near where a roadway to the right went to a cottage situated in the wood, and there was some amount of open ground, a portion was surrounded by wire-netting that left a space for the passage of the track in recognition of its being a public way. Within the netting were hen-coops dedicated to the use of pheasant-rearing, and a number of chicks, as yet quite young and about the size and appearance of quail, were running in the grass or answering to the cluck of their foster-mother hens.

The keeper was near at hand to object to anyone leaving the track-way, were it but to examine the specimens of "vermin" that were hanging to the wire-netting that separated the woodland from the path. Gibbeted there were hawks of both the common species that had met their death from the gun whilst hovering suspiciously in the neighbourhood; also a crow or two, a magpie, a jay and a weasel. All of these had paid the penalty of their character, which, though natural, is but too well known to be inimical to the welfare of young pheasants.

A little further on and upward the rude track-way changed to a made road of whitish-yellow colour, some six feet broad. Beside it, on all sides, grew the species of willow-herb commonly called "rose-bay"; its magenta petals and ruddy flower stalks producing the colour in this woodland which is so noticeable towards sunset when viewed from the distant ground of opposite hills. In places the red was intermingled with the violet of cranesbill, giving the roadside and the more open ground between the trees a fine appearance. On the right there was a thick wood composed of tall and straight-grown larches, and wood-pigeons were cooing there, the scolding tones of one father-pigeon being prominent amongst the rest. A little girl was gathering wild strawberries in an open part of the wood. Near the road in this locality the ground was partly covered with a wild tangle of brambles, briars and furze. To the left there was a pretty view down to Winchcomb and beyond, over a fallow of finely-coloured clean earth, the bright red-brown being strewn with buff stones, and on the ground adjacent were green crops, a patch of charlock of brilliant yellow, the crimson of sainfoin and the purple of clover, the neutral drab of the hay in cocks that was being carted, the blue-green distances of hill and vale, and the quiet blue and white of the July sky.

Proceeding, I passed an old roadside quarry on my right, whose high top was closely surrounded with dark green firs, some of the roots of which were showing through the yellow soil where they overlapped the quarry's upper edge and there was but a small interval between the masses of exposed buff Oolitic rock and the full-flowering rose-bay.

Only a little farther on I discovered Corndean Hall. I looked down on the house which lay below on the left where it is hidden from the vale by a belt of large trees and is overlooked by the tree-covered hill behind. It is a plain-looking house and presented its back towards me, with numerous farm out-houses which gave it the character of a grange, or house of a gentleman-farmer. High above the house and near where the road I had traversed makes junction with another that comes up from Winchcomb, I found a corner of banky ground covered with rough grass and bunches of rose-bay plants, with the gaudy heads of black mullein showing not far off. From here a fine and extensive scene presented itself, including the best distant view of the town of Winchcomb and of Avon Vale that can anywhere be obtained. On the left, part of the top of Cleeve Hill,

Woolstone Hill and Alderton Hill can be seen, with a beautiful view of the whole side of Langley Hill just opposite, and of the rising ground on the nearer side of Langley Bottom, where stands Postlip House showing prominently and facing this way, no doubt for the most pleasing view which this Corndean Hill presents from its windows and garden. Between the slope of Langley Hill and the Cotswold hill-line up from Sudeley Castle, extends the open vale as far as eye can see, with Winchcomb town stretched out broadside at the mouth of the minor valley that bears its name. This corner of ground, in fact, is one of several such corners upon the Cotswold Edge where you may stand entranced by the beautiful view. As the view is chiefly towards the North-East, the afternoon is a good time to come here, whilst the sun is yet some distance above the top of Cleeve Common and shining up into the vale and on to the hills that limit it. The direct and softened rays fall at such a time upon the houses and old church of Winchcomb, and shine straight on the walls of Sudeley Castle, which stands out with distinctness in its green surroundings, with its several towers, battlemented walls and ruined great hall.

From here I had a choice of roads to Belas Knap. The one that goes straight up above Corndean Hall by the spot where the view above described is obtained is continued through an avenue of firs on towards Wontley Farm ; but, before getting so far, it passes a barn and comes to a gate which is within a field's length of the Knap which lies away at the top of that field on the left. By descending, however, this same road in the opposite direction towards Winchcomb, within a distance of 250 yards from the junction of the road by which I had come along to Corndean, a second road is found on the right, passing along the side of Winchcomb Valley and, from this road, the Knap can be approached from below. I found and took this latter road.

As I proceeded, parts of the lovely Valley of Winchcomb came into view between the trees, and I looked across and up and down it at the objects I have already mentioned and the numerous fields and farms that lay in view upon the opposite hillsides. A field up the slope on my right had many poppies in flower amongst its green wheat, and the roadside was finely decorated with countless blossoming plants. A stretch of woodland began to show forward on my right towards the hill-top, and this I knew to be Humblebee Wood.

On my left some cottages appeared, a little off the road, at the side of a cultivated field in the middle of which I saw a small copse surrounded by a stone wall. The field being in fallow, I crossed it to the little copse and, climbing the wall, leapt down into the tangle of the undergrowth and the shadow of thickly-standing trees which appeared to have been planted to form a hiding-place and protection for the ruins of the Roman house, called Wadfield Villa, that had been discovered here.

I found these enclosed in a square building, erected for the purpose, with a thick stone wall and stone-tile roof. This building was immediately surrounded by interbranching sallows and, in luxuriant growth, there were in the copse a varied growth of trees, shrubs and herbs including a self-set pear. On the bough of a spruce fir, at a height of not more than 9 feet from the ground, a wood pigeon sat on her nest and, not liking to be watched so nearly, flew off it with a good deal of noise which was startling in the silence of the place.

The door of the building was locked, but a small peep-hole had been cut in it, through which a portion of the mosaic paving, which was what the building covered, could be seen; but I knew the better part of this had been removed to Sudeley Castle. Outside the building were the exposed foundation walls of several other chambers built partly of stone and partly of square Roman bricks.

I climbed back out of the coppice and recovered the road, and, after a further short walk, I came to an old quarry, just where Humblebee Wood extends from near the top of the hill on the right almost down to the road. I knew that Belas Knap was at the top immediately above this end of the wood and that, by going straight up to the highest corner of the wood, I should find a path that would lead me to the tumulus. But first I entered the quarry, seeing that it was a regular garden of wild-flowers. I counted five-and-twenty species of flowering plants upon its rough bottom and sides.

Going up to the top of the wood by the path that exists at the edge of the field, I made a diversion to a gate that gave entrance to the wood, and I found there that the wood was traversed by a road, or ride, that was rendered quite dark by the dense foliage of firs and other trees that grew at its sides and overlapped so thickly above as to shut out the daylight. The wood seemed full of pigeons, and a pair of hawks came out of it within my sight. Near the woodside I saw some large specimens of the clustered campanula. Then I went to the top and along the path that I found there, past the quarry from which some of the stones required for the barrow may have been taken, and now I quickly arrived at my destination and passed round to the South end of the great mound in order to enter its enclosed space over a stile. I looked at its various parts and noted the stone-walling of its entrances and the great flat slabs of unworked stone that had made its cells. Presently I sat down on the dry surface of the mound.

Amongst the stones that formed the barrow, in the course of long time, a little mould has collected, which accounts for the fact that the mound is no longer a bare heap of stones. Herbs and shrubs have grown up on its surface and about its margins. There were patches of blooming rock-rose and horse-shoe vetch, and beds of yellow bedstraw and blue speedwell, and the wild thyme, which seems the more odorous the less so[illegible] has to grow upon, gave out its strong scent of savoury herb and purpled a part of the ground. Forget-me-not, rose-bay and mullein, also sallow and elder and hazel bushes, with tangled clematis and other plants, were here, resulting from seeds dropped by birds or carried from the neighbouring wood or field by the force of the wind. It is a lone spot, situated high on the hills, to which but few curious visitors resort, but which has been taken into possession by Nature, who has made it a habitation for many of her creatures.

As I sat amidst the flowers, taking note of their presence, a pipit, that, undoubtedly, had a nest somewhere on the barrow, perched himself upon the low wall that divided the space from the field. From time to time he flew up into the air to utter a little song, not unlike that of the lark, as he wavered down again back to the exact spot on the wall from which he had flown up. A yellow-hammer gave me the secret of her nest under the clematis bush, as she had young whose necessity to be fed was imperative and required her to carry worms or grubs to them repeatedly. The song of the skylark and the cry of the peewit came from the field and the coo of doves from Humblebee Wood, whose fence is narrowly divided from that of Belas Knap. A very big bee hummed his way about the flowers. Butterflies flitted round; a multi-spotted fritillary settled very near me, and several marbled whites were about, and burnet moths with emerald and crimson wings.

Contemplation of the pleasant natural scene, with the thoughts slipping back at the same time to the prehistoric past, in which fancy was free to conjure up scenes of ancient Britain, was conducive to a long rest at Belas Knap. I thought that hill and vale were probably much the same in those ancient times as I saw them now, and that the flowers, birds and bees of to-day were only the successors of many following generations of almost exactly similar types to those which existed in the days of the Druids. According to the appearance of bones and skulls found in the Barrow, man himself can have changed but little, if at all, physically, in the few thousand years that have elapsed. Perhaps he is a little less prone to superstitions now than at that time, having by the study of Nature and her laws acquired a better understanding of the material things and forces around him, and so become a better judge of the likelihood and unlikelihood of supernatural things and events. But these thoughts were ponderous and little in keeping with the pleasant touch of present time. It was agreeable to sit still listening to the sounds of Nature and looking at the scenes around. The sun was low down and the fine July day drawing to an end, and four miles lay between me and Cleeve Hill. Consequently, I took up my walking-stick, climbed over the stile into the great field and directed my steps down towards its further extremity where the road passes from Corndean to Wontley Farm and Whittington.

Down the field I noticed that the soil was poor and in the thin grass there were a number of wild strawberries ; I picked up some of them and refreshed my mouth with their faintly acid juice. On reaching the road I turned along to the left, and came to Wontley Farm, where there is a farmstead and cottage a little over a mile from the Knap. Here a rough road to the left goes down through West Wood, and the road straight on goes over the narrow part of Cleeve Common called West Down and on towards the village of Whittington. A footpath and bridle-road through the gate on the right, which I followed, also leads from Wontley Farm to Cleeve Common at the top of Padcomb Bottom, through a couple of fields. The second of these extends up to Breakheart Plantation and is covered, in great part, with furze and thorns. In this furze I heard the rattle of a night-jar and stepped some way from my path amongst the bushes towards the sound. The bird flew out and, after passing me, dived amongst the furze and returned, not altogether unlike a great bat in his mode of flight. He settled on an outside spray of a thorn-bush and I looked at him with my field glasses at a distance of twenty-five yards and, though it was ten minutes to nine by the time of the sun, there was enough light to see him plainly. He left his perch and flew in my direction, passing almost near enough to have been hit with a stick. I now noticed that his spread tail was partly fringed, or tipped, with white, whilst his body was mainly of speckled brown colour, and he had bristly whiskers near the angles of his beak. He settled on the ground not far off and then went further away and his noise went on almost unceasingly. His *whur-r-r-r-r-hurrh* is difficult to represent in writing ; it is approximately like the sound of a mowing-machine, with a deeper note towards the end of each repeated measure, as when the machine strikes into a bunch of thicker grass ; but the sharper rattle begins again immediately and goes on incessantly. He only makes this noise in the nesting season, which may last for about six or eight weeks on the Cotswolds at this time of year. After I had left he went back to the thorn and sat upon the self-same bough, where I could plainly see him with my glasses from the slope on the common that leads up through the furze out of Padcomb Bottom. Whilst I was watching he flew round, making a sharp, flapping sound, as if hitting the backs of his wings together, and then again returned to his thorn and went on making his noise—it can hardly be called music or song. I walked away, up the common, and could hear him faintly still at a distance of half a mile—until a hill-top, in fact, intervened between him and me.

I was now well up on the common, with my face towards the distant cliff, and keeping to the left to avoid the dips of the other two combes. My face was also towards the place of the sunset. The cool, soft grass of the common was beneath my feet and the cool, hill-top air of the mid-summer evening, advanced almost to night, met me as I walked. Beyond the long and upward-sloping stretch of greensward that I was now covering with quickened stride, and which was growing misty and dim, the sky showed in saffron and amber, green and blue, in which last the silver stars were appearing. Other twinkling lights were also shining down in the darkened Severn Vale when I came near enough to the cliff to look into it. Presently I struck the deep-rutted road whose bed is on the solid rock and which, beginning near the Punch Bowl Quarries, leads down the edge of the great common to the houses of Cleeve Hill.

CHAPTER VIII.

TO PRESTBURY BY THE UNDERCLIFF AND QUEEN'S WOOD, AND BACK BY BENTLEY LANE.

I WENT along the Undercliff on the edge of Cleeve Common and passed successively the entrances from the common to " Malvern View " Hotel, the Golf Club Houses and several private dwellings. The old Winchcomb high-road that I was following, with my back now towards that town, crossed the rough track that comes up on to the common from the main road by the " Rising Sun," and I saw the white gate where the short Rising Sun lane opens into the common, and the aggregation of small houses placed in that lane, or on the side of the old highway. This old road, reduced to foot-path dimensions, goes by a fine spring that fills a drinking-trough and passing off the common, immediately begins to descend towards Southam parallel with the main road which it joins towards the bottom of the hill. My route lay along the edge of the common.

The surface all along this undercliff was made interesting by its irregularities. In the course of long time there has been a considerable natural movement of the more superficial layers of ground. The hard rocks and basement gravel of the Oolite are underlaid by the clay of the Lias, which crops out at about this altitude, forming the lower slopes, and causing several springs to be thrown out where the clay passes up under the porous Oolite. The clay, in certain conditions of moisture, assumes a slippery soapiness and, unless the Oolite layers above are held in place by their natural adhesion, or by the fact that the dip of their strata is in the opposite direction to the cliff-face, there is a distinct tendency for these rocks to slip down over the soapy clay, portions of which may also slide over one another, as one becomes more fluent than the other by retention of water.

HUDDLESTONE'S TABLE AND A PORTION OF THE CLIFF ABOVE IT.

CLEEVE COMMON.

VIEW OVER QUEEN'S WOOD TO CHELTENHAM AND THE HILL EDGE BEHIND THE TOWN.

There is also some natural breaking-off of portions of the rocky face of the naked cliffs that, in places, top the height, and further irregularities are caused by quarrying at the face of the cliff, or below it, for the displaced stone, and the casting aside into heaps of the spoil that has to be removed in order to come at the useful stuff.

Having passed by some portions of the undercliff and across the deep-rutted and rocky track that ascends the steep from Rising Sun Lane, I found myself upon other billowy ground, with many grassy knolls, delightful to scramble up and over, and giving other views of the cliffs and the distant Severn Valley, as well as of the foliage of the near Thrift Wood, the entrance gate of which was down in a green corner on my right. About this point the face of the common, having made an angular turn, is directed less to the North and more to the West than before, and Nottingham Hill has passed out of sight. Along by the Thrift the cliff above presents its most rocky aspect and some large boulders of rock, partly separated from the cliff-face, add to the ruggedness and invite anyone of mountain-climbing proclivities to scale them. Running my eye along the cliff, I saw these rocks and the white-beam bush that grows out of them overshadowing a part that is most prominent. I also saw the elder-bush, some distance further along, that marks the entrance to the cave that there exists, high up towards the summit of the cliff. This cave is a crevice in the rocks and has never been authentically explored with thoroughness, but there is danger within both from the steepness of its floor and from water.

Past the spring of water situated above the houses of Nutter's Wood and immediately at the base of the cliff that faces the Roman Camp, narrow paths lead across the broken ground of the undercliff or, rising up the cliff face slantingly, by out-jutting rocks, gain the top at the extreme corner of the common where grow the three beeches called the Three Sisters. I did not ascend the cliff, however, but, passed along beneath those rocks, where stands the great cube of stone a short distance away from the base of the cliff and which is called "Huddlestone's Table." From here, extending downward and to the confining wall of the common, there is an expanse of grass-covered banks with many little hills and bottoms and a considerable portion of bracken-grown surface. Amongst this some young cattle were lying comfortably chewing the cud, and in the neighbourhood a flock of sheep were grazing.

The history of Huddlestone's Table is not known with certainty, but there are several legends concerning it. It would appear to be named after Sir John Huddlestone, builder or re-builder of Southam House in the 15th century. Some say, however, that it has existed since Saxon times, dating from the dedication of Winchcomb Abbey in the year 811.

I found a gate in the wall of the common from which begins a footpath that passes through the grass field situated at the top of Queen's Wood. In the middle of this field is a pond and on the cliff face at the top of it a bit of rough woodland. At the edge of Queen's Wood I saw several pheasants in fine plumage, which ran into cover at my approach. Where the wood and the field helped to make an interesting corner a bridle-gate gave me entrance to the next field, and here the footpath turns sharp to the right down the side of the wood and, afterwards, passing away from the wood, descends the slope through several other grass fields, over stiles. Near the bridle-gate just mentioned stood an oak tree on the side away from the wood, and I had a good sight of a nut-hatch running up one of its branches. The field into which the gate leads was a picturesque one, with cattle grazing amongst the old thistles and thorns that decorated its upper part. On its further side I noted a great hedge, which is really a double hedge enclosing an old track-way and now entirely hiding it by the interlacing of the branches of thorns, euonymus, holly, blackthorn and ivy-clad trunks of higher growth. There was the sound of many birds in the field and the sight of not a few, for, though the period of song was past, the cries of magpie, woodpecker, field-fare, horse-thrush and starling were all heard in the wood or in the field. As I passed down the woodside a large number of woodpigeons rose from the trees within the wood where they were probably collecting to pass the night.

I looked over the broken hedge into Queen's Wood, where some of the leaves had already fallen from the trees, whilst the rest showed in autumn colours. The teazles, burdocks, thistles, St. John's Wort and spurge of the undergrowth were in decay among the stumps of hazel, ash and oak, whose renewed shoots were all ragged of leaf; but the brambles in the thick hedge of the wood were yet green, and the holly bushes were virile in leaf and berry, and some great thorns that, in the spring, had made a picture of white blossom, were now darkly crimsoned over with haws. From the great hedge a short distance below me a drove of redwing got up, and two or three thrushes flew along the hedge when a commotional blackbird disturbed the tranquil autumn air with his sudden outcry. Where the path left the woodside and went to the left of it towards the stone stile, a runnel of water, coming out of the wood, ran parallel to my path by the great hedge. A pair of marsh-tits were flying along the hedge there, easily distinguished from the more common cole-tit by their having no white mark at the back of the head, and by their darker and richer colour.

I climbed over the stile and descended the slope through two or three other grass fields separated by stiles. Before and about me the country appeared to be heavily planted with trees. There were magnificent elms in the field through which I was passing, and pollard ash, and an apple-orchard to the left, whilst beyond there were other large trees standing in the hedges or in the fields in such numbers as to make a dense woody foreground to the further view, which only partly appeared between the branches, and which consisted of portions of the hills beyond Charlton Kings and Leckhampton on the left and some of the buildings of Cheltenham directly ahead.

The last stile brought me into the top of a lane running up thus far into the fields towards Queen's Wood. Near the junction of footpath and lane a row of houses called Queen's Wood Grove, situated here, together with a villa or two, represent a part of Prestbury which in the olden time, when the village was of greater relative importance than Cheltenham, extended into this locality. Down Queen's Wood

Lane I approached Prestbury, the lane being pleasantly bordered by hedges, where I saw a fine show of garlanded scarlet berries of the white bryony, and much clematis now exhibiting the white, fluffy hairs of its fruit, from which one of its names is derived, namely, that of "Old man's beard."

Queen's Wood Lane brought me out on the high-road between Prestbury and Southam, and I turned back towards the latter place, not caring to enter Prestbury on this occasion. As I did so I looked down the lane opposite to where I had emerged into the high-road and saw it was overshadowed by fine elms rising on either side, from which many of the leaves had fallen, though enough remained to brighten the avenue, which, with hedges and trees and fallen yellow leaves, made a vivid autumn picture.

The road between Prestbury and Southam is at any time one of the most picturesque miles in the neighbourhood. The hills run along almost parallel with it, growing constantly nearer until, at Southam, the slope begins immediately from the road. The eye ranges the hillside and the fields on either hand as one passes along the road. These fields at first form the park-like grounds of a house of some importance called The Hayes, where grows a variety of very fine trees, and afterwards are spread as rich meadow-land, some of them occupied by the large milch herd of a Prestbury farmer and others by the sheep, cattle and horses of other owners. Luxuriant hedges, a couple of meandering brooks, a roadside cottage with cherry-trees and a well-grown ilex, a large orchard and thick shrubberies with over-topping wych-elms that surround and hide from the view of the passer-by the big old "Southam House," presented themselves in turn for admiration as I proceeded. Between the trees on the left I could see away to the Malvern Hills, where, upon many a summer evening, I had viewed the sky reddened by the sunset. But the object which appeals most to the eyes in passing this way is Queen's Wood, which at first appears on the right front a mile away and is more nearly approached further along. I saw it now, hanging to the hill-side dressed in its most brilliant and elaborate colouring of late October. The white cliffs of Cleeve Cloud rose above it. The foliage of the trees, already a little thinned, allowed the better view for that of its underwood, and the wood glowed in greens and yellows, browns and reds in many shades. Towards Southam the oaks that spread down from the wood-side to richly adorn the adjoining irregular slopes of the field had resumed the golden-green shades with which they had begun the year last May. Some pears in the orchard at Southam had put on a flame-red colour, and the footpath and road under the trees there were strown with a shower of golden elm leaves.

Opposite the entrance to Southam House the open track, named Bentley Lane, begins to rise the slope straight up, and, being covered at first with the interlacing branches of trees that grow beside it, it has the air of a charming woodland way, such as will invite any one of inquiring mind to ascend it, especially when it be known that it is a public road on to Cleeve Common. I took this way.

Above the lower part of the lane which is hedge-girt and over-hung by branches of trees, the ground of the old track-way was moist and soft ; more so now than in summer-time, though the rushes growing there indicate the near presence of water at all times. In the bottom of the lane, or on the bank at its sides towards the roughly growing hedges, were the remains of a summer growth of willow-herb and other flowers, with straggling bramble-bushes, nettles, docks and clematis. In the sloping grass fields that border the lane stood many fine specimens of oak and elm, giving a wooded and park-like aspect to this part. As I rose higher the old road track was so deep and rough as to render it almost inconceivable that any cart could get up it. Turning to look back, I found the view finely decorated by all the tree-growth that lay below and around, and between and over the many branches were pretty vistas towards Prestbury and Cheltenham and the Severn Vale.

I reached a gate the post of which, on one side, was over-hung by an old thorn. The gate was to prevent the animals on Cleeve Common from straying, for the common here sends down a narrow stretch between two portions of enclosed woodland, dividing, in fact, the greater part of Queen's Wood from a smaller portion. The ground above the gate, which is part of the common, forms a broad and beautiful glade between these woods. The central part of this glade is overgrown in great part with bracken, betokening a drier soil than that in the lane below ; but, on one side, towards the main part of the wood, the ground has been cut or eroded into steep banks and deep hollows, and beech and oak trees are growing here outside the wood enclosure, helping to make a fine bit of open woodland, the banks all mossy and covered with brake. As I stood there I heard the acorns of an oak whose branches were above my head dropping, sometimes giving a branch a resounding blow in the fall, and some Welsh sheep were assiduously searching amongst the bracken and fallen leaves for the acorns, which I could hear them crunching when they had found them.

The old track-way here, I noticed, passed up through a deep gulch, and this and other dykes near by were partly filled up with fallen leaves.

I passed the gate giving entrance to the wood where a sign-board gave the usual warning that trespassers would be prosecuted. The break in the hedge occasioned by the gate gave a view into the wood, where, however, there was at the moment little to attract beyond the bracken fronds and some decaying maple and elder, now showing red and yellow respectively. The bracken of this glade, in which Bentley lane ends, is continuous with the bracken on that part of the common below the Roman Camp and Huddlestone's Table, and I soon came within sight of these objects and turned along below the houses of Nutter's Wood. Here the ground is covered with numerous boulders of rock that must, at some distant date, have fallen from the cliffs, and from the neighbourhood of which a footpath goes down through a couple of pleasant fields just to the point at which the tramcar stops at Southam. Rising then to the corner of The Thrift, I came back along the undercliff.

CHAPTER IX.

DOWN WOODMANCOTE LANE TO BISHOP'S CLEEVE.

THE lane passes down from the high-road near the great common by a steep gradient. The houses that are in the lane straggle through its length for more than a mile to constitute the old village of Woodmancote. At the top is the cluster of stone houses of modern erection known as Cleeve Hill, but it is below these that the remote, inconvenient, old and interesting part of the village in the lane is to be found.

The houses down there are hidden away by the fact of the lane curving shadily down between apple, pear and plum orchards, with great elms, sycamores, ashes and willows by the roadside—all very umbrageous and secluded—and the approach is in part difficult, whether from the hill above or the vale below, on account of the steepness of the road, which affords, in addition, but a rough surface for the foothold of the wayfarer.

The deliberations of the District Council have been known, from time to time, to result in the road being remetalled and rolled smooth; but the surface is soon again reduced to rutty roughness. The rain storms wash out the softer parts, and leave the larger stones bare and loose, and the loaded carts that come down to bring coal, building material, or what else of weight, require to put a slipper on the wheel, which rips out the stones and further damages the fairway.

Perhaps, originally, the whole hill was forest-land, when hereabout stood the cottage of a woodman as the sole or chief residence; else why "Woodmancote"? There is also the hamlet in the bye-lane whose name is Bushcomb, further suggestive of forest, and the clearing by the original farmers has to be supplemented, even now, by the occasional destruction of bushes which, in these hillside fields, propagate themselves with great persistence.

On one side, through breaks in the foliage, the outlying Nottingham Hill presents its green side in several aspects, handsomely and diversely decorated with trees, and from the lane several footpaths go off to ascend this hill or pass along its flank, making delightful walks through the sloping fields.

The better houses in the lane are the old farm-houses, with their accompanying yards and outbuildings ; the rest are cottages, each with its distinctive, if humble, style of build. It must needs be a dull person who could walk down Woodmancote Lane without being interested in its ancient buildings and in the wealth of green and flowery growth that surrounds them, and in all the accompaniments of natural occupation that are there associated. The rill, which starts at the top in a spring and rattles down the side of the lane, has become a brooklet opposite Sibley's Farm and flows through a little bog where bunches of marsh-marigolds and smart flags, with sharp sword leaves and yellow flowers, ragged robin, meadow-sweet and other flowering plants, bloom in their season. It represents the bottom, still very moist, of a mill-pond whose dam has been destroyed ; for at the end of the marsh is the cottage and what remains of a little, old water-mill where the corn of these villagers was wont to be ground, before such local independence was put an end to by the invention of steam-engines.

The inhabitants of Woodmancote aggregate populously in two chief centres of the lane, situated not far apart, and which bestow a more general distinction upon those parts than is to be found elsewhere through the length of it. First, that spot where the "Apple-Tree" Inn and the Chapel, together with several cottages, oppose their united dignity to the Manor Farm.

The chapel advertises itself upon a board near the door, and elsewhere high upon the stone wall of its gable front, as being of that sect known as Lady Huntingdon's Connection. The title is picturesque and should not be altered, for the reference to the Countess seems to indicate a personal

COTTAGES IN WOODMANCOTE LANE.

SIBLEY'S FARM.

WHERE THE FOOTPATH BEGINS FOR BUSHCOMB.

IN WOODMANCOTE LANE.

leadership which has an appealing distinctiveness eminently suited to the lane, and an attachment that is creditable in its loyalty. I have often heard the tintinnabulation of the bell of this chapel, hung in a little turret above the gable, calling in the flock of parents and children ; and on peaceful Sunday evenings in summer, when the lane was chequered with sun and shadow, I have heard a voice in prayer or exhortation issuing through the open door into the lane, to mingle with the noise of tinkling brooklet and song of swallows.

The neighbouring inn, haunt of cider-drinking idlers, stands a little to one side of the lane in a bye-way leading to a large orchard and is itself appropriately named the "Apple Tree" from this juxtaposition and the fact that the chief liquor there consumed is apple-derived. The house is further recessed to leave in front an open forecourt, where tables and benches are set for the use of the rustic company that there foregathers, when the weather and the hours of leisure coincide to favour such open-air resort to cups and conversation.

As to the Manor Farm, this is situated, like the inn, a little off the lane, and presents a side towards the roadway which shows a pointed gable and a large chimney built outside the house-wall to accommodate originally a broad, open hearth within the chief room of the house, convenient for burning wood. At the back the house presents an irregular appearance, with several odd projections and small windows, and the original door of the house. The front wall has two tall gables similar to those at the sides. Above the point of the angle of each gable is placed a round stone ball which gives a finished appearance to the top of the house. The windows in the house-front are of plain, rectangular shape ; two of them, in the second storey, being very slightly bowed, break the monotony of the flat wall. Between their stone mullions the window casements are filled with leaded panes, and some of the casements are guarded by strong, vertical iron bars. The front of the house has now an arched doorway in its centre, and a passage from this admits to several old-fashioned rooms, the chamber situated at the end of the passage being the most important of these apartments. The dark oak panelling that covers its walls all over is intact. Over and about the wide fireplace the panelling takes the form of a chimney-piece, and the coat-of-arms carved in the middle bespeaks a former owner of condition.

Behind the house is another building with walls half of brick and half of timber ; this was originally a pigeon-house, as the hundreds of recesses left in the internal walls for nesting-places plainly denote. In Tudor and Stuart times it was the custom to keep large flocks of pigeons as a ready means of supplying a well-relished dish of one mode of cooking or another. This building helps, with a large and dilapidated thatched barn, some stabling and a cowshed, to enclose a yard behind the house, which is entered from the lane by a pair of wooden doors near which some horse-chestnut trees bestow their glory of flowers in the spring, the shade of their thick foliage in summer, and drop from prickly capsules their fine brown kernels later in the year.

On down the lane, below the chapel, there are other old farms and cottages, some situated upon the elevated bank that, in places, borders the road, where they are in part hidden behind trees and shrubs that grow in the gardens, and, in some cases, they are approached up flights of steps.

But the second distinguished locality is at Woodmancote Green. The green is of small size, being but a triangular bit of grass that lies at the junction of the main lane and a branch that here joins it. Several foot-paths from across the fields come in here from various directions which make it clear that this is the centre of the village, wherever be its bounds. Upon the green is a commemorative chestnut tree, not yet large enough to dispense with its wooden guard.

Near the green there are several houses ; it would not be correct to say many. Most of them are old, thatched cottages with gardens in front, and rudely pitched paths leading away from wicket gates through the garden to the front and back doors of the house and flanked with overhanging fruit-trees, lilac and laurustinus bushes, flowers and growing vegetables, which can be seen over the dry-stone walls that fence the gardens from the road. Some sweetmeat bottles and other articles placed in the windows of one of these cottages, as well as the characters above the window, where you look under plum-tree boughs to read, "The Woodmancote Stores," denote that here is the village shop, where, doubtless, many of the most needed comestibles can be bought.

Opposite, and a little further down the lane, is the cottage converted to "The Woodmancote and Bishop's Cleeve Institute."

Woodmancote Lane is all the time trending to another and larger village called Bishop's Cleeve, and soon you arrive there. Here the great old church stands the centre of all things, showing its Norman doorways, buttresses, turrets, and very fine south porch without and, in one part and another within, its great pillars and circular arches, its old oak gallery and church chest, both far gone in decay; also the elaborate tomb of Richard de la Bere and his wife with carved stone effigies, very finely wrought and preserved, the figures of the couple being dressed in the mode of over three centuries agone; as well as the tomb, with its cross-legged figure, of "Gilbert the Bold," a knight of traditional prowess of much more remote date, as may be judged by the fact that he lies in effigy under a canopy decorated with the globe flower.

Around the old church are farms and foldyards, cottages in stone and brick, and houses approaching to, or reaching, the size of what, in times past, have stood for mansions, several of them being fine specimens of ancient architecture of Tudor time and older.

Whereas the houses of Woodmancote straggle in the lane discretely—here a house and there a house—Bishop's Cleeve is compactly arranged, with but few outlying houses down the roads that lead, according to the finger-posts, to Cheltenham, to Stoke Orchard and Tewkesbury, to Bredon, Pershore and Evesham, to Gotherington, Gretton and Winchcomb, besides our lane that leads to the hill, down which we have come and up which we must again return.

The old stone church centres the village itself and the history thereof, and the chime of the bells that hang in the square, white stone tower, resounding through and beyond its brief streets, seems the centre of its animation. Perhaps the villagers forget, through long custom, to listen to those chimes and to the stroke of the hours that denote the passage of time, and are even but little moved by the tolling and the peal, dolorous and joyful, when these send forth their messages of the events and periods of life. But, for the visitor, the church and its chimes exercise a powerful monopoly of interest over the population and its occupations, as represented by the little inns, the general shop and post-office, the police station, and the farmyards and gardens, about which there is always some slight movement of village humanity itself.

The society of the village, besides being affected by the tenants, for the time being, of "The Cleevelands," "The Priory," "The Grange," "The Rectory," and other greater houses, is more mixed than of old. The truly native life, descended from ancient local stock of cheorl and villein, bordar and hind, is represented in its modernised form in farmer and peasant proprietor, and labourers of various grades, still attached to the land in more or less complete degree. But a greater modernity, due to touch with the fashionable town that lies but three miles away, shows its influence in sons and daughters who have lived there and have returned, or who go to and fro daily by bicycle or train, bringing back with them innovations of dress and ideas, manners and speech. This influence, however, is too superficial to alter or spoil entirely the virtue that attaches to the relative simplicity of rustic existence. On a Sunday the great old church in its congregation sparsely combines these elements, ignoring, as it has done in former ages, the superficial differences which do not touch the essentials of human character.

In Bishop's Cleeve and in Woodmancote the life, like the scene, is still essentially rustic, and, in returning, instances of this may be noticed, for, besides the houses, we meet with many things in our lane, in and near the orchard-begirt roadway. A shepherd driving a flock to turn out upon the great common up above, or, if descending, bringing the sheep back to the fields for the winter ; or perhaps, if in summer, to be shorn after having been driven first to the wash-pool.

WOODMANCOTE GREEN.

AGE IN A SMOCK-FROCK ADMONISHING THE YOUTHFUL CROWD.

Kine also pass in the lane and through the doors or gates of the farmyards, to be milked, or for leisurely return to the field, staying for mouthfuls torn from the rank growth of the underhedge, or from low-hanging boughs of elm trees, till again moved slowly forward by the approach of the driver or his dog. But sometimes the milking is done without such journeying from field to farmyard, the cowherd sitting on his stool by the cow's flank under the hedge in field or orchard, when you hear the milk splashing into the pail from the yielding udder as you pass; or you may meet the man bearing the pail with its white, foaming contents, or carrying home the full yield by a shoulder-yoke and pair of buckets. Horses you sometimes meet harnessed to various waggons, carts or agricultural machines, ridden, or occasionally turned loose, when their work is finished for the day and their harness has been removed, to find their way up or down the lane to the open gate of their owner's field. Startled and resentful if too nearly approached, suspicious of possible further curtailment of the enjoyment and liberty that awaits them there, they draw away from a human stranger as far as the fence will allow in passing.

Some of the human inhabitants of the lane may also be met with in the roadway, or seen in their gardens or by their cottage doors or garden gates; some busying themselves about the farms and cottages in the duties of daily life; some smoking or gossiping together. The baker is met, with his horse and cart; the postman, in blue uniform with brass buttons and peaked cap, on his rounds, carrying a great brown letter-bag of Government provision slung over his shoulder; and the very old man, bent and crippled with some past or chronic ailment, his life's latter days assisted now by a State pension paid at the post-office up the lane upon the day of every week appointed in due accordance with Act of Parliament; the grandfather peasant proprietor also, wearing a smock-frock, that garment of ancient and eminent service, erstwhile worn by every herdsman and follower of the plough, and now gone out of rustic fashion so completely as to be obsolete in this locality, saving for this wearer and one other. The old man believes in spells, such as are used in the time of cutting of lambs' tails, when bleeding supervenes and the lamb seems likely to die. It is necessary for you to gain his confidence before he will tell you of that. The spell is a sort of prayer, uttered mutteringly and in an undertone, over the lamb, which, though previously too weak to stand, will be running about with its fellows next day. Was it due to the spell or to a natural recuperation? Human prejudice leans towards the miraculous in preference to the sophistry of probable explanation, and the spell takes the credit to the exclusion of Nature in the old man's mind.

The lane, its houses and its people, fit each other very well, no matter what the season. It is all very natural and rural visit it when you will, as upon an evening in early spring when the first promise of reviving Nature is seen in the budlets, which begin to break again upon the hedges, and in the fruit-trees, which are promising both leaves and blossom, when the golden saxifrage is blossoming by the brooklet, where it flows in a deep-cut course, and the daffodils are beginning to appear in the orchard, the snow-on-the-mountain on the rockery and the snowdrop and crocus by the cottage path, whilst the breath of an early flowering-currant is wafted lanewards to revive old memories as such odours do. The robin is still a chief songster in the lane, though the blackbird is essaying an early pipe from orchard bough and the thrush a fuller note from a higher tree-top. Young lambs are at play upon the bank adjoining the road, suddenly bounding as to beat of drum—a habit noticed by Poet Wordsworth. And children, human lambs, with their elders, are making life and adding to the colour that is greedily welcomed by eyes tired of Nature's too sober winter scenes.

One group of children are chasing each other round the wall of a cottage home and another group amusing themselves where the brooklet gurgles in its course by the roadside. They are swimming objects down-stream beneath the culvert that passes under the road at Woodmancote Green, and watching at the further end for the re-appearance of the floating stick, after its dark and adventurous voyage.

As the year is reviving in the lane, so humanity is renewing itself in these children who represent the first season of human life, which, like the year, returns perpetually to its spring. There is a blue-eyed, chubby child in the improvised perambulator, and another that can just run, and another, an elder girl, wearing a hat too big for her, from below the brim of which straggling strands of fair hair appear. There are other older children, too, in coloured garments, red and blue. Beyond them, out westward, behind the trees, the sunset shows colour on a grander scale, and there the crescent of the youthful moon is seen, and, in ascending the lane past the cottage, a glance through the open door upon this evening of March shows a comfortable red glow from the fire within. A star also rises over the hill-top in front, which can be identified as the Dog Star, Sirius, brightest of all the stars, when the dimmer lights above him appearing in the darkening sky spell out the constellation of great Orion.

Later in the year the lane is beautified by many blossoms, especially those of its orchards, when the migrant birds have come—the willow-warbler with his little song at top of tree, "*Chu - chu - chu - chu - chay - chay - chay*," and the chiff-chaff, minute fellow but very cheerful, with his continuous "*Chiff-cheff, chiff-cheff, chiff-chiff-cheff*," and the cuckoo, who is always in force at Woodmancote from the third week of April till towards the first of July. Then the foliage of hedge and tree is fresh and sweet, even as the blossom. Later yet the boughs are loaded with fruit, plums and damsons ripening amongst the green leaves; then pears and apples, sweet summerings and sourish cider fruit, which yield their juice to the mill and press in measurement immense. The prevailing odour about the farms in the lane is then the acid and peculiar scent of the refuse apple-pulp that lies where it has been thrown out of the press-cloths in browning heaps. About the same time the blackberries are ripe upon the hedges within reach of the children, and the ivy is in flower upon the pollard ash, putting forth so much nectar from its small green and yellow flowers as to attract the bees and other insects in quite a swarm for a last carouse, for it is autumn then and the coming frost and rain must soon drive all insect life into winter hiding or perpetual sleep.

CHAPTER X.

ALONG GRINNELL LANE AND BACK THROUGH THE WOODS.

Upon the high-road at Cleeve Hill, where the tram-line finds its terminus, the steep slope of the great common rises straight above, whilst the green side of the opposing Nottingham Hill runs out peninsula-like from the range, affording at the distance of half a mile a verdant and pleasing spectacle. Everywhere to the left of that opposite hill the great valley of Severn stretches away league on league, but, for the moment, this uprisen nearer green object monopolises the regard and is surveyed exclusively for the simple beauty of its display of fields and trees, its farm-house, copse and stone-quarry, and the footpath that can with difficulty be traced up its side zig-zagging through the large, rough field, where bushes and ant-heaps cause frequent deviation from the straight course.

I proceeded up the high-road that edges the green combe in its upper part between Cleeve Hill and Nottingham Hill, and came to the highest point attained by the road at the neck of the outlier. Here I left the main road by the wide lane that runs between stone walls on the left along the top of Nottingham Hill. Over the ridge of the hill a breeze was moving, bringing up trooping clouds out of the South-West, that sailed under the blue sky high above both vale and hill—dense, white, separate, well-defined clouds, quickly moving before the smart wind, with clear patches of bright blue between them.

I looked across to Cleeve Hill, obtaining now the opposite view from that which I had had at the point whence I started. I saw the tramcar had again arrived with other persons who had come to join those who already dotted with specks of dark or light colour the great unfenced area of Cleeve Common which rose over there, up a steep grass slope, to a summit bold and bare of trees. The clustered houses situated just below the common seemed to be clinging to the hillside, and the white roadway of the lane that goes down through Woodmancote appeared of impossible steepness and is, indeed, of uncommon gradient.

Over beyond, I saw the houses and spires of Cheltenham, mingled with the foliage of its many parks and avenues, and, further over, the cathedral tower of Gloucester stood up plainly, and the valley below Gloucester was limited upon its further side by the tree-covered hills of Dean Forest. A little column of dark smoke, over twenty miles away but distinctly seen, rose from one of the Forest collieries. Below Gloucester, in the vale, a patch of white light marked the place where the Severn widens as it approaches the haven of Sharpness to make a small preliminary sea. At low tide this shows wide stretches of sandy ooze that glistens iridescent as an opal when the sun shines upon it, and here swimming and wading birds of sea and river resort to feed upon the delicate diet of silvery elvers and other fry that, in season, swarm the remnant waters. Here, also, the salmon fisherman casts his net, remembering always the rush of seething water which comes at turn of tide, forced back by the rising sea of the Bristol Channel up the funnel-shaped estuary, to swirl suddenly over the wide sands and pass up between the narrow banks of the river as a wave of sudden and irresistible force.

Not these details, but only the gleaming white patch of water showed as a mirror lying upon the distant land from where I stood, but I knew the effect of that radiant river-bed as viewed by Fretherne and Gatcombe and from Tidenham Chase.

Directly westward over the Severn where it flows with its water invisible beneath deep banks, the country extended into Herefordshire, to the Woolhope Hills and further, over where the city of Hereford lay beyond those hills and out of sight, by the beautiful Wye, to the mountains of Monmouthshire and to those that form, and lie within, the Welsh border. The whole sixty miles to the furthest visible parts of the mountains of Brecknockshire lay in view.

A quarter of a mile along I found a patch of rough ground

open to the lane, where former quarrying of stone had left many dry pits and hollows, now for the greater part overgrown with hill grass and its accompaniments, inviting to a dry and airy seat. Pink restharrow was blossoming in the grass and blue harebells on the sides of the hollow where I sat down, with yellow carline thistles and ploughman's spikenard. The odour of wild thyme rose from my elbow where it touched the purpled surface of an old and forsaken ant-bank. There were numerous butterflies flitting abroad, those of the brown heath species and many blues of a tint that very nearly matched the campanula bells that only wanted to be set tinkling to convert the scene to one of fairy-land. Dun-coloured spiders made their way through the grass blades, diving hurriedly into unknown paths amongst the loose stones at their base. Grasshoppers were chirping as they clung to the green stalks above and were making their long-legged leaps from stalk to stalk, and a number of humble-bees were sucking with feverish haste an inebriating liquor from the purple flowering ends of great cottony and swollen thistle-heads that blossomed above their strong and prickly grey-green stems at the bottom of the pit. A larger butterfly, coming from the neighbourhood of a bunch of nettles, flapped himself into the midst of this delightful company and settled upon the dingy, yellowish-pink flowers of the spikenard and had there need to continue the flapping to balance himself, in that way showing alternately the fine, peacock-plume spots upon the upper surface of his wings and their undersurface, dusky as a foggy night. Cleverly he essayed to sip the highly flavoured syrup, whose fragrance had affected his finely perceptive smell sense and interrupted his sunny flight. Upon a bunch of more distant thistles that had gone to seed some goldfinches were also making festival under the summer blue sky. They clung to the thistles that are so painful to touch without seeming inconvenience, and pecked the downy seeds so much to their liking. Decorated in red and gold, they too shared the artistic touch of Nature and were gilded to an equality of beauty with flowers and butterflies.

This tender life was all unconsciously happy in its passive

THE FATH THROUGH BUSHCOMB WOOD.

LANDSCAPE VIEWED FROM GRINNELL LANE

SHOWING PART OF THE NORTH COTSWOLD ESCARPMENT TO MEON HILL.

acceptance of Nature's gifts. I plucked a head of spikenard and rubbed it between my palms to get the aromatic and peculiar odour it yielded and, in so doing, frightened away the peacock butterfly and the goldfinches, and so broke the charm of the scene of small things that lay around me.

I stood up and noticed that there was now more blue sky and less white cloud, for the clouds were dissolving into air as evening advanced. A kestrel hawk was hovering over the hill-side, scanning the ground with strong, searching eyes for his prey, which was probably not greater than a grasshopper. He partly closed his wings and swooped straight down, but stayed his velocity by stretching them out again to meet the resisting air which checked his fall. He lightly touched the ground and, rising again, hovered anew, resting for some moments in the same place. Then, seeming to stop the flapping of his wings, he shot upward without apparent effort. Instinctively he knew the position needed for each separate feather of his wings and tail, and how he must hold his head when, leaning into the wind, he took advantage of its force to be blown upward. Then he swept round in a half-circle and sailed away sideways over the valley. A born flyer, the perfected product of natural evolution, where weight and force are exactly graduated to suit each other, and the whole mechanism of nerve and muscle and feather are developed to work in co-relationship with every possible assisting and resisting force, the hawk literally rides upon the wind.

The rough track of the lane along the top of Nottingham Hill is continued through a gate at the central portway of a long line of fosse and dyke that here runs across the neck of the outlying portion for a length of half a mile, to end upon the steep slope on either side. The further part of this peninsular hill is thus guarded by these deep entrenchments thrown across for ancient military defence. They call it a Roman Camp, the whole top of Nottingham Hill being, in this instance, the camp, which must be approached up the sides of the hill, which fall away steeply at every part, or by way of the entrenchments. Amongst the very numerous fortified places to be found upon the Cotswold Edge this is by far the largest. A footpath passes along the bottom of the deep fosse to right and left, at right angles to the lane, which is continued straight on along the top of the peninsular hill, between confining stone walls as a wide, rutty track representing an unmade and original road, old as the entrenchments just described, or older. It is Greenway Lane, changed for easier and rapid pronunciation to "Grinnell Lane."

I tarried for a minute by the stone stile where the footpath passes into the fosse of the Roman Camp on the left, which, with its occupying mounds and enclosed stone quarry, was planted as a larch copse and, as such, was the most delectable spot of my acquaintance. For the footpath wound its way through the well grown and sweetly perfumed larch trunks, by brambles and briars and bushes of travellers' joy, where several common birds found a nesting haunt and even the burr of the night-jar was heard in season, and the wind roared well there in the larch tops in stormy weather. But, on a day, I came to find the crop of wood had been harvested, the larches having been cut down like the flowers in the mowing-grass and the corn in the field. The regret lasted a little longer in the case of the larches because it takes so long for trees to grow to so large a size as these. The fine trunks lay stripped of their branches, very neatly and accurately piled in heaps, plainly by a woodman well acquainted with his craft. The branches, just as neatly cut into equal lengths and corded into faggots, lay near by. The growth of a century had been taken in a businesslike manner.

I proceeded along Grinnell Lane between the walls that fence it from cultivated fields on either side, built of loose stones without mortar, like all the wall fences of the Cotswold fields that exist, in the aggregate, to a very great length in miles, all set up by rustic experts in the local art of stone-walling. I met a number of young horned-stock wandering leisurely down the lane towards an open gate that led into a sainfoin field, from which a heavy crop of coarse, brown hay had been carted and built into a rick in a corner near the gate. There were some lapwing settled in that field within gunshot of the wall, but when I stopped to look at them they rose and flew further off, settling at what they judged to be a safer distance. On a patch of ploughing were settled a number of turtle doves: I counted nine within plain view.

In another field the barley crop lay in yellow swathes over half the field and still stood unmown on the other half, with the long awns of the beard pointing downwards, showing the ears to be heavy and ready for the machine which rested where the driver had recently brought his day's work to an end. Some linnets rose from the cut barley and flew twittering across the lane.

At the next field I leant over the gate to look at a flourishing crop of swedes. The leaves made a fine broken surface of cool, blue-green shade, with yellow flowers of charlock intermingled. Other weeds were growing between the purple tops of the roots that were in culture—pimpernel, chickweed and spurge, field myosotis, basil thyme, wild lettuce, white campion, reseda, fumitory and Good King Henry—vulgar plants that might have been in part removed by better hoeing from the farming point of view, but otherwise flourishing here by right of being in their proper place; for the cultivation of the earth is generant of such weeds. The rough grass that covers the stony soil, when left to itself, has its proper companion weeds, which are not these.

I came to the end of the hill-top where the lane is barred, before its descent, by a couple of gates, and looked about me at the view—most wide and beautiful—that here presents itself. To the left I saw the Brecknockshire mountains and to the right, along the escarpment line of the North Cotswolds, the landscape reached to the outlying Meon Hill and over Stratford-on-Avon to the rising ground of North and East Warwickshire. The whole range of view from West to East measured a full hundred miles and took in one half of the distance right over the middle of England from Wales to the Wash. Across the North-West lay the Malvern Hills, familiar to residents of vale and hill. To the right of them rose the Abberley Hills in North Worcestershire, and beyond these the Clee Hills in Shropshire. Further to the north the view extended expansively over Worcester and Kidderminster for sixty miles or more, towards Shrewsbury and the Wrekin, which last showed its rounded back in the dim far-away.

Some portions of the view were blocked by a number of near hills that outlay the Cotswold line like a group of green islands in the vale. Each of these island hills, unlike its neighbour in form and lying in various positions apart from the others, beautified the nearer distance after its own manner. Stretches of vale were visible, extending in the intervals between hill and hill, each height being marked out with fenced fields and with holt or coppice occupying a part of its side, or showing over its summit or shoulder. Immediately on the right was a banky grass field set about with numerous thorn trees, with a sloping view to an avenue of wych elms, flanking a rough way to Prescott, whose house and farm were sunk in a nest of variously tinted foliage. On that side the eye slipped through, as it were, between hill and hill, into the Vale of Avon and to the ultimate blue-blurred horizon beyond.

I sat on the wall-fence of Grinnell Lane facing the thorn, grown slope and gazed over Stratford way trying to distinguish the steeple of its church, which was, however, undiscernible in the maze of trees at that distance. Stanley Mount was on the right and the Alderton-Dumbleton Hill lay across the vale, with Bredon Hill on the left and the smaller and lower Dixton Hill between the last two. I leant over the gate and looked at Bredon Hill, which showed its bulky side seven miles away, and at the green many-fielded side of the nearer Woolstone Hill and, beyond, to those vaster distances up and across Severn Vale already mentioned. I viewed the countryside broadly.

The spot is a lonely one, for not once in twenty visits will anyone be met treading this ancient highway—Grinnell lane. The scene was silent, too, until a dull, metallic roar grew from the indefinite to the distinctly audible and gave notice of the approach of the little local train whose engine came puffing down between the hills, stopped at Gotherington Station, close to where Grinnell Lane joins the road straight down below, and quickly went off again for the greater village of Bishop's Cleeve. I followed it with the ear when it had turned under the hill out of sight, heard it stop and start again and whistle as it approached the tunnel that carries the line through Marle Hill into the Borough Beautiful.

The green lane is continued down the slope, between hedges, through the right-hand gate, but the left-hand gate opens into a grass field through which runs a rough road down past a farmstead, which is in view, where a short row of larches standing on the edge of the steep screens a portion of the long view North-Westward, and part of the sky that at midsummer is streaked with the colours of the sunset. That track also goes down to Gotherington and to the road that runs along the base of the hill there to Gretton and Winchcomb, the hill in this part being called Gotherington Hill. The track lower down the slope passes Gotherington Manor, a fine old farm-house with an old detached pigeon-house. In Gloucestershire the Manor Houses are commonly accompanied by such old dovecotes.

I was out for only a short walk of five miles, or so, and to descend meant remounting. The wood named Gotherington Grove was on my left-hand, with a path running through it that would lead me back by another route. Entering the field on the left from Grinnell Lane, I passed along the top of it until I found the gate where the footpath and bridle-way goes through the Grove. I found the path closely flanked with the almost impenetrable undergrowth of the wood, that was springing up from the permanent root-stocks of maple, cornel, ash and hazel, whose twigs were interlacing below the branches of oak, fir and other trees that made the larger growth ; whilst the ground was clothed with herbs, where there was room and light enough for them to grow. About half-way through the wood I turned down a side track, merely to see what was there. It led down a stiff slope to a gate at the bottom of the wood. Climbing up by attachment to any growth that its tendrils could reach, I found the large wood-vetch still bearing a few late flowers. Where the underwood had been cut a year or two ago, the growth of herbs was prolific, especially about a moist place where a spring issued and made a trickle of water. Here burdocks spread their large leaves and the great umbels of angelica rose seven or eight feet high, and tall teazles and marsh thistles seemed to be emulating them. The blue-bells that in the spring here cover the ground between the ash-stumps were fruiting now, their leaves grown large. On drier ground on the other side of the path, a thick growth of St. John's wort, whose flowers I knew had earlier made a great show of yellow colour, was now going off into fruit. A swarm of flies in this locality caused me to beat a retreat before them, back to the main path. I left the wood by a stile that would lift off at one end and swing round on a simple pivot-hinge to allow a ridden horse to pass.

I passed along the top of the banky grass field into which I had come, by a rabbit warren, to find the entrance into a second wood through which the path was continued. This is Bushcomb Wood. I turned at the bridle-gate before entering it to admire the beauty of the hilly field I had just crossed and the view of the great valley with the villages of Gotherington and Woolstone showing nicely in the nearer distance—Gotherington with its brick cottages at the bottom, half lost in the leafy orchards, and Woolstone on its little hillside with the church tower and rectory showing prettily. The atmosphere, which had been clear, was now clearer still. Perhaps rain was coming. Over beyond the Woolhope Hills in Herefordshire, the Black Mountains, that had shown as a lightly-shaded line, now stood out distinctly, though fifty and more miles away.

I entered Bushcomb Wood by the bridle-gate, passing under the branches of some large beech-trees, and the path then dipped down under high, spreading nut-bushes, whose thick foliage made a covering that hindered the movement of air. It was a relief to come from out of their oppressive atmosphere into a part where the wood had been cut and where there was room for the great mullein and marjoram and musk-mallow to bloom. Under the hazels the purple fruit and quadrate leaves of Herb Paris and the yellow-green spikes of tway-blade were seen, along with the reddening fruits of the arum. I passed a group of beeches on my right, whose spreading branches made a shade across the path, and, a little further on, near where grew a store of valerian, I looked for the one plant of helleborine that had come up in the same place during a succession of years.

I left Bushcomb Wood through the gate to enter another field on the side of Nottingham Hill where Cleeve Hill was again in sight and where a pleasant air was moving over thymy banks that invited to sit and rest until the sun had sunk low far over the great vale. By a cottage called "The Slades," situated on the hillside there, I reached the lane that comes up from Woodmancote through Bushcomb and passes on by Longwood Farm to the top of the Cleeve Hill main road. Opposite The Slades, at the side of the lane, I found a stone stile where a footpath began that leads to the Cleeve Hill Post Office, by a shorter, though more arduous route down the irregular side of Nottingham Hill to the brook at the bottom of the combe and up the steep opposite slope. I took this path, which is a pleasant one in dry weather, and at this hour of the day the houses of Cleeve Hill, lit by the westering sun, show to great advantage from it. There is a bit of moist meadow to cross at the bottom, before the path reaches the dry bank that brings one to the V stile and gate in Woodmancote Lane.

I reached the top, from whence I started, as the sun was setting. All the clouds had now vanished from the upper sky, but the hollows of the great landscape were filled with soft blue mist, with the further views still plainly visible over and beyond. The declining sun shed a golden light over part of the vale, in front of the Malvern Hills, making more prominent their dark and sinuous outline, and the Welsh mountains were bathed in the same yellowish rays. The long, straight line of the Forest of Dean, passing away to the South-West, was flanked by the blue mists rising from where Severn flowed, but still the cathedral tower rose, a conspicuous object, above Gloucester city and those evening mists. All the innumerable fields of the vale lay exposed in the last light of day. Darkly green stood the trees of the foreground, edging the brighter green aftermath. Coloured cattle and horses grazed peacefully in some of the fields and, immediately at hand, the crumpled slope was dotted with reposing sheep. The white-towered village church of Bishop's Cleeve and its contiguous buildings lay not far from the base of the hill, whence again came the rumble of a train that passed with a trail of white steam where, a mile away, a length of steel rail was fired by the setting sun. The yellow light was presently turned to red, when the whole landscape, over the green of the foreground and the indigo of the distance, took on a ruddy glow. The sun passed through a roll of low, lavender-coloured cloud, crimsoning its edges and, wholly visible again, touched the top of the Malvern Hills a glowing fire-ball, and gradually sank from sight. Then the land grew less distinct under a cloudless but hazy dome of sky, high up into which were shot ascending rays that reached a bright intensity, being marked fan-like through the rose-red blush which suffused the heavens and which yet for some brief minutes bathed the darkening world below.

CHAPTER XI.

TO BUSHCOMB AND GOTHERINGTON BY THE FIELDS AND BACK BY HOLDER'S HILL.

I STARTED down the lane and went by the rustic post-office whose situation is too far down for those who live on the Cleeve Hill high-road and too far up for those who live at the bottom of the hill in the lane, because the hill, both above and below the little house, is of extraordinary steepness. The rockery at the back of the post-office had been covered for some weeks with the massy white blossoms of snow-on-the-mountain, giving it a very brilliant appearance. Immediately below began a succession of orchards flanking the steep slope, and several little stone houses stood on either side with gardens spangled with spring flowers. At the junction of the two roads into which the lane divides towards the top I noted a Blenheim apple-tree, that had never failed to produce a good crop since I first made its acquaintance, was again in a promising state, being covered with blossom. By the side of the next cottage below there was a gate into a field and a V stile beside it, with a couple of pear-trees overhanging the wall near where begins the footpath that goes straight up the green side of Nottingham Hill towards Bushcomb Wood. From this point the lane descends even more precipitately until it has passed the quaint house of Sibley's Farm and the fine group of elms that heads the green bottom which once formed a mill-pond but now only provides a moist setting for the brook that flows through its centre. The lane makes a shady corner here with an old barn by the gate that leads to Mount Vernon and Holder's Hill. At the end of the moist bottom the remains of the little old mill and mill cottage stand where the water makes a fall under the boughs of a fine walnut-tree, whose grey branches were now sprouting with bronzy leaves, and some late primroses were still blooming on the high banks of the brook below the mill.

So, on by more orchards and cottages situated up the steep banks on the roadsides behind their garden hedges, until I had passed the Manor Farm and the "Apple-Tree" Inn, and come to Woodmancote Green, where there is a path to the right up the slope of Nottingham Hill, beginning between two cottages, and yet another along by the brook to the left, making an alternative way to Bishop's Cleeve. Here there is an orchard on the left containing a pear-tree with a very large trunk.

In another quarter of a mile I reached Bushcomb Lane which goes off on the right to ascend Nottingham Hill and which will bring you, if followed to its ultimate end, back by Longwood Farm to Cleeve Hill at the highest part of the main road.

I turned up Bushcomb Lane, where the greening hedges were closer upon me as the road is but narrow. In this bye-lane lies the hamlet of Bushcomb, its two or three small farms and several cottages lying a little back from the road amongst plum and apple trees, in the most rustic way imaginable, and several of the thatched cottages are of quite artistic effect. Sloping green fields stretched away on the right, back towards Cleeve Hill which gave an open view that was enlarged as my bye-lane began to ascend the steep. Some way up, where the main group of cottages of the hamlet straggle along the right-hand side, upon the left was a most entrancing orchard with a strong, hingeless gate opening to the lane, over which begins the footpath for Gotherington. I leant upon the top bar of the gate for a moment to contemplate this blossoming orchard, which at present presented a most bridal aspect, as if it represented the Spring in essence. A nanny-goat that was staked near the lane-side within reach of the young herbage under the hedge raised her head to give me one enquiring look whilst she continued to eat a mouthful, and then resumed her browsing. The growth of grass under the trees in the orchard was well advanced and of brighest green flecked with the yellow of dandelions and the white of daisies and hedge

THE WAY THROUGH THE ORCHARD.

THE COTTAGE BY THE STYLE.

BLOSSOM TIME AT BUSHCOMB.

VIEW OF CLEEVE HILL FROM HOLDER'S HILL.

parsley. The tree-trunks of varying thicknesses were leaning for the main part one way or another out of the perpendicular, and one trunk rested partly on the ground, its head turned upwards ; green moss, cool and damp, grew about its base, and on the larger branches and upper parts of this and other trunks grew lichen that caused the bark to look more grey than brown. There were apple-trees of various kinds, the variety being notified by the difference in habit of the tree, the abruptness or comparative slenderness of its branches and the colour of its blossoms. Some of the flowers were nearly white, some pink-and-white, some a delicate mauve-and-white, and together they exhaled an exquisite odour. The general effect, where the trees overhung the footpath that went from the gate where I stood straight through the orchard, was snow-like, only the snowflakes were, for the greater part, rosily tinted and suspended on the branches, though some also lay in a little fallen shower upon the path. The blossoms were mingled with leaf-buds now bursting rapidly into fuller leaf. A pear-tree, distinguished by its upright stem and less straggling pyramidal top, showed its leaves more advanced with only a few of its bunches of flowers remaining, many of its petals lying upon the grass beneath, where they strewed the ground with small and fragile shells of milk-white hue. The hedge at the side, where the blackbird and hedge-sparrow had their nests, showed its fresh young foliage just passed from bud to leaf and only half hiding the thick and dark stems and branches of the thorn above the ditch where young nettles of a dark, virile green and fresh, sticky goosegrass were flourishing. A cuckoo was close at hand in the orchard, perhaps seeking a convenient nest in which to place her egg, and I heard the notes of a score of birds there and saw many of them—the starling, tit-mouse, chaffinch, chiff-chaff, robin, wren, martins and swallows, and the blackbird from whose yellow bill came a varied song in deep tenor tone to which the thrush sung an obligato and others of the birds joined in to make an accompaniment.

I climbed the bars of the low gate and walked through the orchard, under those blossom-burdened apple-boughs, and passed out at its other side by a small house whose surroundings, at this time of year, are of the nature here described. In the field beyond this house I found myself behind a high hedge, whitened with hawthorn blossom, on a little-used footpath that passes along half up the slope of Nottingham Hill. A second path from this point goes down the slope to join the road near Bishop's Cleeve, which village, from along here, being a comparatively near object in the vale, itself appeared exquisitely embowered in its blossoming orchards. From its white church tower floated up the chimes as the hands of its clock came round to striking time. Tall elm trees, whose foliage was not yet darkened to summer shade, stood in the hedges of the fields and orchards near the village, and its tower, whose aspect and surroundings changed as I passed along the hillside from field to field, showed amid the trees. The greater view extended across the Severn Vale to the Malvern and Forest Hills, and back to the nearer and darker hills behind Cheltenham. Along this hillside the fields were all in good greensward. The footpaths went across them from stile to stile, though often so weakly marked as to make it appear almost a trespass to tread the long flower-flecked grass where the field was closed for mowing. Ewes, with their lambs, were in one field, adding to the effect that was of the year's awakening, and in others mares with their foals and young cattle were grazing. On the slope above were occasional views of the rugged ground that ascends to Bushcomb Wood and Gotherington Grove by great hedge, and outstanding tree and bush, the frequent nesting-place of magpie and woodpecker, and where owls fly at night and the fox hunts for his supper about the rabbit-holes. I passed a fine horse-chestnut tree in full blossom on my right hand, in the shade of which some young cart-horses were standing; and later, shortly before the footpath began to descend, I found the stile in the hedge broadened to a swing-gate over whose barrage the village of Woolstone on the slope of Crane Hill was framed into a picture by portions of the hedge on either side. A little further on the path descended to the railway, which is crossed there without bridge, and this crossing can be seen from the last stile on the slope above. Climbing the high step stiles in the railway fences, I got across at the level of the rails and then passed through two or three flat fields into Gotherington village. In one of these fields stood some feeding-troughs for a small flock of tegs that were being fattened there. Their feeding time must have been due, or, perhaps, overdue, since they came to me on my entering the field appearing to expect as much from any man as from the one who was in the habit of bringing their feed. When I stopped they even came close to me, snuffling at the lappet of my pocket and touching my hand with their damp muzzles and breathing out their warm breath upon me, with their ears stretched forward and their big eyes staring.

An eminently rural place is Gotherington, with its several considerable farm-houses and farm-yards, orchards and fowl-runs and old thatched or tile-roofed dwellings of shepherds and ploughmen and keepers of hens and bees. There are orchards on all sides and running chicken and waddling ducks everywhere, and cottages with outhouses and stores of fire-wood, with flower-beset paths leading to the doors. Also ricks of corn on staddles in rickyards, yet unthreshed, which seem to indicate no hurry for ready money; and horses and cow stock in field or paddock that, not having yet slipped their winter coats, looked rough and uncouth at the moment. There is a sign-post where the roads meet which points to Cleeve and Cheltenham, Gretton and Winchcombe, Ashchurch and Tewkesbury, and so informs one where one is when in Gotherington. Up one or other of the roads there is a house of public entertainment called the "Shutter" Inn, whose name must be nearly unique; also "The Gotherington Village Hall and Reading Room," and the general shop which combines the public business of post and telegraph office with its sale of stores. There is a school-house and a chapel, but no church, at Gotherington. You see the churches of both Woolstone and Bishop's Cleeve beckoning respectively across the fields from North and South, and from the latter you hear the chimes advertising the correct time, or near enough, every quarter of an hour. You know, if country-born, what a delightful thing it is to walk a mile, more or less, to church across the fields ; indeed, the right and option enjoyed by the Gotherington folk in two churches, both situated within easy walking distance, is more than most villages have to offer and would not be compensated by a single church close at hand.

Some few hundred yards up a bye-lane at the top of the village I found the Manor Farm. The very rough road that passes it goes on up Gotherington Hill to meet Grinnell Lane near the top, at a point where there is a broad view already mentioned in a chapter describing a walk along Grinnell Lane. The Manor Farm stands a little way up the slope away from Gotherington Village ; it is a fine farmhouse of ancient style, with a long front showing an extensive moss-grown stone roof with a range of dormer windows. The narrow lane by which I approached it had thick hedges and passed under the railway before arriving at the gate that enters the field, or, rather, thinly-planted orchard, in which I found the house stood. By this gate was a barn of considerable size, and, in the same orchard and before reaching the house, I passed close to the stone dovecote, which still had a few columbine occupants, though none to compare with the great number for which the house was originally built and intended. To-day many of the nesting and perching places within the building were either vacant or occupied by sparrows ; I noticed the interior was rather in imitation of the natural conditions attending the life of the rock pigeon than that of the wood pigeon, which is appropriate, since it is from the former that our domestic varieties are descended.

The immediate neighbourhood of this farm is at all times attractive ; trees and hedges grow luxuriantly about it, and orchards, which were now all in beautiful blossom, surround it. The wood called Gotherington Grove stretches down the slope towards it from the top of the hill above, to add to the richness of the vegetable growth on all sides, and the view to the side of the near Woolstone Hill is broken by elms and other treees, though the higher part of that hill shows through these and gives the impression of a surrounding of hills. It is, in fact, a wild and natural spot.

As I stood near the house my ear caught the cry of a hawk—"*Cheek, cheek,*"—that instantly afterwards dashed past me, bent upon making a prey of something, and there was a variety of small game about affording a fair choice for his hunting.

Returning down the bye-lane, after I had passed back under the railway, I found a footpath over a stile on the left, from which I could again see the tall white tower and pinnacles of Bishop's Cleeve church, and I came back, without re-entering Gotherington Village, to the place where the path makes the railway crossing. From here, instead of ascending to the stiles along the hillside by which I had come, I took another path that runs for some distance near the railway at a lower level and ends in a narrow, metalled byelane in which stand a couple of remote country cottages called "The Woodlands" and "The Croft." This byelane is very narrow and partly avenued by elms whose branches meet above and is closely begirt by hedges. Over these, or, where they are too high, over the field gates, more orchards were in evidence and the sloping grass fields of Nottingham Hill, or Bushcomb Hill, if you prefer so to call it on this side. The bye-lane presently brought me back into Bushcomb Lane, and at the corner I noticed a considerable erection of glass-roofed tomato-houses, built as a seeming speculation some time since by those who, presumably, had knowledge of the business in which they were embarking.

I turned up Bushcomb Lane for a dozen yards and saw a stile in the hedge on my right, over which I passed to find another stile immediately round to the left that brought me across an orchard and so to the green sloping fields at the back of the cottages of Bushcomb. A part of Nottingham Hill up on the right front, that presented a steep face covered with undergrowth, I knew to be called Holder's Hill, and I made for the corner of that enclosure at which point the footpath enters it, and, in ten minutes' slow walking, found myself arrived there.

I admit this place had a fascination for me, and I had often walked there from Cleeve Hill of an evening, and a fine summer evening, towards sunset, is the best time to be there. From my window at Cleeve Hill I could see this scrub-clothed bank, lying beyond the little house called Mount Vernon, which is distinguished by the red tiles of its roof, and sometimes I directed my glasses upon the pretty cottage with the red roof, and the rough patch of steep hill lying behind it which is Holder's Hill.

The bracken grows thickest at the end of Holder's Hill where I entered it, covering the first part of the steep slope; but at present the fronds were only in the act of unrolling; the stems, however, had shot up from the perennial root-stocks already to a foot or more in height above their mossy bed and the remains of the brown leaves of last year's growth, now broken and far gone in their decay. By the hedge at the bottom of the enclosure was a remarkably fine crab-tree covered with pink blossom, and the furze further along the bank was yellowed over with flowers, whilst the thorn bushes which neighboured it were white with may-bloom. Briars, brambles and thistles assisted to make the self-set brush which had grown and mixed itself into an impassable tangle here and there, so that, in passing through it, I had to make little detours, though there was no need to be amongst it in passing through the enclosure as the footpath ran along the more even ground towards the lower hedge. But what is wild is attractive to some, and it pleased me to be near the furze and the thorn. I startled some ewes who, with their lambs, were also amongst the bushes, picking out the more edible herbage from between the thyme-covered ant-banks and nibbling the sweet grass that grows about the base of the bushes. I also disturbed several birds which, no doubt, had their nests there. I watched at a distance a pair of shrike; the cock bird in particular, who appeared to be very angry, whether on account of my presence or for other cause I did not know, so I did not trouble to approach him very near. If he had his nest there, which seemed probable, he was welcome to it for my part. He sat on the spray of a bush with waving tail and spread wings, uttering a rapid and urgent cry of "*Tchit, tchit, tchit, chuck-chuck, tchit, tchit, tchit.*" In another place a white-throat was almost equally excited with his warning note of "*Tchirr, tchirr,*" although he could not help breaking out from time to time into his little song of "*Chick-a-chee chee chee chee chee.*" I was standing quite still at that time by a railing that made part of the fence, and presently my presence was ignored by the hen-bird, whose maternal duty needed the conveyance of grubs to her callow young as fast as she could find them, and so she betrayed the place of her nest in a low part of the hedge, which fact my curiosity caused me to verify by a slight parting of the bush, into which she disappeared, with my hands, when I saw the four soft bills raised together in wide, expectant gape. In climbing to the top of the close I saw the badger earth that some months before had been dug out. I had rather the badgers had been left alone, and, for all the harm they did, I believe they might have been left. Wonderful it is that so many badgers should exist in this part of the country with the continued destruction that is practised, though, on account of their strictly nocturnal habits, they are never seen unless it be by watching very secretly on a moonlight night.

I had walked round and had now come to the top and back part of Holder's Hill, above the furze and brake, where there is some clear grass near the top hedge and the altitude permits of a good view. It was late evening now, with the sun far down in the direction of the Malvern Hills, and his lengthened rays, glinting across the pale young fronds, the golden furze and the snowy may-bloom, fell directly upon Cleeve Hill, which stood out distinctly with its every detail visible. The village, hanging to the hillside, looks lovely from here in such a soft evening light; every white wall and blue slate roof showing clearly, the broken, dazzling beams of the sun being reflected from the windows. The tram-car coming and going on the road half a mile off and motor-cars and other vehicles passing along it give life and movement to the scene. The bare common with its human visitants lay above. To that not remote distance I looked over a part of the rough ground of Holder's Hill and the orchards that lie about and beyond the red roof of the house, "Mount Vernon," that shows beyond the hedge on that side.

Straight in front is a landscape of different kind; it is across the lane of lower Woodmancote, whose cottages are hidden in a thick growth of tall trees. Over the tops of these, past more blossoming orchards, the hills could be followed to Leckhampton and beyond, and in the intervening valley, about which the hills were circling, rose the spires of Cheltenham and the tower of Gloucester. From the maze of tree branches and tall hedges in that direction came the loud chorus of many birds who were singing their evensong as the sun went to rest.

And so you may come to Holder's Hill and find it on any clear evening during the half-hour before sunset. Should you come in June or early July, if the may and furze blossoms have gone, you will find instead the roses covering the bowery briar branches with their pink-and-white buds and petalled cups. The bracken will then be in its fullest green growth and swallows and swifts flying to catch the moths that hover over it. Even later in the year, when the birds have ceased to sing and the blossoms have turned to fruit, the evening outlook is uncommonly fine at Holder's Hill, and you can find the footpath back, where it passes at the top of Mount Vernon garden, across an orchard and through the meadows where the brook flows, and so to the gate in the lane with the V stile near the two pear-trees, when you are well up towards the post-office and the last stiff pitch that brings you to the Cleeve Hill high-road and the tram-car—in fact, to the place that you were just now viewing from the distance of half a mile.

CHAPTER XII.

A WINTER WALK TO PRESTBURY AND BACK BY MILL LANE.

A HEAVY fall of snow had taken place and hill and vale were deeply covered with a white sheet. There had come a partial thaw, but this had been followed by another fall, and now a sharp frost rendered temporarily permanent the wintry scene. I descended Cleeve Hill by the high-road, which, for the time being had been rendered very difficult for the passage of vehicles, though the wheel marks of His Majesty's mail van showed that a motor of so great a strength as that had at least been able to pass over the obstruction, though the snow upon the tram line had stopped the public cars. For the rest, so many foot passengers had passed up and down the road as to have made a trodden track upon which further travellers might walk with tolerable ease and with dry feet. On the roadside footpath and elsewhere where the snow had drifted, this was by no means the case, for there the snow lay in such depth as to have easily buried a man. As I passed the "Rising Sun" they were busy removing the snow from the steep flight of steps by which the front door of the inn is approached, and a group of soldiers and some men with horses were loitering in the space of ground that lies in front of the inn, where the real sun, which at that moment was shining brightly, cast strong shadows upon the snow-covered roadway. The fields that fell sharply away to my right and the vale beyond, far as eye could see, presented great stretches of white but little relieved by the black forms of the trees and the tops of the leafless hedges. The greater distances were rendered more indistinct by fog that in the farther and lower parts seemed to be thickening, and I found the air much more misty at the bottom than at the top of the hill.

At the corner at Southam, upon the bit of green towards which fronts the old gabled house, a merry party were engaged in a battle with snowballs, and some white missiles followed me as I passed near where the tram-car had halted.

Opposite the tram station there is an orchard, with a gate opening into it from the road, which at one time of year and another entrances the vision with displays of blossom, fruit and foliage, and which now was of woe-begone aspect. At the corner of this orchard a bye-road opens on the right, called Southam Lane. At its very entrance is a drinking-trough for horses and smaller animals, a hand-post giving the directions for the three ways, and a view down the lane, between hedges and under boughs, of a couple of cottages pertaining to the hamlet of Southam, whose great house and other cottages, farms, church and barn stand not far removed from this junction of lane and high-road. The view down Southam Lane makes a picture at all times, and the tableau upon this occasion represented as winterly a scene as Nature could depict.

On the corner opposite to that made by the orchard, and over the road from the drinking-trough, a clap-gate led me into the oak planted paddock adjoining the grounds of Southam House, and the footpath went across beneath the bare boughs of the oaks. A miscellaneous collection of birds were hopping about around the hen-houses, seeking any sort of food that might remain from the last feeding of the Wyandotte fowls, whose plumage was even whiter than the snow upon which they stalked or stood in a huddled throng. In the bare branches of the elms on the side towards the house were a number of rooks' nests, which being well protected by neighbouring trees had not been blown out, and one of these was of remarkable form. It had been begun low down and each year an additional nest had been added on the top of that last used and, the whole persisting, now made a long column of twigs, representing several successive nests erected one over the other in so many years. The branching of the tree above the nest was of such sort as to allow of this as a possibility.

Passing out of the paddock by a second clap-gate, I came into a grass field set park-like with oak, wych-elm, thorn and crab, and with a line of very fine elms passing down the length of it on one side. Beneath an elm I noted

"THE RISING SUN" AFTER A SNOWSTORM.

THE CLEEVE HILL HIGH ROAD.

PRESTBJRY HIGH STREET.

WINTER SCENES.

WINTER IN SOUTHAM LANE.

that the snow was broken in surface and holed by the droppings from the thawed burden of the boughs caused by the mid-day sun and, beneath a thorn, the branches of which were very thick, the ground had been protected from the falling snow and showed the grass that was only somewhat whitened with frozen dew ; elsewhere the ground was snow-covered, though there was not half so much snow as upon the hill. This park-like field was no doubt intended to adorn the great old Southam House that could be seen within its garden, separated from this field by a double hedge. Gables, roofs, towers and windows of various sizes of this early Tudor mansion were showing where left unscreened by the foliage of deodars, firs, yews and cypresses.

The footpath here forked, the upper path being directed straight for Prestbury Church, the lower more towards the side of the village known as The Burgage. I took this lower path to-day and soon came to a gateway dividing this first field from a second of similar kind. During the wet weather of the early autumn the gateway had been much trodden up by the horses that had spent a summer in idleness and plenty upon this fine pasture. In wet weather the gateway would have been almost impassable for mud, but this was now frozen hard and the deep holes made by the hoofs were filled with rotten ice from which the water had sunk away. The snow upon the path, though now crisp and crunching, showed few marks of human feet, as the path is not greatly used in winter, though in summer it makes a favourite and much-used promenade. To some of the oaks, with which these grassfields were set about, the dead brown leaves still clung persistently, whilst others were quite bare. Some fieldfares were flying from tree to tree uttering their cackle, and the caw of rooks and daws could be heard from a distance. At the end of this field my footpath brought me to a small brook by the side of which grew a great hedge that went away along the border of the field to the left, following in and out the curves of the brook's course. Fieldfares and redwings were feeding upon the hedge fruit there. I came near a small pool partly surrounded and protected by a growth of bramble bushes and pollard ash, but its water was frozen, none the less, to rough white ice that had consisted in part of snow, half melted and frozen anew.

The path passed by two stiles over a corner of another field, and, for this distance, the brook ran beside it. The water, not long derived from its springs, was not frozen, but, moving on quickly between the snowy covering of its banks and weeds, looked very cold. Climbing the second low stile I noted how beautiful the frozen moss looked about the base of the pollard willow that had been recently lopped of its boughs. My path now passed along a hedgeside, whose branches were all prettily covered with frozen dew. Some birds, or other creatures, were moving in the base of the hedge, from whose top rose two large crab-trees that I had known at other seasons beautiful with ruddy fruit or pink blossom, but which now showed only their close, bare, black branches. From some palings in the hedge a number of rabbits had passed over the snow towards the field, whose white frozen surface presented little prospect of their finding food there. The footprints were in fours, separated by a clean leap, the two hind feet being marked nearly parallel to each other, the two fore-feet being one behind the other almost in direct line. That is evidently how the rabbit runs, throwing his two hind feet forward while he rests upon his two fore-feet, held one in front of the other.

I halted a moment and turned about to take stock of my surroundings. The sky above was pale blue and the distances around were obscured by mist, though it was very fine. As to wind there was not a breath, it was absolutely calm. The sun at no great height shone in front over Prestbury, some of whose nearest houses could be dimly discerned; but he could be looked at straight in the face and his heat was incapable of breaking the continuing frost. Backward and to my left the hills were showing high and dimly, with Queen's Wood making a dark blotch down one side, and the distant undivided large trees towards Prestbury were greyed and only partly visible in the mist. A slow-flapping crow and a quick-flying wood-pigeon flew at different heights across the sky. I listened again for sounds. There was the dulled roll of cart wheels on the road a couple of fields off and the distant hum made by the tram-car, and low, undefined sounds from the side of the town that were temporarily lost to the ear as a result of the sharp and startling bangs made by a double discharge from a gun. The clock of the neighbouring village church of Prestbury very sweetly chimed the hour, that being 2 o'clock.

I now followed my path along by a narrow ash spinney, where all was silent and desolate, and by the edge of a ploughed field, whose brown turned-over earth was covered with snow upon the ridges, whilst the furrows between were brown in places and elsewhere full of ice where the water that had lain there had first melted the snow and then been overtaken by the frost. After passing through a gateway near which a pollard oak thrust forth some boughs half clothed with brown leaves, and a second brook, coming from springs on the side toward the hills, gurgled icily through a culvert, I passed from the fields into a lane guarded by thick hedges, which brought me in a couple of hundred yards to the first houses of Prestbury. On the flat tops of these hedges, not so very long ago cut, there were loads of snow which were specially well maintained by the brambles, because these retained many of their leaves. There was privet also in the hedges, whose leaves, like those of the bramble, are nearly evergreen. Over the hedges were gardens and orchards with plum and apple trees, whose leafless branches, like those of the hedges, were all coated with sparkling rime. A robin was flying along before me, allowing me to approach him closely, and a starling on the top branch of a pear tree made a little thin music as he sat with uplifted bill facing the cool sun, whose rays were just sufficient to show the fine green gloss of his feathers.

I crossed where a number of small new houses have been built upon what is called the "Prestbury Park Estate," to provide rural residences outlying the village, for any immigrant who might fancy the location. A little further, I came to where two back roads of Prestbury Village, called Mill Street and The Burgage, make junction at their ends. The last mentioned is an old street with a row of quaint ancient houses on one side, beginning with the little Manor House at the top corner, and with the "Royal Oak" Inn in the middle of the row. Opposite stood the big square stone Prestbury House in its grounds with its shrubs and trees around, and a line of fine trees flanking the street on that side beyond, where beech and horse-chestnut, leafless and frosted now, might still be recognised by their bark of greater or less smoothness, and by their twigs of abrupt or tapered termination.

I turned down Mill Street from The Burgage, where I found the ancient rusticity of the village well maintained, and suggesting in its old houses and inns the history of a far-reaching past. The Prestbury brook was by the roadside, and by the bank of the brook the old mill, now only in use as a dwelling of odd architectural appearance. I passed by two other small inns, the "Vine Tree" and the "Plough," from the eaves of whose snow-patched thatch and stone-tiles, respectively, long icicles were hanging. There were winter scenes about the premises of the Home Farm and the Church Farm, both of which find a place in this lane. A man was cutting milk-producing fodder from a clover rick, over beyond which, in the foggy distance, toward The Hayes, I could see some white poplar trees with bunches of mistletoe in them. I looked into one of the farmyards and saw a snowy scene and a number of fowls expectant of being fed by the girl who stood outside the back door. Some cows were streaming out of a shed in another yard, after milking, and were passing into the neighbouring paddock, notwithstanding that it was snow-covered. Their breath, exhaled into the chill air, steamed before them. The brook, where visible, though not entirely frozen over, had ice at its sides and snow on its banks and the roadway was itself full of trodden snow.

An elm tree, with a very large bole, reared its naked branches aloft, where it stood just over the railing of the close adjoining the old Tudor house known as the Priory. A few steps further along, Prestbury Church came into view, for it stands by the wayside of Mill Street. At this point a footpath coming across the fields from Southam gains

Prestbury High Street, across Mill Street and through the churchyard. On the triangular bit of grass at the junction of the path and the lane I saw the healthy young tree, whose guard is labelled King Edward VII.'s Oak, having been planted, as I suppose, at the coronation of that monarch. The base of its straight trunk near the ground was nearly a foot in diameter, and its slender top had reached a height of over thirty feet, which seemed to point to its being a quick-growing species.

I stepped into the churchyard and glanced at the exterior of the fine church, noting the tower with its early English base partly overgrown with ivy and possessing a double-faced clock, and protruding gargoyles at each corner of its summit. A good peal of bells hangs in the belfry of the tower, whose tone is the sweetest of any I know, and in a little cote standing over the joining arch of nave and chancel is an additional bell. The churchyard is well filled with gravestones, amongst which I noted a restored stone cross capped with a crucifix beneath a gabled top. These, together with the evergreen foliage of yew and arbor vitae, were now more or less covered with snow. A horse-chestnut, growing in the churchyard near the wall, overhung the lane, and, although now bare, I remembered how much in another season its foliage and blossoms added to the view of the church and made a shady patch across the road of Mill Street. The black and white half-timbered front and thickly thatched eaves of the "Plough" Inn stood in the lane opposite the church and the chestnut tree. As I passed by the open porch of the church an emanation of incense struck my nostrils not unpleasantly, advertising the nature of the service.

Further along this back street of Prestbury, I passed a quaint old stone house of, perhaps, Early Stuart age, called "The Cottage," and other residences; and, where at one point High Street and Mill Street were separated by a very short bye-road, I stepped through and looked up and down Prestbury's village main street, with its houses of size, which one might well desire to own, or to have to live in if it could be done without breach of commandment. Its thatched cottages of most antique appearance, and houses separate or in short rows, such as those down where the road makes one of its corners, are of an age, without doubt, that runs into centuries of years. The "King's Head," chief of all the inns, with its gable in front and partly wooden walls, stands in the middle of this main street, with the post-office combined with village shop on the opposite side. I know of no other village that is more village-like, although the hand-post at the lower end of the street declares the distance to Cheltenham to be no more than one mile five furlongs.

Returning to Mill Street, I proceeded to its end where it joins the Southam road, across which it is continued as Mill Lane. The first part of the lane goes by the garden wall of Prestbury Court, and beyond the small houses opposite this wall I saw the remaining overturned stumps of several great elms that were blown down in the early spring of last year, in the great gale and snowstorm that did so much damage to trees in this part of the country. A thick setting of fine trees hides the Court from Mill Lane, whose direction is towards the hills, and the brook still accompanies the road as it ascends, first very gently and afterwards with stiffer gradient. The tinkling stream is indeed a companionable and beautifying object, whether to the wayfarer or to the inhabitants of a trio of pleasant dwellings that have been built one beyond the other upon its course up Mill Lane—Burnside, Brookfield and Whiteshill—whose gardens and fruit trees flourish upon the banks. Where the brook was at the roadside it contained a good volume of very clear water, with thick, bludgeon-like icicles hanging about its edges, attached to blades of grass and old leaves and sticks, that hung just above the flowing water. On the roots of the hedge, that here grew close to the stream, were moss and small-leaved ivy and the much-divided leaves of an umbellifer, all damp and fresh, notwithstanding the frost. Higher up the lane, where the stream is a good deal overgrown and the water nearer its source, the icicles disappeared, and the growths for next year were shooting up amongst those of last season, which were not yet wholly decayed, such as dog's mercury, nettles, ground ivy and violet leaves, with other foliage of hedge and ditch. Upon a prominent site, I found an enlarged residence called Knoll Hill House, created by modern additions to old buildings. It stands well, if somewhat inaccessibly, at the top of a steep and sudden rise. In front of it, just over the low wall fence, the brook is widened and made to fall over a succession of stone steps, and bulrushes have been planted in the shallows above and pampas grass on the bank that forms part of the house garden, but these, with the buff withered grasses, bare elder sticks and brown oak leaves, that surrounded the pool above, could only suggest a delighting summer scene, for the general aspect now was winterly and lifeless, but for one little wren, which was threading her hungry way rapidly in and out of the crevices of the stones by the water.

From this point Mill Lane rose more steeply and continuously, passing some roadside thickets, and, the roadway being cut a little through the banks, exhibited under its near hedges the yellow soil and stones of the Oolite, proving that I had surmounted the clay at that part. From this I divined that the origin of the stream must be at hand. At a higher level, on the left-hand side, just above a brake consisting chiefly of elder bushes, I came to a range of shedding and a sheepfold, in front of which, at a very short distance in the field, I found the originating spring of the brook. The water issued tamely from the bank-side, passing widely over a number of loose stones, but gathered itself into a decided stream as it went down through the middle of the elder brake.

Mill Lane, from this point, is reduced to a rough track. I had reached the altitude where the snow was deeper. It had been trodden before me by only one man, who, however, was doubtless a shepherd. Through the gate of the field where the spring rose he had driven a number of sheep up the lane and was accompanied by a dog. The footprints of the company were all clearly marked. The man, with his hob-nailed boots, had trodden the best path, avoiding the deep ruts of the track. The two-toed footprints of the sheep and the almost circular tread of the dog, with its four toes and a palm or pad, were very clearly marked. I passed through a gate, when the fence on my left disappeared, and here a path went away on my left towards the Roman Camp on Cleeve Common. Presently, on my right was a beechwood, the trees beyond the stone wall fence occupying a slope that fell steeply away from the side of the lane, hereabout very rutty and deep cut and sometimes bordered by a small stone quarry. The attenuated boughs of the beeches overhung the low wall, their brown colour somewhat whitened with hoar frost, and bearing their tightly rolled and elongated leaf buds at the end of every branchlet that enclosed the sure hope and true prophecy of a leafage of tender and lovely green. The rough ground of this hillside away to the left, now all snow-covered, is particularly delectable in summer-time, with its stimulating air and splendid views to Cheltenham and beyond.

Past the beechwood, and after some steep and rough walking, where even the shepherd had sometimes taken short and insecure steps in the snow, I at length came to the top, and, with a larchwood now upon my right, I passed through a gate that brought me on to that wall-enclosed track which runs along there from Cleeve Common for Whittington and the Hewlett's Hill. One side of the larchwood ran along the side of this top road, and I stepped towards the wall to look into it. Below was a tangle of brambles, briars and other underwood, with a fallen larch all heavily loaded with snow, which also covered the ground, burying all smaller growth. The tops of the standing larches were covered and weighed down with a similar heavy white burden, and the snow had evidently come with a gale from the east and been blown directly into the larches and against the wall fence of the wood, where the drift reached a height almost equal to that of the wall. Large icicles and agglomerated snow crystals depended from the larches, or lay on the ground beneath them in the discoloured snow, showing that some thaw had also taken place here followed by frost. I wondered if the snow-storm had been in the night, and was almost appalled at the thought of what a bad time any one would have had in this exposed and lone place had they been obliged to face that storm.

The time was, however, now fine. I was above the fog and

pleasantly warm from the exercise of climbing up through the snow. The air was here brisk, moving slightly from the North, and through it above was pale blue sky. Over the track that ran along between its two walls, and over the adjoining stubble field and all around, lay the still white snow. I listened, but there was no sound—the silence was perfect—the loneliness complete.

The footprints of the shepherd and his sheep and dog went along to the right. I turned in the opposite direction; and, within three hundred yards from the gate where I had struck this upper track-way, I reached the gate opening into Cleeve Common, near the part where the Ordnance Surveyor has placed the mark of its highest point. The snow lay in a broad and even sheet over this part of the common, perfectly white, excepting for a few old tall thistles that showed above it. It was unmarked except here and there where a bird had settled leaving a light trail of footprints, soon brought to an end by the bird rising again upon wing. One was a small bird that walked, perhaps a lark or pipit; one had hopped—a finch of some sort. I bore across through the snow towards the Punch-bowl Quarries and came to the cliff of Cleeve Hill about sunset, when the sky was showing yellow cirrus clouds with intervening pale blue stretches of sky, the yellow being tinged to more coppery tone down where the mists of the vale rose over the snow to affect the clearness of the view.

CHAPTER XIII.

BY LANGLEY HILL TO STANLEY PONTLARGE AND BACK BY PRESCOTT.

WHEN, after passing the highest point of the main-road at Cleeve Hill, you begin the descent to Winchcomb, you have Langley Hill on the left. It presents its broadside, half in grass and half in cultivated fields, towards the road, and, varying in colour and aspect in different seasons and by different lights, is always a beautiful hill. In this respect it vies with Nottingham Hill and, perhaps, exceeds it. It is an outlier whose position is close up to the general mass of the hills, being separated only by a bottom or combe from the side of Cleeve Hill, where the main-road passes down, and by a similar narrow bottom from the Nottingham Hill and Prescott side. That combe which runs down between the Winchcomb high-road and the hill is Langley Bottom, and the brook which rises in springs on the higher part of the combe is accompanied through its course by a growth of trees and bosky underwood.

I walked over the hill-top by the road and began the descent and came to the farm, erstwhile called Stoney Cockbury and more recently Cockbury Court. The house lies near the roadside up a steep bank on the right. Opposite, across a couple of fields on the left, Rushbury Farm, formerly Rushy Cockbury, was in sight, and, in the bottom below, a cottage and small farmstead called Cockbury Butts. Over beyond the Butts rose the first portion of Langley Hill, at the top of which, to the left, could be just seen the trees that extend down the further and more abrupt side of the hill where it is called Stanley Mount.

Below Cockbury Farm I found the lane on the left, which passes over the side of Langley Hill, by the farm of that name, making an alternative route to Winchcomb. It descends first between thick hedges to Cockbury Butts. I noticed in these hedges nut bushes from which the nuts had been gathered, or had dropped, but the brambles were still bearing ripe fruit, and the briars showed a good crop of finely red hips. There were also red, luscious berries of guelder-rose and blue, bloomy sloes upon the blackthorn, whilst the leaves of the neighbouring maple had turned red. From these signs the season of the year may be easily guessed.

Past the Butts the road turned sharply and rose, still hedge-girt, to a higher level under boughs of roadside oaks, now well covered with acorns, and some of the crop had been shed and lay upon the road. Through a gate, where the field on the left was only separated from the road by a bank, a flock of sheep were picking a scant living from among the bean stubble, and, in the hedge on the right, the black fruit upon some elder-bushes was sagging, over-ripe, amongst leaves that were changing from green to yellow. By the gate-post were some docks, now of a bright rust colour. The road gave a view across the bushy bottom to the high-road on the opposite side, above and beyond which rose the higher hills extending from Cleeve Common, along by the fine woods about Corndean to the heights overlooking the Winchcomb Valley.

At the next gate I found myself close to Langley Farm, and, leaving the road here, I turned up by the side of the farm-buildings and went through the gate into the large field beyond, avoiding as I might the muddy ground I found there. I struck diagonally across this field, sometimes catching sight of the footpath and sometimes losing it in the maze of thistles whose glory was past. Always bearing a little upward with the intention of reaching the top of Langley Hill, a little round to the right, I passed by a gate into a second field more thistly than the first. Sheep and cattle were grazing these sloping fields, and a number of thorn-trees growing there gave some colour to the scene from their haw-covered branches. Over the ploughed field above, on my left, a flock of rooks and jackdaws were in noisy flight, their cries being intermingled with those of pee-wits, and, as I stopped to listen to them, I caught the sweet, thin music of a number of linnets that were nearer to me in the forest of thistles, to the browning stems of which still clung a rich supply of downy seeds. In the warm but misty blue-and-white sky above, some late martins were winging a perpetual flight. Avoiding the corner of the wall that divided the field I traversed from the arable ground above, I passed round and upwards by a rude hedge, where there were many rabbit-holes, and came in sight of some farm buildings, and leaving the ricks and sheds close to my right, I went through a little copse by a bridle-gate. A fallen larch lay amongst those that were standing in this coppice and blocked the path; but, pushing through, I came out on to the rough road that comes up directly from Winchcomb to the top of this hill. Following this road through a gate and round to the right, I had the ground of the hill-top in view 150 yards ahead and passed into it through a further gate near which a shapely but hard-grown beech shaded a corner where a strip of larch wood borders the fence on that side.

The cart-trackway brought me along one side of the hill-top, where there was some trenching, suggestive of the idea that here had been a fortified "Roman Camp," which was to be expected on so prominent a hill. The ground at the top of Langley Hill, which has a highest altitude of 900 feet, has a very irregular surface, presumably the result of much quarrying, and an open stone quarry, still more or less in work, yet forms a part of it. The banks and hollows of the rest of the ground are well covered with a fine turf, affording an extremely pleasant surface to walk and sit upon whilst enjoying the fresh air and the views. That side of the hill-top where I followed the cart-track by which I had come directly overlooks the town of Winchcomb, which lies open to view from end to end, with all the flanking hills of its valley, that passes away beyond Sudeley. At the corner where the track begins to sink down into the vale towards the village of Gretton that village lies in view amongst the trees close to the base of the slope, and beyond there is an extensive outlook into Avon Vale, otherwise called the Vale of Evesham, with the North Cotswold edge going up to Broadway on the right, and the Alderton-Dumbleton Hill lying across the valley in the middle distance, with a

LANDSCAPE SHOWING OUTLYING HILLS OF THE COTSWOLDS

VIEW FROM NEAR PRESCOTT.

part of the town of Evesham showing, as well as the fruit plantations and great house and spire of Toddington. The slope of the hill upon which I stood, on that side called Stanley Hill, or Stanley Mount, sank down by billowy banks and mounds to Gretton and the road and railway that pass through that village. As you look along the flank of Stanley Hill you see it to be picturesquely covered by the wood from whose borders a number of bushes straggle out into the greensward fields. A bridle-road passes along the edge of the hill, and the view into the valley is soon hidden by the wood that stretches upward to the hill-top. Facing along that way I saw that a large patch of Cleeve Common was visible away back on the left. My path lay along the hill-top above the wood at the edge of a couple of cultivated fields. The first one was in sainfoin, upon which a flock of weaned lambs was folded; the second was in a weedy and neglected state, its last plant having probably been a trefoil which, having been allowed to run a year or two too long, had become replaced by dandelions and wild plants of less virtue.

At the corner where the wood on my right came to an end I found another bridle-gate, and, passing through this, I struck down the grass field towards some buildings that I knew must constitute the hamlet of Stanley Pontlarge. Some way down the slope of Stanley Mount I found a cart track, which I then followed. The hanging fox-cover was on my right, and the fields outside of this were partly overgrown with thorn-trees, with furze and brambles and much white-bearded clematis. A newly-arrived immigrant flock of fieldfares and redwings rose, with much cackling, from the thorns that neighboured the wood and were covered with crimson haws, the great crop of which promised bird fare in the coming winter should there be much frost and snow to shut off the provender yielded by the ground. Many pigeons and starlings also were about, and the cry of the green woodpecker sounded harshly before he was seen in undulatory flight. The neighbourhood is very lone and natural, and in little-disturbed possession of such wild things.

On the left there was a near view of Dixton Hill, effectively grouped with a part of Woolstone Hill, with Bredon Hill to the side and Dumbleton Hill lying beyond flat arable fields in front. A woody bottom, or dingle, descending away down towards Dixton Hill, added to its apparent height and gave a foreground of October foliage to a fine landscape in that direction, while a thorn-tree down that way was more brilliantly crimson than the rest.

I passed a substantially-built stone cottage situated in the field some distance up the hill, and from here quickly descended to the brick-built buildings of Stanley Pontlarge, passing a large orchard *en route.* I found the place to consist of a couple of farms and some cottages with a little ancient, towerless church. Its two bells were visible in a small open cote that rose above its roof at the junction of nave and chancel. Its doors and windows were all in Norman style, the north doorway, at least, being a genuine and original example of this mode, its round arch finely decorated with zig-zag ornamentation. The church has a quaint and ancient aspect in its little churchyard, flanked with the heavy foliage of yews and with an artistic cypress-tree rising tall and with heavy top near its south doorway.

A short road led me from the hamlet under the railway and on to the road coming from Winchcomb through Gretton, and, turning to the left, I followed this closely-hedged, lane-like road, with Dixton Hill continually before me, and passed a lodge cottage at the corner of the road leading to West Stanley Farm. Another side lane presently led to yet another farm that counts to Stanley, and then my road, making a rise and a dip, got past Dixton and Stanley Hills, and, rising again to a corner where there was a cottage on one side of the road and a farmstead on the opposite side, I knew I was nearly opposite Prescott and the end of Nottingham Hill, and a few yards further on I saw the white road for Prescott House leading up through a large orchard on my left, and I turned up that road. The orchard boughs were now bare, the fruit having been gathered, and the apple-trees, scattered abroad in the long, damp grass of the aftermath, looked thin of leaf and bereft of the riches they had carried up to a time that was not long past.

At the top of the orchard the road entered the ornamental wood that lies immediately below Prescott House, and, still rising in a sharp ascent, I went through the thickly set trees by several winds and corners. I noticed that the trees were of very numerous species and in many tints of foliage, the original variety due to the diversity of species being rendered yet more varied by the change that precedes the fall. There were sweet chestnuts, ashes and oaks, dark firs and other conifers, with undergrowth of nut and elder, and some yews towards the top overhung the road and made a very deep shade. When through the wood, the road brought me past a thick holly hedge which fenced off a garden, and very soon I saw the top of the stone dwelling—Prescott House, which is a nice residence placed upon a well-chosen site on the descending slope that is there called Prescott Hill. The surroundings are delightful ; the house, together with an adjoining farm-house, stands alone in the midst of as charming and rural a setting as any lover of the country and of Nature could desire.

Where the road by which I had arrived turns into the house an avenue of wych elms descends the slope that is straight on above, and it appears as if this had been planted as a suitable approach from the Cleeve Hill direction. But the road beneath the trees is now in an ill-made state and but little used, another and better-made road that passes by the farm-house, to the top of the avenue, being more suitable for wheels. I, however, walked up the avenue and then by the road that passes through three or four gates to arrive at the Cleeve Hill high-road by a farmstead called Prescott Hill Farm.

The fields between Prescott House and this farm and the whole slope of Nottingham Hill on that side command a series of beautiful views. At Prescott one looks straight down on to Dixton Hill at near view, with its manor house and trees and curious top. The view of Stanley Mount, the Dumbleton-Alderton Hill, Bredon Hill, Woolstone Hill, and the North Cotswold line with Avon Vale, also enter into the scenery in one direction or another. The fields on this hill-side are banky and irregular of surface and set with thorns and other trees and, together with the steep slope which goes down to the bottom that divides Prescott from Stanley Mount, are grazed by sheep, cattle and horses which often assist the foreground of the landscape.

Leaving the avenue of wych elms behind, I found myself upon a better road above. Beyond Prescott Hill Farm I was close to the end of the trench of the Nottingham Hill Roman Camp, and afterwards my road ran by a narrow, sweet-smelling larch plantation and was there parallel to Grinnell Lane, from which it was presently separated only by the stone wall, and a stile in this allows communication between the two ways. Ultimately my road reached the highest point of the Cleeve Hill main-road by the side of Grinnell Lane, from which it is distinguished by the gate that closes its entrance, the entrance to the lane being unclosed.

CHAPTER XIV.

A VISIT TO WINCHCOMB AND SUDELEY CASTLE.

BY the path up the alley where the tram-line terminates I gained the edge of the common, along which, to right and left, runs the rutty track of the old Winchcomb road. Such a road it is as used to suffice before the coming of Macadam, with his creation of an industry for all the roadside stone-breakers that have since existed. A hundred years have passed since the general condition of the country roads was as it is to-day exemplified by this particular old road. The going was slow in past time, as, indeed, it was imperative it should be over such a surface. The fine main-road being now so near at hand, with its much easier gradient and level surface, the old road has naturally fallen out of use, and it is now, practically speaking, never traversed excepting by the foot-passenger. Even he avoids the track, which, on account of its ruts, provides but a stumbling path, and walks by preference at some convenient distance from the road, where the grassy surface affords a more level and superior foothold.

I turned Winchcomb-wards and went by the back of the last houses that are built by the side of the main-road, along the undercliff of the common, by the first and second links of the golf-course, where a number of men were commencing play, it being Saturday afternoon, and up the steep bank adjoining the racing-stables and by the rails that guard the top of the big old quarry known as Milestone Quarry from the fact of the milestone on the road being near its entrance. I leant on the rails for a moment or two and looked over to Nottingham Hill and down into the quarry into which I had at times wandered. Its refuse heaps were all grass-grown, and, from where I stood, one could descend into it over the sides of some of those heaps by narrow and precarious paths to arrive at its bottom, where there are secluded spots to sit or linger for a space. At its further side and where it joins the garden wall of a house called "The Mount," the removal of the stone has left a yellow, precipitous side of bare rock.

Where the old road goes along over the open common I continued my way, crossing the other ancient track which comes up Wickfield lane from the highest part of the main-road and enters the common through a gate close to which I passed. I was here at the highest point I had to attain, and being able now to see behind the neck of Nottingham Hill, an entirely new prospect was opened up. I looked over Rushbury and Cockbury Farms and could see portions of Alderton, Bredon and other outlying hills in the distance, with parts of Evesham Vale and the North Cotswold line.

The slope of the common in this part is gentle and affords very nice walking on soft turf. Some arable fields now lay between me and the main-road, and I noticed how healthy the swedes looked in one of them, though the surface in parts appeared almost covered with flaky stones that had been ploughed up from their bed below the thin covering of brown soil.

I came down to a gate through which the road passed into a field that had been plainly stolen from the common, its wall-fence going up the green hill slope and, after making a couple of corners, returning to the general limiting line taken by the cultivated country. In this field the wheat was being carried. There was an empty waggon passing up in a leisurely way between the shocks of corn and a full one higher up the field with two horses drawing it among the yellow sheaves, a stretch of green common over the wall beyond and a fine summer sky above. I heard the man who was pitching the corn to his mate at the top of the load swear loudly at the foremost horse, which, in the absence of a boy to lead him, was taking the waggon too far to one side.

Arriving at the further gate of the field, I entered again on to Cleeve Common at a corner from which there is a remarkable outlook into the Postlip Combe. The hillside comes down very steeply into the hollow which is seen running up into the common, and the refuse tipping of old quarrying

GLOUCESTER STREET. WINCHCOMB

RUIN OF BANQUETING HALL.

CORNER OF INNER QUADRANGLE.

SUDELEY CASTLE.

operations stands out across Dry Bottom, breaking the regularity of the combe. The fine old Postlip Hall, with its adjoining larch woods, is directly overlooked, and over beyond is the Warren with its wooden cross, the woods at Corndean and the triangular orchard enclosure belonging to the great house, on the further slope, with the valley of the Isborne below going down by the Postlip Paper Mill. To the left Winchcomb is also in sight from this spot.

A branch of the old road descends here to the right to encircle the Hall and form a public track to Corndean and to the villages and places situated in the Winchcomb and Coln Valleys. My road to Winchcomb, however, now turned sharply to the left, and I passed off the common through a gate that led me by scented larch copses and high hedges down a steep lane to the main highway in which the ancient road that I had been following ends at about one mile from Winchcomb.

As I descended through this last mile I had some glimpses of the town, with its church, lying beyond the fields upon the left front, and its aspect is prettier from here than from any other side. The last bit of the descent is down a stretch of road that is steeper than the rest, with a right-angled turn at the bottom and a stone wall facing dangerously up the hill, near where the Corndean Lane opens out of the main road and the Isborne flows.

I entered Winchcomb by a long street of small stone houses which brought me to the church that is situated by the side of this street near the centre of the town. I stopped a few moments here to survey the building, that is distinguished outside by its long line of clerestory windows, surmounted by pinnacles and battlemented parapet, its very numerous and prominent gargoyles and the large vane in the shape of a gilded cock, whose chanticleer-like attitude may be distinguished a good way off. Then I passed on, reserving until another visit the more particular inspection required for this church's description.

Beyond the church the street widens into a market-place, flanked on the one side by a high stone wall and a raised footpath, known as the Abbey Terrace. The ancient Abbey of Winchcomb once occupied the site behind this wall which now encloses a garden. Of this Abbey there are no remains above ground, the old ruins having served the district as a source of excellent and already masoned building-stones for as long as any were available, and these stones having suffered a sort of transmigration, may now be found in many a neighbouring house and barn and bridge.

Beyond the square the street is contracted to its narrowest part, which is also the busiest, being filled with shops. The chief inn is also there, bearing the sign of "The George." From this part a long street goes away from the left or north side, and Winchcomb chiefly consists of these two streets, one passing nearly at right angles to the other. A lane on the right of the main street at this same part leads steeply down to the Isborne, reaching and crossing the river in a short distance. Over the river this road is continued to Sudeley Hill, which it ascends. Near the base of the hill Sudeley Castle is approached at a distance of three-quarters of a mile from Winchcomb, by one of its entrance lodges, an arched erection with gates, all of befitting design in stone.

There is nothing vast or vulgarly pretentious about Sudeley Castle ; no sky-scraping elevation that must cause you to lean back your head to see the top ; in fact, there are but two storeys to the main portion of the house, one at the ground level and one above. This necessitates a large ground area for the site and several long, straight passages within the walls for service to the chambers, the dwelling being in three main extensions that form three sides of a quadrangle, and all the buildings are in the native stone. That part now known as the inner quadrangle is completed on its fourth side by a wall that divides it from an outer quadrangle which pertains rather to the past than to the present time, one of its sides being open and another formed by the ruin of a great banqueting or entertainment hall that had a high roof and a gallery, after the manner of such halls that are found in grand houses of the epoch, and of which a number still exist intact.

The inner quadrangle is a building of appealing architectural beauty and, in this respect, compares favourably with other buildings of Tudor and pre-Tudor period remaining in England. It encloses a circular grass plot bounded by a stone kerb and with a stone fountain in its centre. The buildings exhibit a fine equality of design. The walls terminate above in a battlemented parapet, and a tower, that stands outside the quadrangle, shows its top over one corner. There are large square windows in both storeys, each containing eight lights with latticed panes. The latticing of some of the windows is of very ornamental design, and some of them contain coloured glass. There are many doors situated between the windows of the lower storey, communicating with the inner space of the quadrangle, besides those placed in the turrets that rise in the angles of the square. A projecting course running round above the upper windows gave sitting place for the white fan-tailed pigeons that were there at the moment of my observation. The walls otherwise were covered with various creepers and wall plants, such as ampelopsis, the larger-leaved Virginian creeper, magnolia, wistaria, passion-flower, clematis, honey-suckle, jasmine, rose and others, which lend their decorative foliage and, in due season, their various flowers and perfumes to the sweetness of the quadrangle. The side of the square that divides the inner from the outer quadrangle has the wall of no very great height, but which is really a double wall, creating a covered corridor that runs across from one wing of the house to the other. Rising close to this and spreading its branches in front of, and over it, is a cedar-tree, which only partly blocks the view to the magnificent ruin of the great hall, and the great tower, that form part of the outer quadrangle.

The western limb of the inner quadrangle is extended along beyond the corridor just mentioned, in front of the old ruined hall, until it ends in the massive block masonry that forms an ancient tower, which appears to have defied the cannoniers of Oliver Cromwell. Some portions of this tower which still stand form a lasting remnant of the earlier Sudeley Castle, built in the first part of the twelfth century. There are other ancient remnants, particularly an old kitchen chimney, and what is left of a great old barn forms a fine ruin that stands some distance off the front entrance of the house, which is on the west exterior side. There is a further tower on that side, and service premises. The more considerable part of the older buildings dates from the great re-erection of the house about 1460. The destruction caused by the Parliamentarian forces in the great Civil War of the seventeenth century, and the order for dismantling the fortress which followed, caused the usable portion of the house to be considerably reduced, but left an ample part capable of restoration, which to-day is rendered more interesting and more beautiful by its adjoining ruins. These, indeed, form an effective adjunct to the effort of more modern time to further restore and beautify the spot. Perhaps it would be more exact even to state that the success of this effort is dependent in great part upon the ruins. At all events, house, ruins and garden together made an admirable *ensemble.* The long past is ever present here, and within the house there are other reminders of the same thing in the articles of local antiquity and mementoes of historic persons and things that are collected there.

On the North front of the house the ancient aspect is assisted by a row of old walnut trees, grown rugged by loss of limb under stress of age and weather. Off the main front, lying a little removed, near the ruin of the great barn, is a yew maze.

At the back of the house is a formally laid-out, but lovely, garden. It is bordered by a broad, grassy terrace that is mounted from the garden by several wide flights of stone steps, and this terrace is itself enclosed and bounded by a wall, ornately built in open balusters, which separates the garden from the park around but does not hide the latter. On one side the garden is laid out in a somewhat Italian fashion, or after the mode of an old English pleasaunce, with a central fountain and clean walks between the beds of flowers. The formal effect is intensified by trimmed box and yew bushes and some most extraordinary double hedges of yew that, having been trimmed and trained for a long time, are now of enormous width, forming green corridors with window holes and doorways cut through their intensely vital, dense, green growth. The flowers in the beds require to be of the brightest hues to set off so dark a framing.

On the other side is a garden of roses and old-fashioned border flowers. The beautiful Tudor Chapel of St. Mary, which is separated by a short space from the house, stands here, adding its distinguished presence to the garden, with its sculptured front, buttressed and ivied walls, embattled parapet, small tower and traceried windows, surrounded by lawn and half hidden by the dark evergreen foliage of cedar, yew and fir.

A length of wall that limits the rose-garden on its outer side, where it runs near the walnut trees before mentioned, is used as the back of a long verandah, or covered walk, which is fronted by rose, woodbine and hop, clambering and trailing from pillar to pillar, and backed by the wall covered with the foliage of several uncommon species of ivy, growing under the verandah's roof. This verandah looks directly towards a stretch of water, which is called the moat, though now cleanly contained within stone-built walls to form a long, rectangular receptacle appropriate to the fine lilies that lie upon its water's calm surface, and a fitting home for its decorative water-fowl. Here are also further stretches of lawn and on one side of the water a double row of deodars. Seats are placed at intervals along the water-side, neatly carved from solid blocks of the same yellow Cotswold stone that has been used for the chapel, house and other buildings, and which is plentifully derived from a quarry on the estate.

The grounds surrounding the house and gardens are in the nature of a fine park and are entered from the public roads that pass on either side by two arched lodges, built in architectural equality with the house. The trees show an abundant variety of foliage in oak and willow, crab, thorn, ash, poplar, elm and chestnut. There are dark stretches of larch and fir woods within sight upon the hills that rise near by and form part of the Cotswold edge and the limiting heights of the Winchcomb Valley. The land immediately surrounding the house is in rich permanent greensward, upon which are pastured cattle and sheep. There is much cooing of doves and singing of birds and, in the evening, comes a chorus of cawing rooks that collect at that time in a multitude where they have their roosting-place in a copse but a little way off.

Formerly the castle covered more ground and was one of the strongest and fairest country seats in the kingdom, though, even as it stands to-day, one would have a difficulty in mentioning a fairer.

At Sudeley Katherine Parr is buried. She married, after the death of Henry VIII., Sir Thomas Seymour, brother of Jane Seymour, another of Henry's wives and mother of Edward VI. Sir Thomas was Lord of Sudeley and lived here with his wife, Katharine. who, however, died an untimely death. He, also, was beheaded as the result of a trial upon many charges, well or ill-founded. Queen Elizabeth, and King Charles I. and George III., each in turn, visited Sudeley Castle, and the old house has passed through many vicissitudes of intrigue and war.*

The evening was advanced when I left Sudeley Castle to return to Cleeve Hill. I came back to Winchcomb by a different route, through a portion of the park, out by the other lodge and over the fine bridge that spans the Isborne where the road enters the town through an avenue of limes. From near this bridge I noticed there was a good view of Winchcomb Church, which stands at an elevation above the brook. Having crossed the bridge I soon found myself in the main street where the Abbey Terrace lies on the right and Gloucester Street on the left, the contraction of the broad space in front of the terrace into the more definite Gloucester Street being caused by a stone house that stands out into the space of the highway to form a corner. It is a little Jacobean house of very distinguished architectural design that seems to bespeak the fulfilment of an ambition, or whim, on the part of its builder to have a house whose style should bear witness to its superiority, if its size did not do so.

Some way down Gloucester Street I saw, on the right-hand side, one of those stone-built inns typical of a Cotswold

* For further information concerning Sudeley Castle, Belas Knap, etc., see "Annals of Winchcomb and Sudeley," by Emma Dent.

town, its front being flush with the other houses of the street and its long, plain, rectangular windows being divided by thick stone mullions. It had the peculiarity, however, of being entered by its front door up a flight of half-circular steps, near which a great stone buttress had been placed against the front wall to prevent any tendency on its part to fall forward. It is a quaint and ancient inn and bears the sign of the "Corner Cupboard."

I turned at the "Corner Cupboard" and, passing by its yard entrance, gained immediately a back road and up this turned to the left to again face towards Cleeve Hill, and so I returned by the road that passes over the side of Langley Hill by Langley Hill Farm, which is the shortest route from Winchcomb to Cleeve Hill. I avoided the lane that presently goes to the right up to the camp on the very summit of Langley Hill and soon came to the first gate, for this road has several gates upon it.

As I began to rise up the slope of the hill I stepped to a prominent bank in the field that was there open to the road. From here I looked back at the little town nestling in its valley, its brown church tower being backed, at some distance, by Hailes Hill with its great, dark-green patch of hanging wood, and the Cotswold line going up further on the left by Stanway. To the right of Winchcomb was Sudeley Castle and Sudeley Hill and, further to the right, the high top of Roel and all the hillside below, with its several important farms pertaining to Sudeley.

Further along the road I was just opposite Corndean and, the sun being low, its rays struck straight upon the hillside there, rendering it beautiful and showing the trees of Breakheart Plantation to the best advantage, where every clearing between the trunks burned red with the flowers of rose-bay. The furzy field to the right of the wood was cut by the bold, bare outline of Postlip Warren, and then a mass of Cleeve Common carried round the high ground towards this Langley Hill, which, however, was separated by the combe called Langley Bottom that bears this road on its one side and the Winchcomb-Cheltenham main-road on its opposite side up towards the higher part of the hill, the rising valley being always between them. As I proceeded I could see stretches of the main-road, and noted with what speed the motor vehicles rushed up and down it, the hum of their engines sounding plainly and frequently as one followed another. The cattle and sheep in the grass fields that form this little valley added to the picturesqueness of the scene, sometimes helping to form a pleasant stretch of foreground for the hilly distance beyond.

At a point where I passed some cottages, built for the convenience of the farm labourers, the slope of Langley Hill went up through rough grass lands in a broad sweep towards its summit and, soon afterwards, I came to the farm-house that bears the name of this hill and is served conveniently by this same road. The house, with its walnut-tree in front and its farm buildings beside and about it, lies just off the road and has the air of a modest and comfortable country house that would be pleasant to live in. The hillside and it plainly belong to one another, as must appear to everybody who, journeying down to or up from Winchcomb by that main-road over yonder, see it from the distance of half a mile across Langley Bottom. Having those travellers in view, its position is not so lonely as it might be. The road I was on, which passes close to it, brings but little company for, though shorter, its gates are hindering to quick transit and it is but a narrow road.

Collected at the gate near the farm several cart-horses were resting, as by mutual consent, from grazing the open field there, the idling in company being, doubtless, as agreeable as the nuisance of flies would permit, and this had probably become too customary to be very annoying to them. I had loitered idly, too, and the day was now near its end. The sun had gone below the top of Nottingham Hill which now lay straight before me. In the sky over there clouds were floating that were tinged to rosy hue and between them were patches of pale, bright blue. In one of these the moon, that had not yet come to her first quarter, showed her pale crescent. In the cultivated field of Langley Hill, that was now on my right hand, the corn was in sheaf. There was a pleasant freshness in the air of the August evening which was more evident by the time I had passed into the hollow at the Butts and had risen again by the footpath that led over a couple of stiles on to the Rushbury Farm road which joins the Cleeve Hill highway very near its highest point.

CHAPTER XV.

A WALK TO WHITTINGTON AND BACK THROUGH THE WINCHCOMB VALLEY.

FROM the alley at the tramway terminus I struck up the steep slope, bearing a little to the right, until I found the white stretch of deeply rutted road that comes up from the "Rising Sun." Past the Punch Bowl quarries it ceases to be a made road, being continued forward for a couple of miles as a mere wheel track over the grass of the common. I did not notice it, being well aware of the direction I had to take, and went more to the right in order to avoid the dip into the top of Dry Bottom. The wall of the common was presently not far away on my right, as I faced towards the West Down, and when I had passed a shallow sand quarry, about which a number of horses were collected, I came to the first gate in the wall along that side. A rough road that communicates with Cheltenham down the Hewlett's Hill and with Whittington by the Ham Hill road approaches the common through this gate; but I did not take that road, knowing it to be a very rough one and that it would be dirty after so much rain as had lately fallen. I continued to walk along by the wall.

From the gate just mentioned, which stands near the very highest ground of the hill, the common begins to slope gently downwards. The green turf is continuous all the way, and half a mile from that gate I came to where the wall comes up from Padcomb Bottom until it approaches within 100 yards of the other wall along the side of which I was walking, when, turning at a sharp angle, its course is directed parallel with the other and the common is thus constricted between the two walls into the narrow slip called the West Down.

I passed other gates in the wall on my right hand that

led to farms, and it is the fourth gate down that way through which passes the road that originates in Corndean Lane at Winchcomb, and, having come by Wontley Farm a mile to the left, crosses the West Down very slantingly through the furze to go towards Whittington. From here I could see the end of the West Down and, therefore, the end of Cleeve Common.

This narrow part of the common, down which I had walked, was for some years used as a racecourse, and on many maps it is still marked "Cheltenham Racecourse." It has, however, for long ceased to be a racecourse although it still continues to be used as a galloping ground by the trainer who keeps the racing-stables at Cleeve Hill. The Cheltenham Racecourse of the present day is in another locality and of another kind, being the fine steeplechase course at Prestbury Park, which is situated much nearer the town.

I passed through this fourth gate on to a narrow, hard road which soon improved considerably in surface, being better in this part than where it passes through the fields by Wontley Farm. By the side of the road stood a couple of cottages pertaining to the White Hall Farm that lay in the fields at a little distance down on the left. I stopped here for some conversation with the labourer's wife, commenting upon the loneliness of the spot and the distance that had to be walked to get to any place where things might be bought. But our talk soon turned towards agriculture, the crops, the weather and the hill land in which she and her husband had most interest.

The road was still open to the fields and occupied a ridge of land that presented a view on either side. To the left, portions of that higher ridge, towards Hawling and Roel, were in view, the hillsides patched with numerous small woods of varying shape. The bottom of the Winchcomb and Colne Valleys lay between me and those hill-tops, out of sight, but I saw the steep road going up through the cottages of Brockhampton and beyond on to the Hawling Downs, which showed as bare, bold uplands at that end of the line of hills whilst, at the extreme end in the other direction, the point of Salter's Hill above Winchcomb could just be dis-

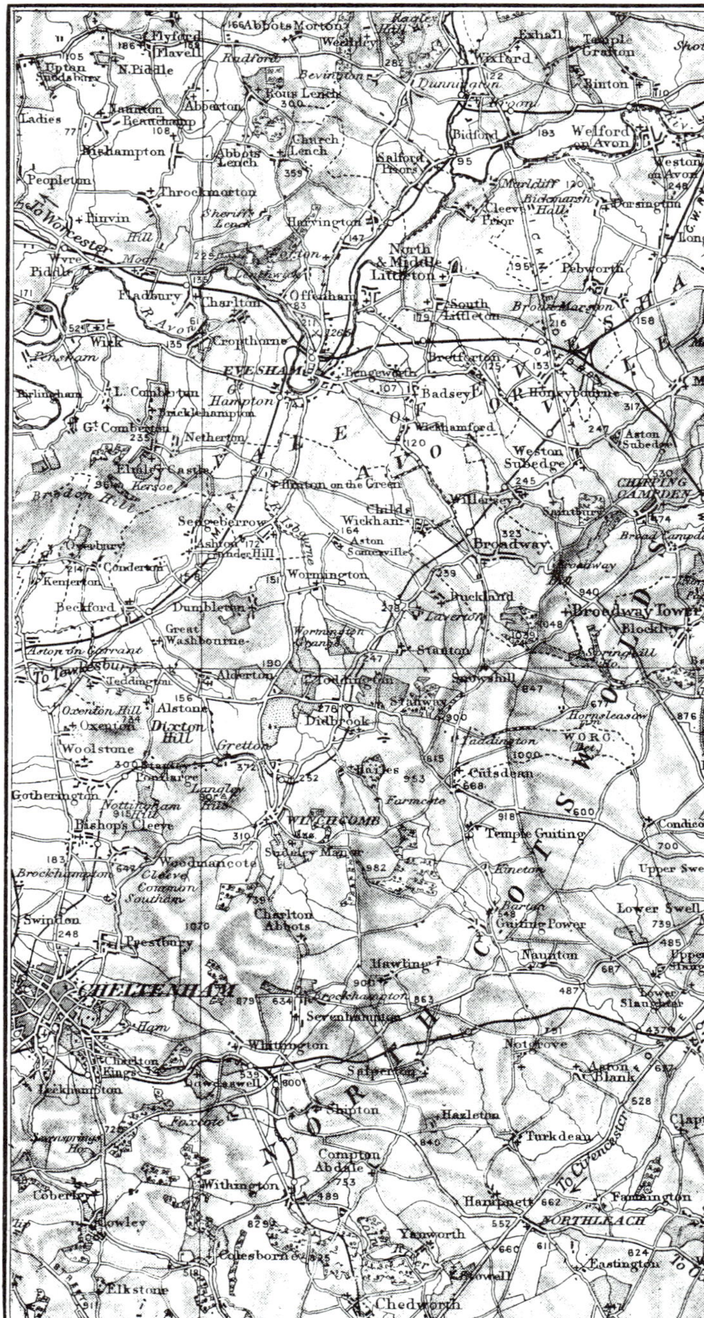

MAP OF THE NORTH COTSWOLDS

(SCALE 4 MILES TO

Reproduced from the Ordnance Survey Map with the sanction

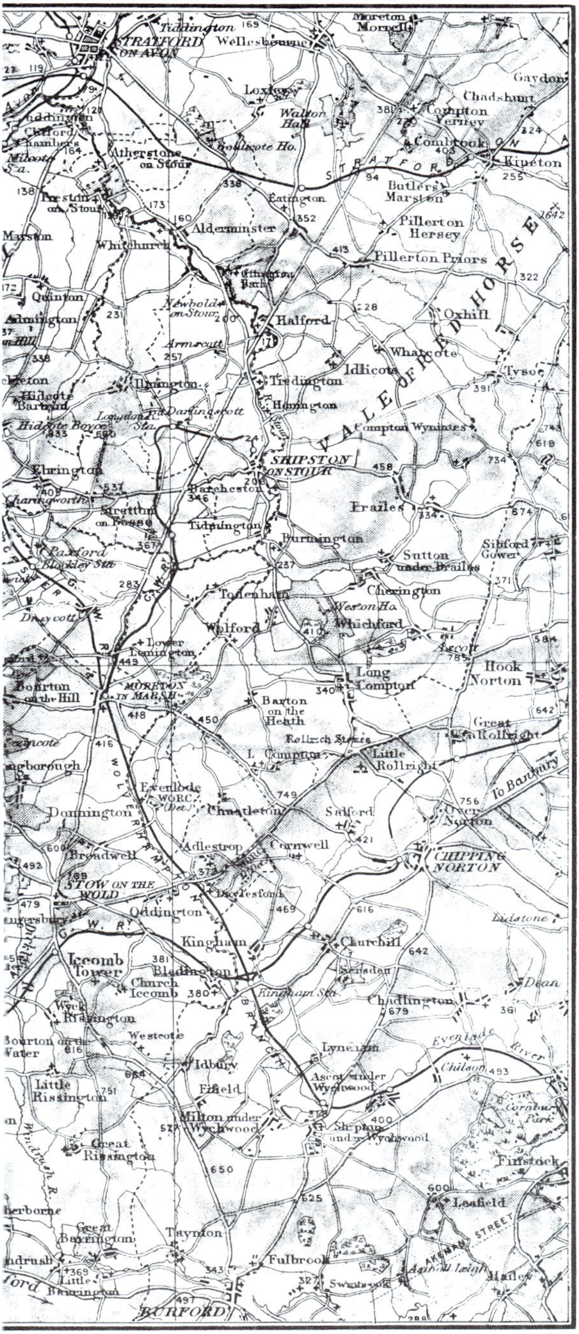

JOHN SWAIN & SON LTD.
LONDON

AND CONTIGUOUS COUNTRY

1 INCH)

of the Controller of His Majesty's Stationery Office.

tinguished when looking over West Wood and by a corner of Humblebee Wood. Above a combe partly covered with brushwood the high location of Belas Knap was in view, with a hill ridge extending back towards Cleeve Common. Close at hand along that side of the road were cultivated fields. At a corner where three fields met I saw one of those ponds which fill themselves by collection of dew. The stone-wall fences dividing the fields went down and made their junction at the bottom of the excavation which, however, was at present dry, some repuddling of its bottom being probably required. In one of the adjacent fields a plough, with two horses driven abreast, was at work in the oat stubble. In another a flock of rooks and jackdaws were hovering over and settling amongst the turnips where they were, no doubt, finding food of some kind for their evening meal. A patch of bright brown fallow lay further away.

The field, along the upper end of which my road lay, was in rough greensward, partly covered with furze, thorn, crab, holly, bramble, briar and thistle, forming a piece of very wild ground open to the road, suitable for the rabbits of whose presence there was considerable evidence. Extending down the side of the hill on this side, to a bottom below, and away towards Drypool Farm on the right, lay Puckham Woods, and beyond these the ground rose again to the Hewlett's Hill that lies towards Cheltenham. I left the roadway and stepped across the rough field to investigate its contents. I found a deep dyke running athwart a part of the field, which might have been an extended stone quarry or a defensive military trench ; it is generally held to be the latter. It was overgrown with bushes and, from its neighbourhood, I traced a wheel-track that ran to and along the upper fence of Puckham Wood. I found an opening into the wood and entered it. The aspect of the woodland was now rugged, damp and forlorn, the glory of the summer being past. Between the oaks, where the hazels had not long ago been cut and were now but of short growth, the ground was covered with fallen leaves, and, beaten down by the rains, dead and done for, were the remnant stems of seeded bluebells, meadowsweet, spurge, sanicle, burdock,

St. John's wort and other woodland plants. Still standing were some tall, gaunt marsh thistles, some weather-stained rag-wort, and some dog's-mercury, rank and overgrown. I followed down a ride in the wood until I heard the dog barking at the keeper's cottage below, when I returned again to my road.

Further along, through a gate on my left, past other road-side cottages, a branch road led down by the wall of Brockhampton Park to the village of that name. On my right-hand a foot and bridle-path led through part of Puckham Woods to the Hewlett's Hill. A flock of fine sheep was in a clover field over the wall on my left, but the clover appeared to have been left too long, its growth being past its prime for fodder ; the flower-heads were quite brown and the stems and foliage looked tough and dry. A line of beech-trees grew along by the roadside wall where I began to go down by a somewhat rugged descent to a main-road, upon reaching which I turned to the right and came to Whittington Village, within three-quarters of a mile from the point where I struck the larger road.

Whittington is a very small village, quite of the Cotswold type. I entered it at the top of its street, and from that point of vantage you can see practically the whole of it, with its church and Manor House lying away on the left, up the side turning that runs past the church entrance to join the Oxford and Cheltenham main-road, which is there close at hand. The old rectory was in view at the other extreme end of the village. It is a sweet tiny village of stone—none of more simple character on all the hills. Some of the stone-walled and stone-roofed cottages that line the street have an old-fashioned aspect, with quaint doors and dormer windows. One has a sun-dial upon its front, and several show the gabled fronts of the local house architecture. Generally speaking there are no regular gardens in front of the cottages, but in the case of some of them a couple of feet of ground against the front wall have been utilised for growing flowers, and roses and creepers that climb up the house-fronts which in summer-time are thus much brightened. The street contains the appropriate barn and spring and, at the further end, the school and beyond it the parson's house. The promise of life here is of the most rustic order and, apart form such of its inhabitants as are to the manner born and neither know nor need a more exciting existence, all the charm of rural retirement is here afforded with an easy relief to possible occasional desire for more company in a visit to Cheltenham, with all its amenities, that lies five miles down the main road. You may go there, in fact, upon any weekday, by rail from the station at Andoversford that is only half a mile along that same main road in the other direction, or more quickly and conveniently by motor vehicle.

The church and old, moated Manor House adjoin each other. From the bye-road the ancient house lies behind the church, some part of its square, latticed windows, grey stone roof and yellow stone walls showing there, its Tudor front facing in another direction. Its walls enclose some rare old wainscoting and a fine antique staircase, with other original features of note. The little church lies in the nearer foreground, a comparatively minor and humble object, but of very ancient foundation. It has two gables facing the roadway, and also shows from there its wooden bell-turret topped by a metal cross. An old stone village cross stands in the churchyard near the chancel window. The approach to the church door is under the branches of a fine yew tree, which spreads its dark foliage to partly hide the front of the church in a half-protecting way, as if to sympathetically screen any defects occasioned by time or the renovations that are but half in keeping with the church's original design. The present windows are chiefly lancets in a square frame. The little chancel window has a pointed arch and with its coloured glass is of artistic effect enough from within. Inside, the effect is generally simple and touching. The small body of the church is divided by a lateral arcade to make a south aisle or chapel of extreme narrowness, being at its Western end only just wide enough to contain the stone effigies of two crusaders and a lady. The arches of this arcade are of Norman design, and a piece of old walling in the West end, with its wide mortar joints,

WHITTINGTON MANOR HOUSE.

is very suggestive of a remnant of an original Saxon church. The rector is proud, as well he may be, to show the church register dating from 1535, its earliest entries being written in a very neat handwriting.

In olden times there was a resident family who bore the name of De Croupes, to whom the monuments in the church relate. The Richard Whittington, Lord Mayor of London, to whom pertains the legendary rhyme connected with church bells and all the pantomimes of Dick Whittington and his cat that have ever been produced in the theatres at Christmastide is not connected with this place. He, however, had origin in Gloucestershire at the village of Pauntley on the Herefordshire side of the county.

I hesitated whether to go out on to the main-road and round by the gates of Sandiwell Park and Andoversford to reach Syreford and the Winchcomb road, which would have meant a slight increase of distance. I rejected this alternative and, having first paid a visit to the Rectory, which is a house of more remote origin even than the Manor House, I passed back up through the village and by the turning for Cleeve Hill down which I had come, and presently dipped to the Coln at Syreford, near the mill and springs of that name. These were beyond a high hedge out of sight, but, at the corner, on looking back up the hill I had just descended, I found the road made an interesting picture there. The corner was made beautiful by the road up that little hill lying between very high hedges in which were several beech-trees, and the latter extended in a line up the Winchcomb road. A white-painted, black-lettered hand-post stood by the roadside under the nearest beech, pointing the several ways. The thick, tall hedges, warmly enclosed the roadway up the little hill, and the foliage of hedges and trees showed in pleasing form and in various rich tones of autumn colouring. Even as I stopped to look and admire the picture was completed by a flock of sheep, followed by a Cotswold shepherd and his dog, that came past me from the Andoversford direction and went up the hill towards Whittington.

I turned along the Winchcomb road up the side of the

valley created by the little stream, which is one of the feeders of the Thames. At the roadside were lines of beech, oak and fir trees. This valley of the Coln forms a little ravine, the hills on either side rising at no great distance, and the road goes along one side at some altitude above the brook, which permits of an excellent view of the valley and the opposite line of hills. These presently rise to a bolder height and show pleasant arable fields where farm work is in progress. The barn and cottages of Sevenhampton Village were soon in view, occupying the hillsides near the stream, some of the cottages extending further up the hills that here made a background of steep slopes and rounded summits.

I turned down the lane by the wall of Sevenhampton Manor, an old house dating from the Stuart era, which stands by the church on this side of the ravine, and I went down a steep incline to the Coln whose shallow water is crossed by a simple ford and foot-bridge. A number of white ducks were enjoying the running water at the ford, and some of the children of the village that lived in the stone cottages above were playing at the water's edge. I noticed how closely united was village and stream, and how inseparable the latter must be from the life of the village and its remembrance. It is the case with several Cotswold villages which are built close to the banks of the streams.

Regaining the highway, I proceeded to the village of Brockhampton, which is but half a mile from Sevenhampton and in the same ecclesiastical parish, having no church of its own. The village is approached, like Sevenhampton, by a short bye-road and has stone cottages by the brook and extending up the steep road that ascends the opposite hill. Its overpowering interest lies in the fine residential mansion known as Brockhampton Park, modernly rebuilt in the gabled style of an old Cotswold house. The entrance lodge to this great house is by the roadside, and the public road practically cuts the park in two. A glimpse of the house is seen through the entrance gate, the stone pillars of which are on either side surmounted by a large stone ball poised on a slender pedestal, a not uncommon mode of ornament in the Cotswolds. The high stone walls which flank the road, hiding the house and park, are intermitted in a stretch equivalent to the width of the front of the house, which can so be seen from the road. The end posts of the walls at the vacant part are ornamented by great stone balls similar to those at the entrance lodge gates. The object of the intermission in the walls is to show an avenue of elms that there stands in the park opposite to the front of the house and in which numerous white and spotted fawn of the fallow deer were straying beneath the trees at the time of my passing. Behind the house is a lake formed by the youthful Coln, where its waters are dammed back for the purpose, and this lake is spanned by a remarkable ornamental bridge, water and bridge lending distinction to the grounds and house on that side.

I continued my way, and in the meadows that lie above Brockhampton Park I saw where the Coln has its origin in the springs and oozing ground that there cause the stream's beginning. In the half-mile of slightly higher ground beyond this, where there is not much in the way of a valley and no watercourse, the fields are cultivated and of true Cotswold appearance. A small road crosses here, going up to Roel Gate and Hawling Village, Guiting Power and other hill places and coming from the West Down, Westwood and Wontley Farm. Immediately beyond this the ground begins to fall Northward and, arriving at the village of Charlton Abbots, I saw I had crossed the summit of the two watersheds and was upon the side of the beautiful and extensive Combe, or Valley, of Winchcomb and Sudeley, which is broader and deeper, the hillsides being further apart and the descent more sudden than in the case of the Coln Valley. Some miles away, beyond Winchcomb, I could see where the mouth of this combe widened out and became one with the Vale of Evesham.

The village of Charlton Abbots presented a few cottages to view. These were mostly approached down a steep road. This village has one fine building, which lay close at hand, in its grange-like Manor House, whose sharp gables and stone-mullioned windows proclaimed the true ancient style of Cotswold house. From the gate opening into the paddock above this house, in which paddock a dozen feeding calves made an animated foreground, stood the fine old house with its extensive farmbuildings and ricks, about which were growing several great trunks of ash and beech. And over the grey tiles of the house-roof and to left and right up and down the valley the steep much-cultivated hills, with their fields and colouring woods, made the completion of a fine rural landscape. Three teams of first-class cart-horses that had done their day's work in the fields followed each other closely up the lane and entered the yard of the grange, down below which I went to find the small Early English church that lies in the contiguous lane, from whose churchyard there is a pretty view of the valley.

Again progressing upon my journey, I passed some ricks by the roadside, where a thrashing-machine was busy at work, and noticed the thick hedges here were covered in part with the fruiting clematis. On the left front Humblebee Wood extended its considerable length along the top part of the hill, its trees now all russet and gold but for the dark green of its firs. Pigeons were flying overhead, and from the wood above, towards the top of which the sun was but just sinking, came the rather too early "Oo-oo-oo" of an owl. The sloping fields below the wood and between it and the road where I walked had been planted with winter-wheat which was already well up in its thick drills in promising plant. Below the woodside I could see a number of pheasants straying into the field, all in very fine plumage. They had passed through one most dangerous month, as pheasant shooting begins with October and November had now come in.

I came soon to where the road forks, the upper road on the left being that which goes by the name of Corndean lane; the other road, to the right, is that which passes by Sudeley Castle and Winchcomb. I pursued this latter which goes through the unfenced grass fields and has several gates upon it. I went immediately through a gate and under the small bit of woodland called Little Humblebee. The road, following the level of the hillside has several steep rises and falls in its course. It goes down steeply first towards where some springs have created a bottom running down the hill-side, with a dribbling streamlet discharging to the brook below. This bottom is converted into a pretty dingle by being overgrown all down its course by trees and bushes. From this point, and from elsewhere along this road, this beautiful Valley of Winchcomb is viewed to advantage. Towards the bottom, below the dingle just mentioned, lies a farm-house near the main brook, called Waterhatch. The Sudeley Brook that courses in the bottom rises over yonder at the top of the valley where lies Spoonley Wood and Farm. Up there are the considerable remains of a Roman Villa. High on the opposite hillside to the left lies another important farm-house and buildings called Sudeley Lodge. The whole hillside, ranging from the valley's head to Salter's Hill, is from here in view and not so far off but that its details can be followed. All its numerous woodlands and trees showed magnificent on this autumn day, from the larch spinney by the brook, whose green had turned to yellow, to the woods that extended along the top and showed russet for the beeches with mingled shades of gold and red and green for the other foliage. How beautiful were the fertile fields of hill and valley, those nearest to me being proclaimed rich by the length of the aftermath and the fleshliness of the red and white cattle that were feeding there. The moist atmosphere of the fine November afternoon was not so misty as to hide any part, but spread over those hills an indescribable softness, lighted by the languorous rays of the declining sun that would soon disappear behind the top of Humblebee Wood and bring the shortened day to a close.

A large part of this valley pertains to the park of Sudeley Castle, whose outer wall lies a long way off on the top of the hill. The whole of the valley and the adjacent hillsides may be considered a great and beautiful park—not less beautiful and park-like by reason of the culture it exhibits.

As I came within half a mile of Sudeley Castle, where the road descends sharply to a gate near the brook, a crowd of rooks and jackdaws rose from the little coppice, chiefly of ash and oak, which is just there, and which has been chosen by those birds as their roosting place. They fly off in the early morning, dividing into numerous companies, and scour the country in every direction in search of their daily food, and return in the evening to pass the night together in this chosen spot. I could not see that there was anything particular about it to distinguish it as specially suitable for such a purpose amongst all the woods, and the fact of this road passing so near to it was disturbing. As I stood there the birds flew up in a crowd of black forms and wheeled overhead, describing many circles and so continuing in flight without flying away. Rooks and jackdaws were intermingled; there were many of the latter. I made a rough, one-glance estimate of the number of the whole flock of both species that were on the wing and told myself it was two thousand.

I stepped to the brookside, which was here close by, and found a foot-bridge with a footpath going over the brow of the green hill towards the castle, the top of whose towers and the flagstaff could be seen over there. From the drinking-place for cattle that had been made in the brook near the bridge a water-hen flew up at my approach and went further along the brook. The road followed the brook's course at a short distance off and here became enclosed as a lane between hedges, though still with several sharp ups and downs upon it. The hedges were brilliant with scarlet hips and crimson haws, of which there was a profusion. Where some stretches of rails intermitted the hedgerow on the right in several places admirable views of Sudeley Castle were available, the view being across the brook to the castle that stood on a slight eminence beyond, surrounded by its trees, two of its several towers, the keep with a tall flagstaff, the ancient chimney and a considerable part of its other buildings showing from this side.

I reached Winchcomb in due course and ascended to Cleeve Hill by the main road, finishing my walk in a leisurely way, but not before the sun had set and the twilight had deepened almost to the darkness of night.

CHAPTER XVI.

AROUND WOOLSTONE HILL AND TO ITS SUMMIT.

WHEN you walk by Grinnell Lane along the top of Nottingham Hill to the second gate, where you look down on the railway and Gotherington Station, the hill over beyond that station is Woolstone Hill. It is rather a little group of hills than a single hill, for it shows several eminences from whichever side you look at it. From the Nottingham Hill side there are three summits visible, and two or three when viewed from its other sides, several of these slopes and summits bearing different names. On the side opposite to Woolstone it is called Oxenton Hill, which fact has led to some confusion in the references made to the hill in different writings. The whole outlier might be termed the Woolstone-Oxenton Hill Group.

I followed down the rough slope by which Grinnell Lane descends between hedges to the vale. The track was almost lost in coarse grass, and it was evident that it had not lately been used as a wheel-way, though the right to use it as such is undoubted. From the gate above there is a slightly better rough road going down on the left to Gotherington by the Manor Farm, which the few vehicles that pass this way prefer to use.

Grinnell Lane opens into the lower road to Winchcomb close to Gotherington Station. Coming into the main-road there I turned to the right and, about 500 yards along this road, took the turning to the left which leads by Dixton to Alstone. I immediately came to a railway bridge that crosses a cutting of the railway, that passes from Cheltenham to Honeybourne and Stratford-on-Avon. Dixton Hill, with its Manor House and farm, was near by on the right front, and on the left front Woolstone Hill presented itself in three eminences, the middle one being the largest, and it was that one I presently intended to scale, though, viewed from here, it did not promise all I found when I got there. I proceeded onward where the road sank and rose to accommodate itself to a small watercourse and, on the rise, passed a farm and some cottages pertaining to Dixton, and the turning by which Dixton Manor House is approached. This is a pleasant ancient Tudor habitation, hidden from the road by surrounding trees. But I was not visiting the Manor House to-day and, besides the farm adjoining, there is little else to see in the hamlet. I presently came in sight of Alderton Hill, away on the right front, and Woolstone Hill, which remained nearly on my left, now presented two summits, the further one with trees upon it, which increased in density further along, covering the top and side of the hill as Dixton Wood, well-known to the fox hunter.

The narrow lane, taking several sharp winds, at a distance of a mile and a half from Dixton, brought me suddenly round a corner into Alstone Village. I was struck by the distinguished agricultural air, gained by evident age, which this village possesses. The Manor House, not a great place, leads the display in black and white, lying a bit back off the road in a garden and near the church. The church, small, simple, five or six hundred years old, with some parts still older, but in very usable condition, turns its little chancel towards the roadside and its little, half-wooden turret heavenward. It affords entrance to the visitor through its open door that is approached through a fine porch ; over the door is a tympanum with Norman ornament. On the opposite side of the road to the church there is a little old barn, and an old black-beamed house occupies a prominent corner higher up ; besides these there are a very few ancient cottages and a farm-house or two.

A short distance below Alstone Manor House I turned to the left along an even narrower road which still kept me in the near neighbourhood of the hill that I was bent upon encircling and which, along here, shows some wooded sides that ascend rather abruptly and, though not high, present a bold background to the scene. At about a mile from Alstone Church, at the hamlet of Bengrove, I found a pretty

THE HIGHEST PART OF THE HIGH-ROAD.

IN GRINNELL LANE.

CLEEVE HILL AND NOTTINGHAM HILL.

LANDSCAPE FROM END OF NOTTINGHAM HILL.
SHOWING PARTS OF WOCLSTONE HILL, BREDON HILL AND AVON VALE.

group of half-timbered, thatched cottages. They stood behind their garden hedges but were not too hidden away to be viewed from the road. One of them had a rambler rose, still in flower, growing over its doorway, outside which the old proprietor was sitting whilst the wife was also visible moving just within the threshold.

Half a mile further on I came to the first houses of the small, straggling village of Teddington with its blacksmith's shop where the hammer was sounding, and the odour of burning hoof which emanated from its somewhat dark interior seemed to indicate a shoeing operation in progress. The church is a short way down a lane to the left, its grey tower being backed by the green of another slope of the hill. This village gives its name to the cross roads known as "Teddington Hands," and, presently, when I came out of the lane in which Teddington village lies on to the Evesham main-road, I made a diversion to visit the crossing which could be seen some 400 yards or so distant. There is an inn there, and opposite the inn is a stone sign-post with six pointers, or directing hands, to as many roads. This is "Teddington Hands." Inscribed upon it are the following lines :—

"Edmond Attwood of the Vine Tree
At the first time erected me,
And freely he did this bestow
Strange travellers the way to show.
Ten generations past and gone
Repaired by Alice Attwood of Teddington.
August 10th, 1876."

The last line of this inscription is out of metre and Alice Attwood should have avoided that and, being a descendant of Edmond of the Vine Tree Farm in Teddington, philanthropist of ten generations agone, she might have kept up the family interest with the following addition to the first rhymes :—

"Ten generations past and gone,
An Attwood still of Teddington,
In year of grace eighteen seven six
Gave me amendment and refix."

The stone, however, for its permanence requires that all succeeding county surveyors shall take it into their care and amend and re-erect it as required. It is true that the line of division of the two counties of Gloucester and Worcester passes over the very spot occupied by "The Hands," but if both surveyors determine to keep the thing in order it should be done.

At the opposite corner to "The Hands" lies a mass of weather-worn stone called "the tibble stone," which appears to have been put here also very anciently, before the roads were made, as a landmark.

The directions and distances in miles indicated upon the six hands are as follows :—

Cheltenham	7½	
Tewkesbury	4½	
Winchcomb	6	
Stow	15	
Evesham	8½	
Overbury	2¾	and Pershore 9

The neighbouring inn bears the sign of "The Cross Hands," which is painted on a board in front of the house as two human hands clasped, in disregard of the other meaning of cross-hands above described, which plainly gave the name to the place.

I walked back along the main-road to where there is a sharp turn to Cheltenham, more than a mile from Teddington Hands, and, turning there, I passed by the longest side of Woolstone-Oxenton Hill, soon to find a short bye-road leading to Oxenton village, which is situated close under the hill. The church is at the top of the road at some slight altitude on the hill, so that from the back of the churchyard the bare, bold hill-top, which one can see there, is near at hand and could soon be gained. I looked round the church and at its tower with its four crocketed pinnacles and ogee arches in its belfry windows. I also looked into its somewhat musty interior, where a woman was dusting in readiness for the morrow's service. There was evidence within of a former dilapidation, made good by the utilisation of old with new material. The most pleasing thing I found about the church was its little avenue of cypress trees grown tall, which winds up the bank to the church door. To light the turn of the avenue on a winter night a solitary old lamp was suspended from a bough of one of the trees.

I returned down the straggling street of inconspicuous cottages that constitutes Oxenton and so regained the main-road and, three-quarters of a mile nearer Cheltenham found a similar bye-road leading into the village of Woolstone. I took this turn to the left and, having often turned to the left since I approached Dixton, I had now almost encircled Woolstone Hill. As I covered the last half-mile into Woolstone Village from the main-road, I noticed the hill on this side presented two almost equal summits, divided by a lower, recessed portion. The pleasant curves of these eminences, varied by patches of wood, were on my left as I entered Woolstone, and the road before me had willows, as well as other trees, beside it, because a streamlet courses by the roadside there. From the farm gate, where there is a large cow-byre on the left, a herd of cows were coming forth into the lane, after having been milked. They made a pretty rustic picture there as they followed each other at a slow pace, some passing out of the road-way on to the green road-side waste and to the hedge towards where the willows grew. I stopped to admire the scene and the cows passed me by complacently.

I found Woolstone a pleasing village, as Alstone is, but it is quite different from Alstone. It lies towards the bottom of a slope of a lower extended part of Woolstone Hill which is called Crane Hill and, looking Southward, gets the maximum of sunshine. Even from the distance of Cleeve Hill it appears a bright place, and from there you can see its church, new rectory and some of its houses quite clearly. The rectory is rather new because the older house was burned down some years ago. The farms and houses of the village are, however, in great part hidden amongst trees which are fruit trees in the main, for orchards here abound which, in blossom-time, make Woolstone a very sweet village. Upon the bank to the left I found Woolstone Church, with its tower and church clock and neat interior, all in the well-ordered condition of a restoration which, although it may have had place nearly fifty years ago, is still evident. Behind it one enters from the churchyard into the pleasant precincts of the rectory.

In passing through this village I saw but three persons: an old woman by a cottage gate, a farm labourer who followed out the herd of cows from the byre, and a sportsman with a gun upon his shoulder who was returning from the fields.

Following the road to its end, I went through a gate, down a short incline and then up a short distance to Woolstone Hill Farm—a house in red brick with a considerable array of farm buildings, standing away from the village. Beyond the farm rose Woolstone Hill—I mean the highest part of this group of outliers. This highest part rises to an altitude of 734 feet.

I made the ascent easily from the farm, passing first through an orchard. There was a fair crop of apples of a variety of kinds at present on the trees in this orchard. A ladder stood against the branches of a tree of an early sort, from which the fruit had been partly gathered and, perhaps, sent to Cheltenham last fruit-market day, as a trial of their present value. In the upper part of the orchard, which had been more recently planted, the soil seemed poor and clayey. There were many thistles, now covered with down. There were butterflies: a peacock, a meadow-brown and a large white. A sparrow-hawk stooped to the thistles at the top of the orchard and, rising again, settled for some seconds on an apple-tree bough. It was the female bird of large size; I could see the horizontal striping of the front of her body and tail and her yellow legs. Higher up I passed a dead hedgehog that appeared to have been crushed. This, possibly, was the attraction to the hawk.

Above the orchard I got into a field of rough and thistly surface and went past a hovel and pond, near where grew a number of thorns and bramble-bushes. Then, passing through a tall hedge-fence, I entered some still rougher ground, with more thorns and brambles, long grass and ant-banks, a splendid cover for wild creatures. There was a sparse sprinkling of sheep of Welsh breed, and some cattle and horses could be seen down the hillside. A rabbit leapt from a lair in the long grass. I heard the cry of the green woodpecker some way off on my right ; in Warwickshire this bird is called the " eckle " ; in Herefordshire " iccol " ; in Gloucestershire, " yaffle." As I crossed the deep trench which guards the summit of the hill on this side, creating a so-called camp on the top of it, eight magpies flew across in front, following each other to some ash-trees that grew a little below the hill-top on the other side and, settling there, made a prolonged and considerable chatter. As I reached the top, a covey of partridges buzzed up from among the ant-heaps and went foolishly downward beyond the further edge of the hill, towards where, from time to time, I heard the discharge of guns. It was the 2nd of September. Several sky-larks also rose from the rough surface of the hill-top.

The top of Woolstone Hill presents a most extraordinary appearance. In extent it might be guessed to measure some six hundred yards in length, with a width of two hundred yards. It is pitted all over by artificial excavations, with as many small mounds between, and the cause or object of these holes and mounds makes a subject for speculation. Some of them are, no doubt, due to quarrying at the surface for road stone ; but some have connection with a sometime resident and extinct humanity. Human bones are still occasionally unearthed here, though there does not appear to be any definite large tumulus. The rabbits have made an extensive warren of it, burrowing into the hillocks and pit sides in all directions, exhibiting the yellow sub-soil and Oolitic stones that show the hill to belong to the neighbouring Cotswolds, though completely separated from them.

Another notable thing about the surface is the number and variety of thistles that grow there, which now, for the main part, were covered with downy seeds, and some of these, being set free, went sailing abroad in the currents of air that moved more or less continually over the hill. The yellow carline thistle, in particular, luxuriates here, evidently well suited by soil and situation. Nettles and ground-ivy and rock-rose also flourish here and flower in season. Down in Oxenton and Woolstone villages they speak of this spot as " The Knolls."

A panoramic view presented itself to my eyes from this hill-top, extending all round the circle. The longest and, at the same time, the most intimate view of the Cotswold escarpment to be obtained anywhere here presents itself. The edge of hills is in plain view through a length of forty miles, including Meon Hill at one end and at the other passing beyond Gloucester by Painswick and Haresfield Beacons, with glimpses of Stinchcomb Hill beyond Robinswood Hill, in clear weather. Standing well off the Nottingham Hill promontory, Woolstone Hill commands a view of all this length of range, as well as, practically, of all the outliers. I faced Nottingham Hill directly and could trace Grinnell lane descending its side, to the left of which Prescott House was seen to be prettily situated, and Stanley Mount, to the left of this, whilst over beyond, the woods of Corndean, a part of Roel Hill, the position of Belas Knap and a stretch of Cleeve Common were visible. Between me and Stanley Hill the farms, cottages and Manor House that constitute Dixton lay backed by a thick setting of large trees, and the bare, grave-like summit of Dixton Hill. Beyond, in that direction, the spire and houses of Gretton Village were showing, and the road that goes to Winchcomb. That town itself was hidden behind the slope of Langley Hill. The continuing hill-line, with the parts named after Hailes, Stanway, Broadway, and the prominent heights beyond, were all showing. To the left of this hill-line the Alderton-Dumbleton outlier stretched across, partly shutting off Avon Vale, large portions of which could, however, be seen up beyond Toddington, whose fruit plantations were conspicuous in the nearer distance. In the bottom, immediately below, was the railway which goes away towards Cheltenham by Bishop's Cleeve in a long, straight stretch.

Looking from the opposite side of the hill towards the North, the broad slope of Bredon Hill lay not far off with several villages about its lower slopes, amongst which Beckford showed most prominently. From this side the various parts and tops of the Woolstone Hill group are best appreciated, and its slopes, as from here viewed, are specially pretty as behind Oxenton, for instance, where the woodland is nicely disposed on a little cliff and on the slopes below, which sweep down gracefully to the roofs and red walls of Teddington and to Bengrove, with its farm and large rick-yard. Behind the swell on the right the village of Alstone is partly seen among the orchards.

The whole view of Severn Vale lies on the other side, passing up into Shropshire and to the Malverns and over into Wales and down by the Forest Hills.

In fact, the views from the top of Woolstone Hill are very striking and could not have escaped remark and apprecia-tion in any era since these parts were first populated, though, to-day, it is a rare thing to meet with any one who has been to the top of this hill.

The place is fascinating by reason of its views, its broken ground, its thistles and other living objects, and its bracing atmosphere. To come here it needs to choose a dry and clear day and to do the journey in a leisurely way, somewhat as here described. At different seasons of the year local appearances will naturally differ slightly. If you do the round on wheels, instead of walking, you must leave your vehicle at the farm below and, at least, walk the three-quarters of a mile up from the farm. Take maps and a tele-scope of some sort, and some light refreshment and stay on the hill-top a couple of hours. Two persons doing it would be company enough. The hill may also be ascended from Oxenton Village by a rough cart-track that goes right to the top, and by a rather shorter route from the Dixton side.

In descending by the way I had come up I saw there was much fruit on the brambles though it was still all green and mixed with flowers. Near the pond half-way down the slope, in the large thorn-trees and pollard willows that grew there, a company of long-tailed tits were flying from tree to tree—quite a dozen of them. I had a good view of several of these pretty little birds as they hung, back downwards, from the willow-twigs; they were in fine plumage and colour. They were uttering a monotonous short twitter, not the "*chick-a-dee-dee-dee*" of the tom-tit with which all are familiar. I could not remember whether I had ever heard the long-tailed tit make that sound. One does not meet with this particular titmouse very often in this neighbourhood, but too often to consider him a rare bird ; when seen after breeding-time he is always in a company that is not numerous enough to be called a drove but really consists of the parent birds and the members of their always numerous family. At the bottom of the orchard, by the farm-house, so many chaffinches were collected together that one might have said there was a drove. Every one showed the white bar in the wing when in flight, which, I suppose, is what gives the bird its second name of pie, or pied, finch.

I came down through Woolstone village to the turning for Gotherington and to Bishop's Cleeve by that way, and re-ascended Cleeve Hill through Woodmancote.

CHAPTER XVII.

AN EXCURSION TO DUMBLETON HILL AND TO SOME OF THE VILLAGES IT OVERLOOKS.

DUMBLETON-ALDERTON-WASHBOURNE HILL, so named respectively at one part and another, is that other outlier lying away on the right of Woolstone and Dixton Hills and showing, as viewed from Cleeve or Nottingham Hill, a long side whose highest part is at the centre, with a lower part at either end. Being not a single, simple hill, however, but rather a little group of hills joined together, like the Woolstone-Oxenton group already visited, its aspect is different at every side, the side which faces Beckford and the Cheltenham to Evesham high-road, showing two well-marked eminences of pleasing appearance, whilst the aspect from Toddington and the road or hillsides between Winchcomb and Broadway is again quite different. On these last-mentioned sides it is always referred to as Dumbleton Hill.

I made first for the village of Alderton that lies on the nearer side of the hill, and took Gretton on the way. If one went by wheel it would be necessary to descend from Cleeve Hill and go by Bishop's Cleeve and Gotherington to get to Gretton; but I walked to the last-mentioned village over Langley Hill, for I was afoot to-day, though the tramp threatened to be a long one. As Gretton can be plainly seen from the top of Langley Hill and be kept in sight whilst the descent is made to it on the other side of the hill, it cannot be missed, even should you fail to strike the footpath, and the walk to this village, down through the green and banky fields, is pleasant and easy enough.

I found Gretton a very ancient village of thatched roofs and part-timbered walls, some of which had fallen to decay, and the general appearance of the place was rather of neglect and dilapidation. A new church, with a spire, has supplanted the old one which now forms a picturesque ruin as viewed from a grassy corner where some cottages, recently rethatched and renovated, made on this occasion an appropriate addition to the scene which was rendered more lively by a number of geese upon the patch of green in the foreground. The depressing effect of decay at Gretton struggles with the pleasing effect produced by the picturesqueness and antiquity of its cottages. These have sometimes been made the subject of pictorial representation upon the canvases of local or other artists.

Having walked to the top of the village, I turned back and, near the modern church, found the turning for Beckford which leads in a mile and a half to a junction with the Tewkesbury-Stow main-road, and Alderton then lies in sight under its hill, with a bye-road reaching it in half a mile. A footpath that lies over a stile passes across a couple of fields and shortens the distance to the village which presents itself prettily enough from the high-road as a medley of small houses with a square-towered church nestling at the foot of the hill to which it gives its name. This view of the village with the hill behind it is, in fact, the most entrancing thing about Alderton.

Entering the village I saw that it was a degree superior to Gretton, more of the old cottages having been replaced by new erections which, if less picturesque in style, make more healthful dwellings. There are a number of very old houses, too ; some down the side of the meadow adjoining the church and others in the village street. They mainly aggregate themselves into a winding main street with a bye-street or two passing round towards the church and the entrance to the rectory. The church, like most of those in this neighbourhood, appears to have been originally in the Fourteenth Century style. It has a nice decorated window with clear glass in its chancel end. Other windows, however, are square-headed, of the Perpendicular and debased Perpendicular type, some of them, perhaps, resulting from rather recent restoration. The chief entrance has a modern wooden porch of good design. The interior walls are neatly pointed in dark cement, the floor paved with tiles, and the

AT GRETTON.

AT DUMBLETON.

AT DUMBLETON.

TODDINGTON CHURCH AND DEMESNE.

whole is in proper order for service, which, in such degree, cannot be said of every church, though such service is the reason for the existence of churches.

Towards the end of Alderton Village, on the Washbourne side, may be found the entrance to a rough road which is passable for a bicycle in dry weather, with some amount of walking; it leads straight over the hill to Dumbleton. I took the footpath near and opposite to the post-office which led me over stiles into the fields and ultimately joined the rough road above mentioned. I left this temporarily, however, in order to climb to the highest part of Alderton Hill. I went up a steep, rough slope where the ground was of poor quality and covered with rank grass, thistles and briars, from amongst which two or three rabbits were roused by my passing. A larch plantation was on my right as I neared the summit. When I got to the top I found the view was much restricted by the large wood that covered a part of the top of the hill and the whole of one side of it. There was a fine view on the nearer side which took in the slopes of Stanley, Nottingham and Woolstone Hills, with glimpses between to the further views of Severn Vale and the hills beyond. The vale below was now smiling with sheaf-full fields. Over the wood-covered spurs that formed the immediate fore-ground lay the plum plantations of Toddington and a stretch of the Cotswold line above Winchcomb beyond these.

I descended a little to rejoin the rough road that goes from Alderton to Dumbleton, where it passes through a small wood, and followed it by Dumbleton Hill Farm and down a green glade between the woodlands, and soon the prospect into Avon Vale opened out in front, with a near and good view of Bredon Hill, with Ashton-under-Hill hanging to its skirt.

I left the road again to climb a high, bare tump on my right that lay below the wood, in order to get, from its summit, a view of the upper part of the Cotswold edge and the vale in front of it which had been hidden by the wood at the top of Alderton Hill. I saw Broadway Tower above the village of that name and the thin spire of Saintbury

Church further along the hills ; whilst, out in the vale, I traced by their spires the villages of Child's Wickham, Sedgeberrow and Bengeworth (Evesham), and the red walls of Wormington, and identified the little hill of Aston Somerville. Further down the glade on the immediate left lay Dumbleton Hall, and the road presently brought me down in front of it, giving me a fair view of the mansion with its decorative lake and gardens, a part of which, with wide, grassy paths, are laid out up the slope of the hill above which a thick wood forms the dark background of the scene, where pheasants were crowing and wood-pigeons cooing.

The road passes on by a farm into Dumbleton Village, which is entered near the church. The tower of the church from afar, upon this early autumn day, had looked as if it were built of red brick, but the colour proved to be due to the reddened leaves of a creeper that covered its stone wall upon one side. It is a massive square tower for the rest ; the base, or first storey, an epoch or two older than the upper portion which, together with the main part of the existing building, appears to be of early Fourteenth Century style. In the North wall of the church, however, there is an interesting late Norman doorway, now blocked up, which has a tympanum filling its round arch, figured with a head, and evidently symbolical of speech and hearing. Many tongues proceed from the mouth of the figure, and a waving line from ear to ear would seem to represent the reception of sounds. In the wall above this door there is a line of carved corbel stones. Similar stones also jut forth from the top of the lower storey of the tower and in each case appear to indicate the position of a former roof. The main entrance of the church is by a stone porch that looks new ; it has a sundial on its front, where the sun, unfailing in its truth, was at the moment correcting the clock situated in the tower whose hands were an hour in advance, marking what we have just begun to call "summer time." The interior shows a miscellaneous display of arches. The original church has been plainly subjected to considerable alteration and repair. There are some monumental tombs, one with kneeling effigies up in the chancel, and there is a fine old carved font inscribed with the names of Richard Ingles and Charles Agg, churchwardens, Ao.Dm. 1661. There are six or eight drooping ashes and elms in the churchyard among the graves, whose appearance is too formal and even lugubrious, to be ornamental, especially when compared with the beautiful trees of the closely neighbouring park of Dumbleton Hall.

The village straggles round and there are some pretty cottages in it—old and modern—besides the ancient rectory which is quite an important old house. Near the church is an elaborate stone drinking-trough, or fountain, and just here is the most distinguished corner of the place. The path to the church lies beyond the fountain, and the church tower with the fountain and some large trees group effectively together. The dominance of Dumbleton Hall, which is approached from near the church by an avenue passing through its fair grounds, and which has some of its out-premises screened from the churchyard by a thick belt of yew and box, is always and distinctly felt.

From Dumbleton to Toddington is a walk along the road of over three miles and you pass through a portion of the fruit plantations and close to the jam factory. The season was past when the fields around are redolent with the odour of strawberries, but the plums in vast numbers were now colouring towards ripeness. I had often seen the spire of Toddington Church in the distance from the Cleeve Hill vicinity and was now bent upon a nearer acquaintance. The village of Toddington is not much to speak of. It consists chiefly of a line of cottages that lie on the side of the main-road to Stow, some distance from the church. The latter is an adjunct of the great house, Toddington Manor, which is a handsome mansion in yellow Cotswold stone, built in imitative Perpendicular or Tudor style. It has a central tower with numerous turrets and decorating pinnacles. The church is of the same material and colour and, practically speaking, stands in the garden of the house; it was of old foundation but was rebuilt in 1723 by a former owner of the estate, Thomas Charles, Viscount Tracy, a fact set out in an inscription on a mural tablet inside the mortuary chapel. This church, however, did not suit the taste of an after owner, the late Lord Sudeley, who pulled it down and built the present one in 1877.

Toddington Church offers a contrast to any other church in the neighbourhood, such as the one at Dumbleton which I had just visited. It has a fine spire and all parts appear in perfect state and of the single finished design adopted by its builders. The building seems to be intended to serve the double purpose of a church and a mausoleum for the reception of the relics and monuments of the family of Tracy and of Hanbury-Tracy. In the chapel situated on the North side of the church there is a magnificent monument in marble with reclining figures of large size upon the top, representing Charles Hanbury-Tracy, Baron Sudeley, died 1858, and his wife. The older memorial tablets on the walls of this chapel to former members of the Tracy family were evidently removed from the older church. Arched recesses have been made in the walls of the chapel seemingly to receive other tombs or cenotaphs. Can any man be so sure of the continuance of his line, or of his property? The Tracys derived their line and dignity from a Plantagenet King, but are no longer owners of the estate of Toddington.

The general architectural style of the church is imitative of the Early English, with modern embellishments. The exterior appearance is good, with its graceful tower and spire, and the warm colour of the stone contrasting with the rich foliage of the great trees that stand about it. The arches of the interior are all decorated with pillars of polished grey granite; the roof of the chancel is groined, and that of the nave is a fine example in wood. The paving of chancel and altar-steps is in marble; the walls around the altar have canopied sedilia, or stalls, the backs of some of them sculptured in screen work. A small South chapel shows effective lancet arches and steep groining. The West end of the nave, beneath the tower, has an arched screen forming a vestry. The edifice compensates in considerable measure for its want of age by its architectural grace. The mortuary chapel, with its big monument, is a part rather for private sentiment and gratification.

In the garden outside, opposite the West end of the church with its beautiful spire, is an old ornamental archway that pertained to a more ancient house. The road through the archway leads, within a short distance, to a bridge over a piece of water formed by a portion of the River Isborne, whose main stream is heard near by splashing separately down a little fall. This water is an additional ornament to the beautiful park. I noticed a growth of water-plants of various sorts upon and about the water, and several water-hen were swimming there. When I made a second visit to this place in June, a guelder-rose and a briar-rose and a great cornel bush were in bloom by the bridge, bamboos and other exotics were flourishing at the water-edge, and white lilies, with their cool leaves, were spread upon the surface. I noticed that pleasant footpaths passed by the water under the mixed foliage of many fine trees, with views between the branches of the great yellow stone house, over lawns and beds of blossoming rhododendrons.

The main road from Cheltenham and Winchcomb to Broadway passes along one side of the grounds of Toddington Manor, and that would have been the nearest way to walk back to Cleeve Hill, which is seven miles away. Toddington Station lies at about a mile's distance from the church and, as the time suited, I caught a train there that brought me to Bishop's Cleeve Station, from which I walked up through Woodmancote and thereby saved myself four or five miles. On my return I had walked about fifteen.

CHAPTER XVIII.

EN ROUTE FOR BROADWAY AND BACK BY ITS TOWER.

I RODE down to Winchcomb and passed straight through the town, crossed the stream known as the " Isborne," over the bridge just beyond, by a double twist of the road, and was then fairly on the road to Broadway.

The Isborne meadows, one of which is sometimes used as a playground by the Winchcomb folk, lay at first on the left, and along upon the right lay the Cotswold line. This main-road is near to the hills and follows to some extent the prominences and recessions of the hill edge. It cannot, therefore, be driven or ridden at a very fast speed, on account of the numerous curves and corners that occur repeatedly to hide the road in front, and whatever may be upon it.

There is no village or place of great interest situated on the eight miles of main road between Winchcomb and Broadway, but several very interesting places just off this road and between it and the base of the hills. At two and a half miles beyond Winchcomb two side roads lead towards the hills, which leave the main road so near together as to require but one sign post to indicate the places to which they go. The first points to Hailes and the other to Didbrook and Stanway.

I turned for Hailes and, within three-quarters of a mile from the turning, arrived there. The place consists of a farm or two and a few cottages, with a small restored church, situated in the green fields, close under Hailes Hill, whose hanging woods of intense green made a sufficiently solid background, and some fine trunks of ash, wych elm and other trees adorned the more immediate vicinity.

The road, passing on through a gate, rose up the hill

towards Farmcote and, in the field on the right, enclosed by an iron paling, lay a little wilderness, where the hummocky ground was overgrown with tall grass and other wild plant-life that half hid the blocks and heaps of stones and portions of arcading that constitute the ruins of Hailes Abbey.

The remaining arches, which stand *in situ*, belonged chiefly to the cloisters and the chapter-house. Though these are much broken and themselves topped and surrounded with briars, brambles and other plants, they are, together with other visible remains, sufficient to indicate the imposing nature of the sacred pile that once stood here. The Abbey pertained to the Cistercian fraternity and was founded in 1246. Soon afterwards it became possessed of what had been officially certified to be a portion of Christ's blood. This led to many pilgrimages to the Abbey, with resulting gifts and contributions to its available funds, for to such relics great credence and reverence were attached in an age when it was less the custom to inquire into the origin and verity of things than at present.

The history of Hailes Abbey and its relic of the Holy Blood, and the more particular description of its ruins, can be looked up by any one to whom such details are likely to be interesting in Mr. Baddeley's scholarly book upon the subject.* The things to be found upon the spot and the suggestions that arise from them may satisfy others. The key to the padlocked gate giving close access to the ruins, is to be obtained at a cottage situated near the church hard by and, whether from within or without the enclosure, it is pleasant to contemplate the rural scene of which the ruins are the centre, and which was so well judged a locality for the practical operations of agriculture, to which the white monks and friars of the order chiefly devoted themselves. At one time a considerable part of the Abbey's income was derived from the sale of its wool. The scene is a pastoral one by nature, of greensward and woodland, flock and herd and cultivated field—a place for feeding and increase of man and beast. The great building was an intrusion into the natural condition of the land, but it is pleasant to consider such

* See "A Cotswold Shrine," by W. St. Clair Baddeley.

institutions as resulting from an instinct acting on behalf of humanity towards spiritual culture, and restraint of evil by disciplinary means. The chief avowed object of Hailes Abbey, however, was for the dispensing of charity, and on that account a considerable part of it was allowed to remain up to Cromwell's time, when the result of an inquiry into its management, and the nature of its "holy blood," which latter was declared from a London pulpit to be no more than a mixture of honey with other ingredients, militated against its continuance. Thus was the Abbey closed, its properties being appropriated to the use of other persons, its chief and minor officials being retired on small pensions, and hence these ruins.

I left Hailes and, rolling back to the main-road, took the other of the two turnings at the handpost, and went by that bye-road under the railway to come to Didbrook at a distance of about a mile. It is a small village of houses of a sort that pertains to the vale rather than to the hills. There is a little square-towered church, some interesting-looking farms and a fine specimen of a half-timbered building, divided now into two or three small dwellings, but probably one house originally. Its present very sound appearance indicates renovation, and chimneys and roof have manifestly been renewed, but it retains its ancient style all the same, and is quite pleasing to the eye.

On another mile and, leaving the farms of Wood Stanway on the right, the Tewkesbury to Stow highway was crossed just as it is about to ascend Stanway Hill, and the main part of Stanway Village, or Church Stanway, was immediately approached down a slope. Turning the corner at the bottom of this little hill, you come suddenly upon the extraordinary group of buildings which distinguishes Stanway among villages. The first of this to come into view, and the most unique from the point of view of architecture, is the gate-house leading to the forecourt of Stanway House—a large Tudor mansion belonging to the Earl of Wemyss. The gate-house is of very original design, said to be the invention of Inigo Jones (circ. 1630). The high garden wall at its side is pierced by oval fenestra, which look as

RUINS OF HAYLES ABBEY.

CORNER OF GARDEN AND GREAT BARN AT STANWAY.

ORNATE GATEHOUSE AT STANWAY.

if intended as a relief to the plainness of the wall rather than as a means of viewing the front of the gate-house from the garden. Through the arch of the gate-house the elevation of the Tudor mansion, with its numerous gables, might be viewed, but this appeared to me in no way so striking as the gate-house, notwithstanding the large double-storey window of its great hall. At the further side of the court I saw another archway of plainer design that leads to the park. The other two buildings of the remarkable group were the church and the great barn, both adjacent to the beautiful garden of the great house, and all built of yellow stone—the church with its fine square tower having its colour less modified by action of weather and attached lichens than the rest, to which one or two ordinary dwellings that stand opposite the church add hardly any evidence of existence, their presence being rendered so insignificant by the greater buildings. Magnificent trees neighbour house and church, and the heavily wooded Lidcombe Hill rises from the park immediately behind.

Through the park I proceeded along the road under an avenue of oaks and, in a further mile, entered the village of Stanton, which has a decided street and is, therefore, much more of a village than Didbrook or Stanway. It is a village of distinctly Cotswold character, moreover, and the majority of its houses appear of the same architectural design, apparently dating from the same epoch—somewhere back in Stuart times for the main part, though some are no doubt older. Inconspicuously situated in a bye-lane, is the remarkably pretty tapering-spired church. It is not of the most ancient order, as it at present stands, having apparently been in main part re-built in the sixteenth century, not to mention extensive recent restorations. It has, however, an appealing and endearing aspect inside and out, with its centre and two side aisles, chancel and two transepts, forming together a regular cruciform design, and the spire rising at the West end. In the front of the entrance porch is a sundial, and there is a little surrounding graveyard, and a backing of thick foliage that hides the big house—Stanton Court.

The main street of the village is directed backwards towards the hills and ascends gently through its length. Stanton is not a village in decay as some villages may be. Looking up the street from the bottom you may always see some slight movement of village humanity, and what pertains to rustic life, beside the still, plain stone houses that present so well-preserved an appearance. In the street to one side near the church, the village cross stands upright and perfect on its stepped base. Church, school, farm buildings and cottages are all in fair repair. The village also possesses an old Tudor mansion in Stanton Court. But whereas at Stanway, if you took away the great house and its belongings, there would be no village to speak of left, at Stanton the Court, fine old stone house as it is, has no such relative importance, being but an adjunct to the village, as is also the Manor House.

I went up the street, the better to admire it, and continued to ascend by the road after it becomes steep, rough and narrow, and passes through a gate into a large rough hill field, known as Stanton Hill and which was formerly common land. At the top of the first high mound of Oolitic rock in this field, below which the rough road winds, I found a fine view was to be obtained, especially of the outlying hills, which, as here viewed, extend in a line from Cleeve Common to Bredon Hill, with a glimpse into Avon Vale to the right, and Stanton lying amongst the trees below.

Returning then to my machine, I rolled forward by the front of Stanton Court and, joining the high road again within a couple of miles of Broadway, I soon saw the houses and yellow church tower of that renowned place in front of me, but before entering it at the base of its long and very broad street, I turned into the village of Buckland, which is half a mile off the highway to the right, up a separate bye-road. Buckland has some interest in its church, in which is a chained copy of Fox's Martyrs.

Broadway, situated in a strip of Worcestershire that here thrusts itself deeply into Gloucestershire, is a place that is much talked about. It is not a town, not quite, only a village that is a larger and more grandiose edition of Stanton. Its street rises up the hill as that of Stanton does, but it is much longer and much wider, and its houses outshine those of Stanton in the medley they make of architectural features and position in relation to one another and to the street and green waste. The church is situated up a bye-road and is, therefore, only adjunct to the main interest, which lies in the character of the village street. This is what I have heard called "Old World." Its air of antiquity is almost unique in its thoroughness. To be appreciated it requires the artistic perception and the imagination that recalls the life that has been associated with such appearances, and the desire arises in a few to live that life in that place. But these endowments are as foreign to most natures as are the modern brick villas that have been built down the Station Road and up the Stratford Road, to the houses of Broadway's ancient street.

As you pass down Broadway the houses of the street group themselves pleasantly in several places. For the better appreciation of these quaint old stone dwellings it is well to go down the street as well as up it. There are better combinations looking down than up, and the street is so wide that it is only in places that you can get the two sides in effective view together. From the bottom, however, you have the general view up a long length of the street, with its houses of various size and prominence, and, everywhere, there are individual examples of ancient habitations of quaintly attractive character. Towards the bottom there is also a considerable village green, and the side-turning for Snowshill that leads past the modern church and afterwards past the original old church of Broadway that lies further up the lane. The "Lygon Arms" has been renovated and furnished after the ancient mode and is a very good hostelry.

From the top of the village I rode up Broadway Hill, or, as it is otherwise called, Fish Hill, by the road that goes to the top of the Cotswolds in a long winding incline, this being the main road from Worcester and Evesham through Broadway, Moreton-in-the-Marsh and Chipping Norton to Oxford and London. At several points during the climb I stopped to look backward at the broad prospect which was opened up as the altitude increased. The road makes several semicircular winds, and the corners thus formed make pleasant stopping places. Just at the top of the hill stands the inn that bears the sign of "The Fish," and a very short distance further upon the right I found the entrance between two pillars to the narrow road that, after passing by Broadway Tower, ultimately communicates with several villages situated in the hills on that side. Turning there, I soon saw the tower in a field upon my right—the tower that, seen from so many places in the vale, marks the position of Broadway. I stopped at the gate of this field and, entering, approached the tower.

The tower on Broadway Hill, viewed from close quarters, is seen to be solidly constructed of stone, its walls forming a regular hexagon and having three strong turrets at the alternate angles, which rise from the ground to a height of some feet above the main roof of the building. The tower is used as a habitation, the entrance door being between two of the turrets on the West side. The external walls show some decorative detail and the turrets are battlemented, the whole building being more elaborated and costly than is usual in look-out towers. The hill itself has an altitude of 1,024 feet, as marked on the ordnance map, forming one of the highest points of the Cotswolds, and the tower adds some additional 50 feet. Having paid the pence demanded by the person in charge, I ascended to the top and took note of the circle of views that one may obtain there. There is a wide surrounding outlook.

First, to the North-East is the vast plain extending over the main part of the county of Warwick, with portions of Worcestershire, and embracing Evesham Vale, or the Vale of Avon. On the left it is limited in the distance by a line of hilly country, including the Ridgeway, running up by Alcester to Redditch in the Birmingham direction. This country includes Stratford-on-Avon, which can be seen, Warwick and Leamington, and Coventry, with its three renowned spires, which are discoverable by telescope. From Broadway Hill a spur of the Cotswold escarpment passes for some distance up into this country, being continued beyond the great mass of Ebrington Hill, which lies at near distance, with the town of Chipping Campden at its foot, and the village of Ebrington on a shoulder of a hill beyond, and so to Ilmington Hill. Lying a little off this line of hills to the left is Meon Hill, which I have mentioned before as the last outlier of the Cotswolds.

Further eastward the great Warwickshire Vale is limited by a long line of hills which from Broadway Tower are seen to extend from behind Stow-on-the-Wold as a virtual continuation of the Cotswolds in that locality. It runs for many miles on the borders of the counties of Oxford and Warwick, behind the villages of Adlestrop, Long-Compton, Brailes, Compton Wyniates and Tysoe to Edgehill, and beyond to the Burton Dassett and Napton Hills. This line of hills bears no name in particular, but individual parts are named after the villages near to or upon them. The part of the Warwickshire Vale that runs in front of this line of hills is called the Vale of Red Horse. Near Edge Hill the soil is of a dark red colour, and formerly a portion of the hill line above the village of Tysoe was kept bare in the form of a horse, which could be seen from the vale below, and hence the name of Vale of Red Horse.

An excellent view of the Vale of Red Horse, looking over Moreton-in-the-Marsh, is obtained on the Broadway-Stow road, from the neighbourhood of Bourton-on-the-Hill and Longborough. The edge of the Cotswolds above which runs this road is in view from Broadway Tower, and at its end, looking South-East, may be seen the church tower and some of the houses of Stow-on-the-Wold. Then the line of hills leading back above Great Rissington towards Burford, by Shipton Downs, where the poles of the Wireless Telegraph Station can be seen.

South and South-West the longer view is limited by the high Cotswold country behind Snowshill, including Snowshill Hill. To the South-West is the beautiful combe near at hand, leading up from Broadway to Snowshill Village, with Laverton Hill forming its further side. The distant top of Roel Hill is seen, and the view then passes round to Cleeve Common, with Langley, Dixton, Woolstone, Dumbleton and Bredon Hills lying in succession to the right and due West from Broadway Tower. In the interspaces between these nearer hills are seen the dark hill line of the Forest of Dean and, further away, the same mountains of Monmouthshire and Brecknockshire as are seen at the nearer distance of Cleeve Hill. The Malvern Hill line is also mainly in view, being partly screened by Bredon Hill. Then, in clear weather, in the North-West and over the Worcester part of Severn Vale, with the towns of Evesham and Pershore in the middle distance, the view is to the Clee Hills, the Wrekin and the Abberley Hills and, more northward, by the Lickey Hills, back to the Ridgeway and the Warwickshire plain that extends to Leicestershire and Northamptonshire.

On leaving Broadway Tower, I continued my way along the minor road by which I had approached it, which presently gave a twist to the left and afterwards arrived at a meeting of roads, where I took the right-hand side one through a gate and found my way, by attention to the sign-post that stood at each cross road thereafter, to the village of Snowshill and, by this, past the villages of Cutsdean and Ford, where I crossed the main-road that comes from Stanway and goes towards Stow-on-the-Wold. A few score yards along this road in the Stanway direction from Ford I turned again to the left by a cross-country road that ultimately brought me on to Sudeley Hill, where I descended into Winchcomb.

The country I passed through was quite typical hill country of the Cotswolds. The village of Snowshill is situated in a hollow very near the edge of the hills, and is a stony, rather decadent little place with no features of any great interest. It requires to pass down a short bye-road to visit Cutsdean, which occupies a morsel of Worcestershire that is completely cut off from the rest of that county. The view of the village from the road at a distance of a third of a mile, with its very small church tower, farm and cottages in grey stone, is more pleasing than the view at close quarters. The hollow, or shallow combe, that begins above Cutsdean, and which is seen plainly from the road, is where the river Windrush originates. There is also a pretty view of Ford from the high-road, which, going in the direction of Stow, here dips suddenly to cross the hollow. This village has no church, but its inhabitants are within half a mile of that of Cutsdean. It is a fine, airy, undulating country up here, with cultivated fields, stone walls and sheepfolds. They were mowing barley in one field near Snowshill and, in a turnip field where hoeing had been neglected, the whole side of a hill was scarlet with poppies, late in the year as it was.

To pass this way one needs not to be in a hurry, as there are many gates upon the road and it is a relief to have done with the last of them on arriving at Sudeley Hill. I descended this hill by its very steep slope that is almost dangerous when the surface of the road happens to be in a broken condition. Towards the bottom I passed the fine yellow, stone-built entrance gate that guards the road of approach to Sudeley Castle on this side, and entered the main street of Winchcomb by a steep pitch from the bridge over the Isborne and round a sharp corner, and so returned up that side of Cleeve Hill.

CHAPTER XIX.

A JOURNEY OF DISCOVERY INTO THE NORTH COTSWOLDS.

Winchcomb Church—Sudeley Hill—Guiting Wood—Guiting Power The Windrush—Guiting Grange—Naunton—Upper Slaughter—Lower Slaughter—Bourton-on-the-Water—Wyck Rissington—Icomb Tower—Stow-on-the-Wold—Alternative Routes back from Stow—Upper Swell—Ford—Stanway Hill.

To propose a visit to the North Cotswolds is like projecting a journey to over the hills and far away. The thought will always be anticipatory of pleasure to those who know the country, and be hopeful of something new and a wonderment of what to others of the proposed company. It needs neither pedestrian endurance nor bicycling attainments when the proposition is to accomplish the tour by the easy means of a motor-car. The whole distance from Cleeve Hill to Cleeve Hill again is, however, not too great to be done in one day by a moderately practised pedal bicyclist, whilst the walker, by reason of the great advantage which his mode of progression possesses in leisure to view the country and in making a halt upon any spot he wills, may rejoice in his really superior method of doing it in a two days' jaunt. He would stay the night at the "Talbot" at Stow-on-the-Wold. A good idea of the general topography of the country is, however, obtained in the motor-car.

We drove down to Winchcomb by the main-road when the side of Langley Hill stood out clearly and as beautiful as at any time, its cultivated fields being coloured with the brown and gold of beans and wheat, and a pale patch of ripe barley half cut and half standing. From where the cutting was in progress the rattle of the machine, which was also in view, came faintly across to us over Langley Bottom. Some two or three miles away in front of us rose the continuing line of the escarpment hills. That part above Sudeley Castle, which bears the name of Sudeley Hill, was made distinctive in the verdant range by the stretch of very steep white road towards its summit that we were presently to ascend.

We soon turned the sharp and dangerous corner at the bottom of the hill and passed up through the street of low, small houses that can hardly be more distinguished than their predecessors of old Winchcomb at the time when the town was accounted a capital of Saxon Mercia. We drew up beside the raised pavement called Abbey Terrace that flanks the little square, or old-fashioned market-place, just beyond the church, and descending here, returned a few yards to examine the edifice.

This handsome church of Winchcomb is a pure and excellent example of Late Perpendicular church architecture, and is one of the best instances of it in a parish church. It was built by Abbot William of Winchcomb, assisted by Lord Boteler of Sudeley, not very long before the dissolution and demolition of the closely neighbouring monastery and buildings of Winchcomb Abbey, being finished in the early years of the sixteenth century. The restorations that have been needed to the church since the time of its building have introduced no element out of keeping with the original design. In this respect the church compares favourably with most of the other churches of the neighbourhood, which, being of older foundation, have suffered much alteration by introductions agreeing with the mode of building in vogue at the time when repair was needed. The unspoiled unity of design in Winchcomb Church produces an effect agreeable to the orderly mind, especially as viewed from within. The virtues of its style are also apparent in the large window area. which renders every part of the building perfectly light. The dim religious light admitted through the narrow window openings of Norman and Early English churches was better suited to the older semi-mysterious Catholic service in Latin.

At Winchcomb nave and chancel are under one almost equal line of roof, and the large clerestory windows are continued by windows at nearly equal height through the length of the chancel. There is a tall tower at the West end whose top, as well as the tops of the walls above the arcades between nave and side aisles, and the outer walls of these aisles, are battlemented and decorated with crocketed pinnacles. Jutting forth from below these battlements and pinnacles is an extraordinary number of projecting gargoyles carved into grotesque figures of men and beasts. The interior of the church is ample and well proportioned. The long roof has a splendid ceiling of oak in square panels. The end window of the chancel is very adorning, and the art of displaying on a window a single broad scene in coloured glass, notwithstanding the interruptions caused by the window mullions, finds remarkably successful exhibition here. The theme includes the broadside of a ship with Christ walking upon the water and Peter sinking in it. Amongst other notable antique objects in the church is an old alms-box terminating a low wooden post. This box is triple locked, one key being intended to be kept by the vicar and one each by the two churchwardens.

Proceeding through Winchcomb, at a turning that leaves the narrowed business street on the right near the "George" Hotel, we descended a short steep hill to the River Isborne, and crossed this by its bridge near where it receives the Sudeley brook. We then began to rise gently, our faces being set directly towards Sudeley Hill. The road was lane-like and much overhung by tree branches, and it was not until we had passed some length of the wall of Sudeley Park and the yellow stone lodge and arched gateway that leads through the park to Sudeley Castle that the hill got steep. This Sudeley Hill is indeed a very steep hill, going directly up to the top of the Cotswold edge. In its steepest part, on this occasion, it also had some ruts, though requiring for safety's sake to be kept of good surface on account of its acute gradient. Our engine being of sufficient power, on a low gear, we surmounted the steep.

Arrived at the top, the road ran straight forward at that altitude for some distance. The view over the wall to the right, which it is worth while stopping to examine for its lesson in the local topography, is right down into the Winchcomb Valley, over larchwoods that on other occasions we have viewed from the other side of this beautiful valley.

The view can be followed up to Charlton Abbots, and to the trees over beyond in the commencement of the Coln Valley, where lie Brockhampton and Sevenhampton. Beyond, in that direction, the view ends in a portion of the ridge that runs from above Withington in the direction of Leckhampton Hill. Immediately opposite, towards the top of the other slope of the valley, is Humblebee Wood, and to the right, Cleeve Common and the extension of the high ground along Nottingham Hill, with portions of Langley, Woolstone and Bredon Hills, and of the Severn Vale, with the Malverns and more distant Clee Hills.

A road to the right goes away along the edge of the Winchcomb Valley to Roel Gate and Hawling, by what is known as the outer park wall of Sudeley Castle. The view just described is enhanced about a mile along this road by a very fine foreground formed of part of what may be called Sudeley Park with a more mountain-like view beyond, the hills from that aspect ranging one behind another.

On the other side of our road we saw the high country lying just to the back of the escarpment line, where it runs up towards Broadway Tower by the camped tops of Hailes Hill and Snowshill Hill. The highest ground further off on our left front was towards the Bourton Downs, whose tops overlook the vale that extends far over Moreton-in-the-Marsh.

Our road now went on by Guiting Wood, which is one of the most considerable patches of woodland in the Cotswolds. The first portion of roadside woodland passed, extended on the right-hand side of the road to form a thick dark coppice of larch and fir, beneath whose deep shade there was little undergrowth, excepting some brambles that bore the white flowers and juicy fruit known as dewberries. The main part of the wood stretched down a slope on the left. They were chiefly beech boughs that overhung the road further along, and there beneath a copious growth of beech and oak in the main part of Guiting Wood grow bracken and polypody ferns, the more open parts forming a hunting ground for Cotswold woodland plants and smaller animal life, as well as for foxes.

Beyond the wood an open pleasant Cotswold country of

cultivated fields lay on either side of the road. A dip in the road brought us to the brook that rises above Roel Farm, and a small road crossed our route near this stream, coming down from that farm and going to Kineton and Temple Guiting.

Soon afterwards we descended into the village of Guiting Power, which has plain old stone houses, some of them clustered round a little green to make a centre space. A small road leaves the centre of the village on the right and passes up the side of a combe by a farm called "Tally Ho!" to rise to the high-located and outlandish village of Hawling.

We continued straight on down the main road and, when past all the houses of the village, saw the church of Guiting Power up a field to the right, approached by an avenue of large elms. We stopped our car by the roadside here and walked up to the church, which exhibits some interesting Norman architecture—a very fine and highly ornamented entrance porch especially, of this ancient order of building, on the South side, and a plainer one of coeval construction on the North side.

The village churches in this part of the Cotswolds very generally show remains of eleventh and twelfth century architecture. They are the historic remnants of ancient settlement, proving that these hills were occupied so long ago by a considerable population that was aggregated into villages and occupied chiefly in tilling the ground, as at present. The old Saxons were good agriculturists, but their religious establishments were greatly assisted by the Norman invasion, which led to the building and re-building within the following century of a great number of splendid churches. The creative art and labour expended with such prodigality upon the buildings of those past times have held for centuries in derision the meanness of a limited and commonplace utilitarianism.

A short distance further on we reached the youthful River Windrush and crossed it by the bridge there, and our road joined another coming this way from Ford and Temple Guiting, just opposite the entrance gate of the park of Guiting Grange, where a portion of this conveniently built and pleasantly situated country house is visible up the drive,

1 2 3

EARLY ENGLISH ARCHITECTURE AT WYCK RISSINGTON. TOWER AND CHANCEL—1 & 2.
PERPENDICULAR TOWER. WINCHCOMB CHURCH—3.

ENTRANCE TO UPPER SWELL MANOR HOUSE.

with an avenue of great lime-trees stretching up the ground in front of it. We turned to the right along the course of the brook and noticed in the boggy ground by its side whole beds of naturalised mimulus, whose yellow flowers were not now so thick as they were a month earlier. Again we crossed the stream where it is bordered by a pleasant meadow which, in turn, is edged and ended by woodland pertaining to Guiting Grange. Then we ascended, keeping to the left at the division of the road, and came up on to the main highway that passes from Cheltenham to Stow-on-the-Wold, and turned along to the left in front of an old roadside inn converted to a farm-house through decay of custom, and kept along the higher of the two roads before us.

We were at Naunton, or rather on the high-road that runs along above the village, whose position, stretched out along the valley of the Windrush, that runs parallel with our road down below, vindicates the longer appellation of Naunton-in-the-Vale, which sometimes attaches to it. The village, with its little square-towered church, chapel and houses, and the woods situated on the steep side of the valley, down towards Guiting Power, the little river making a serpentine course through the meadows below the village, and the cultivated Cotswold fields that rise to form a background to the village on the other side of the vale, now sheaf-full and glowing in their harvest dress, made together a striking picture. In fact, this is, perhaps, the prettiest bit of scenery to be found in the North Cotswolds. We stopped for a few minutes at two or three points along the road in order to fully appreciate it.

It is only six miles to Stow-on-the-Wold by the main road from the point where we struck it near the roadside house that was formerly the "Naunton" Inn. They are, however, very hilly miles, as the road dips deeply three times to cross as many streams before ascending Stow Hill. We made the first dip and crossed the Windrush below Naunton. On rising to the top of the following hill, we crossed the old Roman road called Buckle Street, which leads, on the right, straight to Bourton-on-the-Water. From this hill-top we looked down the main-road and saw the woody screen of

Eyeford Park on the left, with the entrance to the park at the bottom of the valley near the stream, here called the Eyeford brook and, a little lower down, the Slaughter brook. Proceeding down the hill towards Eyeford, we found another road to the right, about a third of the way to the bottom, where the handpost points to Upper Slaughter and Lower Slaughter. Here we turned and, from the higher ground, got a glimpse forward of the inner ridge of the Cotswolds, extending from near Stow towards Burford by the villages of Rissington and Barrington. This ridge begins on the left at Icomb Hill, that has a look-out tower upon it, which we could now see and to which we were presently coming.

Our road brought us to the stony village of Upper Slaughter, and we turned in on the left to explore its farms, cottages, stream and church. The church stands on a height above the brook, which passes picturesquely below it, being crossed by two or three primitive little bridges, with a farm and some cottages built on its further side. The rectory is down by the brookside, and you look to its level green lawn from above, whilst from below you look up at the fine church with square tower effectively grouped with the trunks and foliage of well-grown sycamore and other trees that rise about it.

The church architecture exhibits interiorly some arches of the late, or transitional Norman type, situated at the East and West ends of the nave, which are pointed and not semicircular, but bear several kinds of Norman ornamental mouldings. In a chapel North of the chancel is the tomb of a former rector, consisting of a mural entablature, overarched in the imitative decorated style with ogee mouldings, forming a much-enriched canopy, in good architectural taste. There are brasses of sixteenth century date to John Slaughter, his wife and son. The tower is a good one—Late Norman below and Decorated above.

As we leave Upper Slaughter to pass on down the little valley, the great old stone Upper Slaughter Manor House is seen on the left. Its architectural features are those of the reigns of Elizabeth and James I., the front doorway being typically Jacobean. It has a fine interior with a good deal of oak wainscoting and decorative fittings that pertain to its era and definite ancient appealing style.

A mile further on, keeping down to the left, we are again near the brook and at the village of Lower Slaughter. This is a pretty and peaceful place, with the cottages situated along the brookside, which is crossed by little bridges at one point and another, where convenience requires. The line of houses begins at an old black-wheeled water mill and straggles down towards the church and Manor House. A footpath at that end passes by the brookside under shady linden boughs. The church, almost entirely re-erected not so very long ago, is now a decent steepled building.

Half a mile beyond the last house of Lower Slaughter, the road from that village reaches the main-road between Northleach and Stow-on-the-Wold, at a distance of three miles from the latter town. This road is the ancient Roman road, known as the Fosse Way. We turned to the right, away from Stow, to find the large village of Bourton-on-the-Water, that lies just off this main-road, one mile along there.

Bourton is a very pleasant place and derives its main character from the fact of its being "on the water." In this respect it is an enlarged edition of the Slaughters. The water is that fine trouting stream the River Windrush, which has meandered down here from Naunton, and makes a straight course through the middle of the village as a shallow rippling stream of clear water, crossed by several stone bridges that have the peculiarity of being without the usual guarding parapet. There is an irregular main street and one or two short bye-streets, with old houses and inns, some of them of true ancient Cotswold type. In Sherborne Street and in the lane leading away from the end of it will be found several pleasing examples of houses of Stuart and Tudor age, as well as the old square "Harrington House," of rather later date. Elsewhere may be found the Georgian rectory and other ancient habitations.

The church is to some extent re-built. Its tower is an original eighteenth century conception. The body of the church, however, forms a fine, airy and spacious place of worship, the windows being of Decorated type. Near the entrance, in the churchyard, is a modern commemorative cross to a former rector, which has sculptural merit.

Anciently there was a Roman encampment, or station, usually marked "Salmonsbury Camp" on archaeological maps, situated at Bourton on ground approached from the lane that leads round to the railway station. It now bears the name of "Camp Field," and we found it after some questioning. Although some years ago a number of relics of ancient Roman occupation were recovered from the ground, as well as a large collection of Saxon arms, there is nothing now in the way of entrenchment to permit of the nature and formation of the camp being followed. There are some rude, irregular mounds, and a portion of the ground is poor and weedy, as if there might be some stone structures below the surface, and a portion of the field over the hedge is still called "The Castle," which also seems to indicate former buildings. But the greater part of the ground has been ploughed into ridge and furrow and otherwise levelled for agricultural use, and the existence of the camp has thus been reduced almost to a tradition. The ancient Roman roads, the Fosse Way and Bughilde Street, or Buckle Street, led to it, and these both still exist, the latter coming across the Cotswolds from the neighbourhood of Alcester, on the other side of the Avon Valley, over Bidford Bridge and up Saintbury Hill.

Coming again into the Northleach-Stow high-road and turning to the right in the Stow direction, a sign-post, half a mile along, on the right-hand side, directs to Wyck Rissington.

Arrived there, we found the village with its houses set about a large green, practically a field, through the middle of which runs the roadway, the cottages being chiefly on one side, some distance away from the road. Domestic animals of various species were on the green—a donkey, horses, kine, pigs, fowls, ducks. There was also a pond and a public water source with an elaborate stone covering. The size of the green made the houses look small and few.

At the further end of the village stands the church,

whose square tower and chancel end offer for observation a very remarkable and pure example of Early English architecture. The tower appears to be unaltered and perfect as at its completion, in the beginning of the thirteenth century. It is solid, plain, with weak, gable-headed buttresses at the corners, narrow single slit openings in its walls, and unbattlemented, pierced parapets with small corner turrets. The chancel end of the church has two pairs of narrow lancet windows, each pair somewhat distant from the other, and having above an angular diamond-shaped light, with a third similar light between the other two, but higher in the gable. These windows are unique; a raised ornamental string course passes above them and formerly was extended round the sides of the chancel without break, to pass over other lancet windows, some of which still exist on the North side. The corners of the chancel are also buttressed in the Early English manner. Square-headed rectilinear windows have elsewhere been inserted and are outrageously out of keeping with the original design of the church, though effectively introducing more light within.

From Wyck Rissington Church we ascended by a very steep and rough lane to the top of the Cotswold ridge at Wyck Beacon. Turning there to the left, we came in a further half-mile to the Stow and Burford main-road. Turning to the left as for Stow, at a distance of a mile from the junction of the roads, we were at the top of Wyck Hill, with the demesne of Wyck Hill House behind a thick belt of trees on the left. A little way down the hill, a lane up to the right led to Icomb, and we turned sharply there to ascend within half a mile to the top of Icomb Hill, where we discovered Icomb Tower, or the "Round House," at the roadside, its lower storeys being used as a cottage dwelling.

Paying the cottager's wife the charge demanded, we climbed by a flight of stairs to the open top of the tower and enjoyed the remarkable panoramic view there obtained.

Icomb Tower commands a most comprehensive view of the North Cotswolds. The hill country through which we had passed to come here from Cleeve Hill lay exposed, with extensions to right and left that embraced a wide area of this part of Gloucestershire, whose very hilly nature is more plainly evident as viewed from here than as viewed from any other point.

Not far off, the small town of Stow-on-the-Wold is discovered, situated upon its hill, which from here is clearly seen to be an outlier of the main range of the Cotswolds. From Stow, the ridge that faces the great Warwickshire plain can be followed by Bourton Downs towards Broadway Hill, and the line of the Cotswold edge that faces the Vales of Avon and Severn can thence be traced, and the highest tops, such as Snowshill Hill and Hayles Hill, be identified, whilst the country that lies between is scored into ridges and valleys by the Windrush and its tributary streams. The Valley of the Dickler goes up from Lower to Upper Swell, winding behind the large house, Abbotswood, that is looked down upon from Stow. The Valley of the Slaughter Brook is similarly discovered, with the villages of Upper Slaughter and Lower Slaughter, as well as Bourton-on-the-Water and the big house in Eyeford Park. The Valley of the Windrush itself goes back into the hills where are the Naunton Downs. The Hawling Downs are further over, and the high ridge of Roel lies in view in the same direction. Stretches of Cleeve Common end the view over that way. Further round, due West and South-West, beyond Hampen and Salperton, the high tops that overlook the Valley of the Coln, beyond Compton Abdale and Withington, pass as a ridge by Foxcote and Pegglesworth towards Leckhampton Hill. A long line of beechwood marks the Northleach road where it goes by Puesdown. The high ground of the ridge that runs straight back from this Icomb Hill, above Little and Great Rissington, prevents the further country by Burford and towards Witney being seen. Behind, however, to the South East and East, the view is immediately into Oxfordshire, being first into the valley of the River Evenlode and to the hill ridge that runs up upon the other side of this valley. The wireless telegraphy installation on Shipton Downs is plainly visible, and, far over, on the other side of the Thames, in that direction, the dim, blue ranging line of the Chilterns can be discerned.

The Oxford and Worcester branch of the Great Western Railway passes up the Evenlode Valley, where several of its stations can be seen and the villages they serve, as well as other villages, both in that valley and on the slopes of the opposite hills. Oddington, Bledington, Addlestrop, Kingham, Idbury, are some of these villages. The town of Chipping Norton also stands plainly in view upon its high site. This opposite ridge of hills beyond the Evenlode is extended along to the North-East to limit the Vale of Red Horse. In that direction the outlying Brailes Hill is seen, standing a short distance off the range. The great Warwickshire plain, further to the North, stretches away illimitably, with Moreton-in-the-Marsh and Batsford Park in plain view on the left of the opening, behind which the hills that are seen are those of Ebrington and Ilmington.

Close below, that is, within a mile or so, is the little agricultural village of Icomb that gives its name to this hill and tower. The saddle-backed tower of its church is but a small object and lies in close relation to barns and farmyards. The little tower is not of much interest, but the chancel of the church is another example of the lancet, or Early English, style that is very appealing in its neat simplicity, and to be found in several churches of this immediate neighbourhood. A mile from the village stands the old Tudor house, Icomb Place.

We came back to the main-road for Stow-on-the-Wold and, turning for that town, passed its railway station at the bottom of Wyck Hill and afterwards climbed into the town by the Fosse Way, which we intersected again just at the beginning of the long hill that divides the town from its station.

This little town of Stow-on-the-Wold is built close to the Fosse, but hardly any of its houses face on to this ancient highway, from which you must turn in and pass round a corner or two to reach the market-place, about which the inns and shops are centred, upon the very top of the hill. The tower of the church overtopping the houses, looks from the graveyard, where its stands, into that same market-place. In an opposite and further corner from where the church tower shows, but in plain sight of it, the ancient wooden stocks will be found in the shade of a couple of large elm-trees. On the other side of the market-place, where the main street begins to go down the slope, stands a stone cross to one side, in a position where things should be able to pass without injuring it, though the local powers that be have surrounded its base with a spiked iron guard of rude construction and dangerous approach. The top of this cross has been restored not very tastefully, and we thought it would have been better to have left the structure as a broken column, standing on the great single stone that forms its base above the couple of steps beneath, and without the iron guard.

In the Civil War of the time of Cromwell, the Parliamentarians and Royalists had a set-to in this neighbourhood, when the former being victorious, crowded Stow Church with their prisoners—a sort of thing that should be prohibited as the worst form of desecration. At the present date the church, which has a traditional history beginning in the reign of Saxon Ethelred, is in a good state of preservation, having been much and often restored. Its architecture is, consequently, various. It has Norman pillars and mouldings, Early English arches and windows, two Decorated windows of fine design in tracery, though filled with unpleasing glass, other Perpendicular windows and a good Decorated and Perpendicular tower, whose parapets are panelled on their outside. An old font of a graceful model, that had been cast aside in favour of a newer one, has been pieced together and brought back into the church. A large, well-painted, gift picture of the Crucifixion by a Flemish artist, dating from 1610, has been placed straight in front of the architecturally fine chancel window.

Stow's wide market-place is the chief part of the town, and that which gives it its character, which is slow, quaint and semi-rural—bright enough in sun-shining times, and its air light and bracing on account of its altitude. It is a pleasing town in its limited way. The space of the market-place, though, perhaps, now too great for any required use, has, almost unfortunately, been partly built upon, the most recent erection there being St. Edward's Hall, which combines a public library and reading room, with an assembly hall. Near the church is the old Tudor school-house, now used by the Freemasons as their place of meeting.

In May and again in October of each year Stow has its great Fair, which formerly included many draught oxen, and sheep of the Cotswold breed, as well as horses. For long Stow Fair was an emporium for acquisition of rams of this heavy, grey-faced, long-wooled breed, which were wanted to produce a cross with the closer wooled Hampshire Down ewes. The resulting dark-faced, long-wooled breed, known as the Oxfordshire Down, is now well established and has, to a great extent, displaced the flocks of the pure Cotswold breed, and become the favourite sheep of the neighbouring counties. Upon Fair Day the market-place is far too small to contain the animals and attendant men, who swarm in from a long radius, and the general approach roads, as well as an adjoining field are called into requisition to supply necessary space. In one spot an auction sale takes place of such horses as have been scheduled for it. Elsewhere, strings of horses pertaining to various dealers are tied up by the wall, or under the trees that line the Fosse Road, to be brought out, one by one, for showing off. Droves of Welsh pony colts, mares and foals, stallions, nags, heavy and light van horses, splendid shires, and gipsy crocks, lean draggers of caravan and travelling show are there, in charge of individual owners, grooms, carters and ploughboys. The chatter of groups of men, who are feeling horses' legs, or looking at their teeth, or only looking on, the shouts of the runners-up with their "Hi! Hi! Hi!" and cracking of whips and waving of coloured flags before the horses to further excite them, creates an animation that is almost a pandemonium in and about Stow-on-the-Wold on Fair Day. The little market-place is further crowded with merry-go-rounds, shows and stalls, and itinerant salesmen of various commodities, ware and gimcracks, calculated to supply the needs of remotely-dwelling countrymen, their wives and sweethearts. The passage ways, yards, bars and public eating-rooms of the inns are filled with a crushing, hungry and thirsty humanity, who talk and drawl and swear in the local lingo, not a few getting drunk before night, according to local custom. If fine, there is dust ; if rainy, mud, and it is wet as often as not at the October Fair and, sometimes, at that in May.

We were now thinking of returning and the question was—by which route ? There is a good main-road to Cheltenham, which is eighteen miles off, fifteen miles of it being over the hills, a very fine, bracing drive. At first you go down Stow Hill to Lower Swell Village and the River Dickler. You immediately rise up Swell Hill and, as soon as you are at that summit, sink down a steep hill to Eyeford. Crossing the Eyeford brook, you rise again past the turning where we left this main-road to visit the Slaughters on our outward journey. You then return along the stretch of road to beyond Naunton, which we have already covered, crossing the Windrush at Harford Bridge and noting again the serpentine course of the little river through the meadow on the right. You pass the road where we came up from Guiting Power, and a second turning to the same village at the roadside " Fox Hill " Inn. On the right is the " Tally Ho ! " combe leading up to Hawling. A large out-of-work stone quarry not far from the road here adds its item to the scenery where over beyond is a nice view to Guiting Church. You are now high up on the Hawling Downs. Turnings to the right lead to that village, and to the left they lead to Notgrove and Bourton-on-the-Water and, later, to Salperton, Hazleton and Shipton. You reach the cottages at the top of Hampen Hill and descend under the railway and down a long slope to Andoversford. At Andoversford there is a railway bridge to pass under that is made dangerous by three roads meeting at the bridge, neither of the other roads being visible until you are close to the meeting point. Passing again under the railway, you go by Whittington and descend further to the Cheltenham Reservoir at Dowdeswell, in the valley of the Chelt, and enter the town through Charlton Kings, having passed diagonally across the North Cotswolds. At Whittington you will have seen a sign post directing to Cleeve Hill. Do not attempt that route with a car. It has been described in one of the walking excursions.

There is an alternative and totally different route from

Stow that you may take viâ Broadway, the distance to Cleeve Hill being about the same as through Cheltenham, that is, about twenty-two miles. It is a good main road. You descend not so deeply out of Stow and, ascending again, pass along the ridge that ends the hills to the eastward above Moreton-in-the-Marsh and the Warwickshire Plain, over which, in the first four or five miles you get occasional views. On the other side of the road are the upland Cotswold fields of the Bourton Downs. You may turn in to the right to visit at distances from the main-road of one mile and two miles respectively, the villages of Longborough and Bourton-on-the-Hill, both of which are of fair size, their buildings being in yellow stone, facing towards Moreton, on the hill slope. Bourton derives the latter part of its title from the fact that it is actually situated on the road for Moreton, where this is in steep descent. Both these villages present certain interesting features that make a visit worth while. Beyond the turning for Bourton, towards Broadway, is an entrance into Batsford Park, the seat of Lord Redesdale. The road is then flanked for some miles on both sides with thickly growing trees, chiefly beeches. Past the turning for Chipping Campden on the right, and that for Broadway Tower and Snowshill on the left, you reach the "Fish" Inn, at the top of Broadway, or Fish Hill, and wind down into the renowned village of Broadway by a long and beautiful descent. Thence you take the much winding road under the hill edge to Winchcomb.

On this occasion, however, we returned by another alternative route, namely by the Stow to Tewkesbury main-road as far as Toddington Crossing and thence through Winchcomb. By this route it is nineteen miles from Stow-on-the-Wold to Cleeve Hill. First we sank down by the wall of Abbotswood Park to Upper Swell, crossing the Dickler by a little stone bridge, just below an old water mill, behind which is a big pond in the course of the stream. Rising from the bottom, the stone buildings of this small delighting village, and some large elm, beech and ash trees make a pretty scene. On the right is the old Tudor Manor House with its very fine entrance and interior rooms. Close to it stands the little old church of Upper Swell, under whose stone porch is a good Norman doorway, with zigzag and lozenge ornamentation around its tympanum. Some old narrow windows were noticed in its small chancel, which is also Norman, there being a nice chancel arch of that style.

By a long, gentle rise we ascended from Upper Swell into the heart of the hills and, looking backward, could see Stow Church topping its wold. As we got higher, we were in a gloriously bracing country of harvest fields and red-brown fallows, separated by stone walls, with here and there among the fields a hard stony farmstead, with neighbouring ricks of corn and of brown sainfoin, or clover hay. Dotted here and there were copses of tapering larch, or rounded beech and dark fir. Sheepfolds were also visible, with shepherds and their dogs, and the ploughing had already begun where the crops had been removed. Many roadside flowers were still in bloom, and sight and odour were of the glorious earth of the Cotswolds.

A beechwood overlapped the road and presently we sank into a deep little hollow at the village of Ford and again crossed the Windrush, not by a ford, as at one time was necessary, no doubt, but by a bridge near where flags and willow herb grew luxuriantly in and near the shallow stream that had risen within a couple of miles above. The village of Cutsdean could be seen half a mile off as we rose out of Ford where a turn to the right leads towards it. A bigger road along the top to the left goes to Temple Guiting. We rolled away by the main-road, straight on to Stanway Hill, from which we got the view into Severn Vale and to those outlying hills of the Cotswolds with which we were now familiar. We had already seen the interesting buildings of Stanway, else they lay but a quarter of a mile to the right at the bottom of the hill. We pushed forward past Toddington railway station, and were very soon at the crossing of the Broadway to Winchcomb main-road, where we left the road we had travelled along from Stow. Turning here for Winchcomb we were soon through that old town, and climbing up Cleeve Hill, with the wooden cross on Postlip Warren showing on our left.

CHAPTER XX.

CHELTENHAM.

ONE of the reasons for dwelling, or for being, upon Cleeve Hill is the proximity of Cheltenham, that Borough Beautiful. The inhabitants of the town have a definite legal right in Cleeve Common, which they utilise largely, since it is the chief place of resort from Cheltenham, not only for golfers, but for all mankind. Nevertheless it may be that hitherto many of the town visitors have seen too little of the glories of the hill and its neighbourhood, having gone up and returned without making more than a very limited acquaintance with the immediately accessible parts of the great common and without acquiring any knowledge at all of the interesting country around.

From Cleeve Hill the town lies in view, not so brilliantly through the middle hours of the day as from Leckhampton Hill on its southern side, because the sun on that side is behind the viewer, whilst from here it is in front of him, shining down upon the houses from over opposite and putting the front of things darkly into shadow, and so reducing the relative definition of buildings and trees and making them appear blended in a sylvan mixture of dark forms. From about the centre rise the three steeples near together with a scattering of other spires and towers, and the two tall chimneys on the extreme border. As the sun gets round further and further towards his place of setting, the details of the buildings are better defined, and white scintillating fires arise at dazzling centres where the angle of reflection from glass roof or window determines the transmission of the broken image of the sun. And often about sunset, in summer-time, a red light overspreads the darkening scene and tinges for a short space the white quarried face of the tree-crowned hill behind. In summer too, at sunrise and for some hours later, the town is more directly lit, and all its chief buildings can then be identified, and the beauty of their setting, and of the general site of the town with its half encircling hills, and the glory of the neighbouring country to the far-off horizons can be fully appreciated.

One knows to what degree a piece of plain brick wall may be haloed when it lies in the midst of a rich and contrasting embroidery of plant growth, and when viewed at the distance that lends enchantment. At Cleeve Hill we view Cheltenham at a distance of three to six miles, where it lies in that green lap of the hills accepted, and undoubtedly greatly beautified, by Nature unassisted by any thought of man, and perhaps experience of other places might lead us to enter this town with trepidation arising from the fear of disillusionment. Cheltenham, however, bears entry, the internal sight at close quarters being hardly less entrancing than the view from afar. In a town of 50,000 inhabitants it is perhaps inevitable, owing to the deficiencies of poor humanity, that there should be poor quarters to be found if these were sought for, but to Cheltenham these, after all, are rather of the import of a small mole upon a soft cheek, or of those black patches of plaster which ladies of a former generation were wont to stick upon their faces as foils to their beauty. Tested by comparison, as upon return after an absence which has entailed visits to many other towns, whether in England or on the Continent, Cheltenham more than holds its own ; and the thought of its being a nice place to return to, by which one so returning is generally struck, does not arise out of the associations and memories of inhabitation so much as out of actual appearances. It is a smiling town, and welcomes you with its brightness and the ease of its gentle gradients, its well-ordered thoroughfares, gardens and avenues, villas and terraces. It is not vulgar or commonplace, not overpowered by money-making industry and the commercial instinct, whether in its buildings or in its population. The commercial interest is present, no doubt, but not aggressively so. It is distinctly after, and secondary to, the artistic and æsthetic, for, look where you

CHELTENHAM

1.—THE ANCIENT PARISH CHURCH OF ST. MARY.

2.—THE ROYAL CRESCENT WITH BROACH OF ST. MATTHEW'S CHURCH.

CHELTENHAM—IN THE PROMENADE.

will, there is design and beauty, man's art being everywhere considerably assisted by natural circumstances.

In its main features the town has a predominating style which is one of terraces and trees. Its architecture is of classic type touched by a Georgian element, with façade, pillar and pilaster, portico and balcony, much in evidence. At its building there was an expenditure on external ornamentation to which our later restricted notions of economy seldom rise. We do not lay out towns and build them after this manner nowadays, and if Mr. Pearson Thompson, who, a hundred years ago, mainly shouldered the financial responsibility for building those parts that give Cheltenham its chief architectural character, lost his fortune in the enterprise, he left behind him a result of lasting value. However, the thing could not have been accomplished but for the very marked architectural talent of one John Buonarotti Papworth, who, whether or not by inheritance from a native ancestry indicated in his second name, was a fine dreamer of design and practical draughtsman, who had not only the opportunity but the rare genius to be successful, and so the two founded Cheltenham, for the village of its first origin, situated upon the Chelt Brook, whence the name of the town, formed the beginning of little more than the shopful High Street.

Thus to-day you may visit Cheltenham to admire its streets, with their houses and other buildings, that make the town a place of quite unusual appearance. Trees and houses go together as if by nature. There are the avenues of the broad main-roads and those of the back roads and bye-roads. The villas in their gardens have many fine trees ; the wide pavements are overhung with tree branches.

The central chief street known as The Promenade takes a double avenue, and a long flower-garden with statues, and a large and elaborately sculptured fountain all in its width, and here the windows of the best shops are shaded by the branches where you look across the garden to the finest terrace in the town, and one of the finest in the world, whose centre houses, without breaking the uniform design of the terrace, now afford good offices for the conduct of the business of the municipality. The Town Hall stands independent of the Municipal Offices in Imperial Square, whose one side is open to The Promenade, and adjacent to it in the square, and visible from The Promenade, is seen the great glass roof of the Winter Garden ; the chief club-house occupies also a corner of the same square towards the street, which rises gently beneath its avenues to the Queen's Hotel, whose Corinthian-pillared front faces down the rise, its position, as well as the impressive order of its architecture, giving it an air of quiet superiority and distinction. Above the hotel the character of this street of streets changes somewhat. A considerable row of shops bearing the name of The Montpellier Walk lies recessed from the highway on the right, beginning with two part circular abutment buildings with a roofed alley between leading on to the side paving of the Walk in front of the shops, which with these end buildings are of equal design, the shop fronts separated by caryatides of more than life size. At the top end of the row is a building with dome and colonnade of very singular but distinguished design, called The Montpellier Rotunda, built by Mr. Thompson from the designs of Papworth, and uniquely suitable for the purpose of a "Spa," or place for drinking the mineral waters for which Cheltenham is famed, and which was the intended purpose of the building, though it was allowed afterwards to fall from that use by want of understanding on the part of those who managed the "Spa." On the other side of the street, opposite Montpellier Walk, the railings of the Montpellier Gardens are against the side path, the broad walks, wide grass plots and effective trees, with a band-stand, stage and awning-covered auditorium, all being in view to tell the tale of Summer games and popular entertainments in the open air. Further, at the very crest of the little hill, the roadway is divided, first by a statue of Edward VII. above a drinking fountain, then by an ornamental standard for the electric light, which centres a meeting of seven ways, and here, near at hand, are several of the finest of those old terraces which give Cheltenham its main character, those called Lansdown Terrace, Lansdown Crescent, Lansdown Place, Lypiatt Terrace, and Suffolk

Square, with numerous large villas belonging to the same epoch, being all well worth inspection. A magnificent avenue of planes and limes in the prime of their growth, and more than half a mile long, follows the Lansdown Road in the direction of Gloucester, and the avenues and garden trees in the neighbourhood of Christchurch, which pertain to this Lansdown quarter, are superb.

There are many other avenues, terraces, parks and gardens on all sides with which the older inhabitant is acquainted. The chief public park is the Pittville Park, which includes the century-old Pittville Gardens with a large modern addition. In the older part is situated the Pittville Pump Room, provided, like the Rotunda, for drinking the Cheltenham Waters. Its design represents a Temple of Health, and though the dream of its originator of crowds of fashionable invalids swarming by its broad approach walks as to a shrine to be cured of their several ailments was not destined to be realised, the great Doric pillars of its loggia, and its domed roof, look exceedingly well at the present day between the tree branches, or from across the lake. A stream runs through the whole length of the Park, filling a couple of lakes, the first decorated by ornamental stone bridges at its either end, and the second, in the newer part of the Park, is of sufficient length and depth for boating and fishing. The trees of Pittville Park are of various and fine growth, those of the older part being largely evergreen, and here between ilex and cedars stretches of old turf provide pleasant courts for lawn tennis by the little clubs and family parties who hire them for the season.

Situated a little away from the shopping centre of the town, somewhere amid the avenued side-roads, are the several Cheltenham colleges and great schools, for if the first interest of Cheltenham was connected with the use of its natural mineral waters, its later main interest has lain in its educational establishments. This educational interest, originating about the middle of the nineteenth century, has since been largely developed. Some of the leading colleges of the country, for what is now spoken of as secondary education, have place here, as well as a training College for Elementary

School Teachers. The Cheltenham schools primarily supply the educational needs of the high class population resident in the town itself, but their growth and recognised importance and success have brought in a large number of pupils from various parts of the country to become resident scholars in the numerous school boarding-houses, which pertain to one or other of the scholastic institutions referred to. It is hardly in keeping with the nature of this book to mention these by name. It will be sufficient to say that the character of the town has received a new impress by this modern development, and the name of Cheltenham in connection with education bears a distinction and credit that is little short of that attaching to the names of our older universities, to which many scholars proceed from Cheltenham, whilst others gain degrees at the open and more modern and democratic University of London. Many also pass into the national institutions for preparation for the army, navy and civil services of the Empire. If it were correct to speak of education as an economical industry, it might be said that the chief and more important industry of Cheltenham lay, at the present time, in the labours of its school and college teachers.

Thus amongst the other erections of Cheltenham, some of which have been already mentioned, the college and school buildings now hold a conspicuous place. There are not only the buildings devoted to teaching the most modern education, with all the laboratories and special apartments this requires, but also the residential houses, some of the later built of which are large and handsome buildings that provide all that is to-day deemed requisite or desirable for the most healthy and active life of their inmates.

Athletics, to which, according to some of our foreign critics, the English idea leans to an unwarrantable extent, naturally find a fine field for exercise in Cheltenham. Public schools without athletic games as an integral part of the educational system would be an anomaly with us, and the remark applies during the last score of years equally well to schools for girls as to schools for boys. It is recognised, perhaps subconsciously, that the development and training of the physical body has an importance that is by no means inferior to that of the development and instruction of the youthful mind. Athletics in Cheltenham, however, by no means end with school life, the enthusiasm for outdoor movement being carried on to old age, so permanent is the habit when once instilled.

Inhabiting the villas and terraces of the town, whether as permanent residents or as visitors, there is a population of retired national service men and their families, amongst whom, as the result of a resort to sport and games to counteract the relaxation of trying climates and the boredom of limited society, during service abroad, athletics have passed into an instinct, whose exercise has become a necessary part of existence, and certainly results in the keenest enjoyment of life. The sons and daughters of this breed follow the custom, being reared in the atmosphere of its practice. Thus it comes to pass that not only the universal games of cricket and football find their devotees in Cheltenham, but clubs have here been formed for practically every game anywhere played by English men and women. Naturally, in fox-hunting England, a pack of hounds would be required conveniently near, and the kennels of the Cotswold Hunt are situated within the town boundary. The Cheltenham Racecourse Company, which came into existence some years ago to provide and keep in order a course that is beautiful from more than one point of view, supplied its object and became an immediate financial success. It was in the height of its prosperity at the outbreak of the great war, when it was able to yield up its large club buildings for the use of wounded soldiers, and in lieu of the smart assemblies of its sporting members, the beauty of the trained horses, and all the pride and glory of jockey and jacket that go to make up a race meeting, was converted to a new and great service and utility as "The Racecourse Hospital." Not less brilliant have been the time-to-time assemblies at Charlton Park of players and spectators in matches and tournaments of tennis, hockey and croquet. At other seasons and places football has claimed hardier crowds, and county cricket has called together concourses, contributed to from near and far, to view the batsman, bowler or stumpsman of renown come here from some other county to meet the best that Gloucestershire could put in the field, by name of Grace, Jessop, Board, Page, Wrathall, Townsend and other men of memory. Oh, but the enjoyment of watching this beautiful game of cricket, taking place in the centre of that green and level lawn of the College playground upon a fine summer day, can be intense. There is hardly another game that exhibits the human body in such a variety and elegance of movement. If you never saw, you ought to have seen, as a sight of athletic grace, Townsend bowling, and the great Grace himself, in his earlier days, with the bat. Upon such an occasion the ladies, dressed in their gala outfits, promenade the space by the College buildings which leads to the full stand, whilst the seats by the rope that surrounds the pitch are filled, and backed by a standing throng that takes long to tire, and goes home to dinner to return in the early afternoon, and stop till the hands of the clock upon the gymnasium front mark the hour of six. Stumps will then be drawn and the game be perhaps won, or defeat just prevented, by bold or conservative tactics, during the last minutes.

Such a cricket match is but an occasional event, but it is the result of the practice of cricket upon many cricket club greens throughout this and other counties, for it is upon the local greens that the cricketer of the select and honoured county eleven has to first prove his prowess.

Day by day, between the trees of this bright town, upon the innumerable lawns of private houses, or in the many public recreation grounds and parks that exist on all sides of the town, and on the club grounds, as well as in the college and school playgrounds, these games go eternally on, and practically every class and age take a part in them. For golf there is the magnificent course upon the great common that exists upon the Cotswold Height from which these notes are written, and which accommodates the two golf clubs that have their separate club-houses there.

Such out-of-door exercises are seconded by numerous indoor entertainments, that are called for and provided to amuse the townsfolk of every class and age. These touch more nearly the social life of the town, as they bring people of different families into close communion, and establish society in its various phases and grades. Social intercourse is greatly aided here by societies, which exist in great numbers, and are the easy means of bringing together people of similar tastes. There are musical, dramatic and debating societies, the Dickens Fellowship, and other clubs and brotherhoods that serve this purpose. The houses of public entertainment are likewise numerous, beginning with the Theatre and Opera House, that has a following of considerable numerical extent in the minor show-house rivals, the Hippodrome and the Picture Palaces. Cheltenham is full of "halls" and "rooms" that are in more or less constant requisition for meetings of one sort and another; for the constant effort and enterprise on the part of the populace, particularly of the feminine half, to find something creditable to do, whether on behalf of charity or instruction, or in advocacy of some special policy, cult or craze, leads to an endless billing of assemblies.

Chief of all the places of assembly is the Town Hall, built not many years ago to replace the original Assembly Rooms. These old rooms had been much and often used for dancing, which in the winter season seemed to have become a permanent institution of fashionable Cheltenham. The architect of the new Town Hall was bidden to bear this in mind, and, in the central greater hall of the building, constructed a special floor with that intent, and put round it a number of apartments, each room varying in size and purpose. These together have provided Cheltenham with one of the finest suites of assembly rooms to be found anywhere, most eminently suited for a dance, a concert, a conference or bazaar, or for other similar meetings or use. Upon what "scenes of revelry by night" have the galleries of the great hall looked down when the dance was in progress that for display of beauty, smartness and vivacity was never, nor anywhere, outshone, and the band of great price and renown played the waltzes for five hundred pairs of feet that moved about each other through the long programme of the ball! Many other festive gatherings have taken place there, some of them truly popular assemblies, as when the Mayor gave his big At Home, or when tea-tables were spread for the numerous little private parties for which they had been bespoken by hostesses for gossiping friends at the afternoon concerts. And the floor of maplewood was never hurt a bit by being stumped over by thick soles, or by having placed upon it the heavy velvet-seated fauteuils, upon occasions when the musical or vocal virtuoso visited the town, but could at call always be polished up again to its dancing form when the ball season returned.

In a corner of one of the corridors of the Town Hall the natural mineral waters of Cheltenham are at present dispensed, and the baths and massage rooms connected with the Spa are in a building a short distance away.

The Winter Garden, with its magnificent glass roof, provides one of the largest covered halls in the country, and is adjacent to the Town Hall. It is not only a handsome building, lending its imposing presence to the outlook from The Promenade, but is a very useful institution, so acoustically wonderful, considering its construction, its large covered space also so adaptable to every new form of entertainment or exhibition that succeeding generations may demand or create.

Cheltenham also has its libraries and museums and its college buildings, in which many will find interest. Its religious institutions are very numerous, being centred by the original little old parish church of St. Mary, which is an architectural gem, lost to view from the busy High Street, from which and from Clarence Street it is approached up one or other of several alleys where it lies looked down upon by house backs, its old surrounding churchyard crossed in several directions by linden-shaded footpaths, which make cool leafy corridors about it in Summer. An ancient village cross, that probably once stood in the street, now stands in the churchyard amongst the many gravestones, some of which have quaint epitaphs engraved upon them. The old church has a little tower in which are hung, by some extraordinary economy of space, its twelve bells. An octagonal, finely fluted spire rises above the body of the church. There are a central and two side aisles and many large windows, all filled with coloured glass. The varied tracery which the windows exhibit and other features of the church form a remarkably fine example of the type of church architecture called Decorated, which was in vogue in the first part of the fourteenth century, to which period the main part of the present church dates, with some portions belonging to the preceding Norman and Early English times, and others to the later Perpendicular order. In the end of the north aisle is a very large circular window containing brilliant glass, the colours being in rather sharp contrast. This ancient temple, whose south door will always be found open, shows within and without much to interest and admire. Inside there is its little gallery, once used as a schoolroom, and its Tudor baptistry, its ancient decorated carved piscina, its sculptured reredos recently erected in memory of a sometime Mayor of the town, to the personal virtues of whose ancestor a memorial tablet may also be found, that bears an epitaph of extraordinary length and grandiloquence of diction suitable to the service he rendered in assisting materially to develop the original Spa.

The earlier history of Cheltenham is the history of its Spa development. People first came to drink the waters, but found the village occupying such a pleasant site, and the country around so enchanting that many desired to become permanent residents, and so houses were built, and the place quickly became populous Many droll coloured prints may be found upon the walls of the municipal museum showing the life in the town in those early days, and the costumes then worn. The drinking of the waters was varied by gay social gatherings in the old Assembly Rooms, in similar style to those carried on under the ceremonial management of Beau Nash at Bath about the same time, and of course the Cheltenham Assemblies had their masters of ceremonies. The local Society of that time supported a good many parasites and hangers-on, who made a livelihood out of the wants and frailties of the fashionable crowd. There were a host of chairmen, grooms and lackeys, and apparently a plethora of doctors, among whom some jealousy made itself manifest, as it is always sure to do, those who have come last to the town envying the reputation of those of long standing. A certain Dr. Adam Neale, who had originally taken his degree at Edinburgh, and who had not been received by his fellow-practitioners and the Cheltenham public with that recognition which was warranted by the testimonials he had brought with him from the North, where the climate is well known to favour the production of flowery letters of recommendation, conceived the evil intent to condemn the Spa by a spiteful innuendo, made public in a pretended correspondence with an Edinburgh professor, to the effect that the waters were not the products of Nature intended for the sure cure of all faithful believers, as had been represented, but were, in fact, of an artificial production connected with a considerable import, as he averred, of Epsom salts and Glauber's salts in dry casks and packages, that ran up to hundredweights, if not tons. It was a contemptible calumny, and though, as may well be imagined, it raised a storm of indignation amongst the honest burgesses and successful medicos, it did not do more than assist the decline of the Cheltenham Spa.

For other and broader reasons, connected with change of fashions that came with change of King, the opening up of the Continent for foreign travel, and the adoption of different social manners and requirements, all the English Spas, which by this time had become rather numerous, were on the decline, and Cheltenham Spa went down in popularity along with that of Bath and the rest.

The decay of the Spa by no means put an end to the town, however, which was destined by sheer virtue of its natural attractions to continue to grow and become a favourite place of settlement, combining in such marked degree the best urban features with the most pleasing of rural appearances and delights. It became the Walhalla of the retired Anglo-Indian and the settling place of many an aristocratic and eminently exclusive army or navy officer, who, taking his pension whilst still in early middle life, came here to hunt and educate his growing family. He spent much of his time at the club, to which he was wont to resort at exactly the same hour every day to do just the same things. There he met his fellows and joined in games of billiards, chess, or cards according to his custom, read his one particular newspaper, and no other, and delivered his opinion upon passing events; or reverted to the experiences of his past life, with his intimate associates, and was always most punctilious upon points of etiquette. That was the sort of club which a new member might attend daily for three months before anyone spoke to him, or he to anyone, unless he had acquaintances made previous to his entry there. The choler of that fine old gentleman may well be understood who complained bitterly to the secretary of the club of the new member who had had the impudence to ask him to drink with him.

The sons and daughters of these proud old settlers, many of the former of whom entered the army or other national service as soon as they were old enough, made a very smart and handsome Society in Cheltenham. It was mainly to them that the winter balls owed their show of feminine beauty, that was so superior and so English in carriage, style and glowing complexion. Some of the men of the same families might be seen, too, walking in The Promenade, or riding off in the morning to the meet of hounds, or back home in the afternoon, in their white breeches, scarlet coats and high silk hats, mud-splashed and temporarily soiled by the boldness and urgency of the chase. The ladies who rode did it in flowing riding habits on side saddles, which, whether less practical or not, was eminently more elegant than the modern imitation by horsewomen of a man's mode of riding.

This smart Cheltenham Society in the end was destined to suffer some dilution and decadence from its original numerical force. A gradual change in the quality of the population led to a decided toning down of the *chic* and *mode*, that had formerly made the chief display, by the introduction of a more sober-minded and russet community, who prided themselves more upon their mental than their physical qualities. These made a Society of their own, which, however, could never mark the place as did that smart set, who cultivated the best appearances of beauty and physique and were proud of their caste, the entry into which was sometimes the cause of envy on the part of unsuitable aspirants. How, indeed, could dusty thinkers and bookworms, whose overwrought wits not infrequently turned to foolishness, consort with the well-groomed human animal, glowing with health and full of animation and well-developed beauty of face and figure, whose first and main consideration was to be, and to look, well, and in and by whom humanity comes perhaps nearer to a normal perfection than in any other class whatever? From their games and sports, balls and wedding parties, the town seemed to borrow an unusual vivacity that laughed from gay hall, green lawn, or leafy avenue with a light "Ha, ha, ha!" But a social change had set in, even before the great war came to knock down beyond restoration the old Humpty-Dumpty pride of the retired officer. What social conditions and appearances are destined next to influence the gay town, who knows? But a prayer might arise for a continuance of all the pleasure, grace and gaiety that has marked the local Society for so long, and that everything of real value that belonged to it may be retained to beautify the new social fashion that seems to be arising from the democratic evolution of modern times.

THE CHIEF HILLS VISIBLE IN THE LANDSCAPES DESCRIBED IN THIS BOOK.

Pertaining to the Cotswolds.

Prestbury Hill (1,040 ft.) adjoins Cleeve Hill immediately to the south.

Hewlett's Hill (900 ft.).—The next green part of the edge beyond Prestbury Hill.

Ham Hill (840 ft.).—Beyond Hewlett's Hill and above the River Chelt on the north side.

Battledown (460 ft.).—The lower green hill extending in front of the Hewlett's and Ham Hills.

Pegglesworth (979 ft.) overlooks Charlton Kings and the Chelt Valley on the south side. The tree-covered front is Wistley Hill, and the Gloucester—Oxford road, where it rises up it, is Chatcomb Pitch.

Charlton Common.—Part of hill edge to right of Wistley Hill as viewed from Cleeve Common. It has a plain scooped out appearance without trees. The road to Cirencester goes over immediately to left of it.

Leckhampton Hill (965 ft.) lies next to right of Charlton Common and has a portion of white perpendicular cliff with a short line of trees above.

Cowley Wood rising by Bubb's Hill to top near Elkstone Village (919 ft.) shows through to left of Leckhampton Hill.

Birdlip (984 ft.).—To right of Leckhampton Hill and beyond it a white strip of road at a high altitude can be seen passing to Birdlip.

Shurdington Hill (850 ft.).—Outjutting prominence overlooking Severn Vale to right of Leckhampton Hill.

Cooper's Hill.—The next prominence showing to right of Shurdington Hill as viewed from Cleeve Hill. Highest part called High Brockeridge (927 ft.).

Robin's Wood Hill (651 ft.), *and Churchdown or Chosen Hill,* are the two outlying separate hills seen to right of Cooper's Hill, the first named, which is furthest away, being close behind Gloucester. The two outliers help to make the wide half circle of hills around Cheltenham.

Painswick Beacon and Haresfield Beacon are the more prominent points of the escarpment south of Cooper's Hill, parts of which may be seen from Cleeve Hill or Nottingham Hill.

Stinchcomb Hill is a promontory hill situated lower down the escarpment line than those last mentioned. It has a curiously-shaped outlier called Cam Long Down on the northern side of it. It can be partly seen from Woolstone Hill and places in the Vale of Severn, and it is a familiar object in the neighbourhood of the towns of Dursley and Berkeley, which are near it.

Nottingham Hill (915 ft.).—A promontory hill jutting forth from Cleeve Hill.

Langley Hill (901 ft.).—Outlier seen at near view from the Winchcomb high-road and from Cleeve Common.

Stanley Hill or Stanley Mount, is Langley Hill on its northern side.

Woolstone Hill (734 ft.).—An outlier of considerable size lying off the point of Nottingham Hill.

Oxenton Hill.—The northern side of Woolstone Hill.

Crane Hill.—The western extended lower end of Woolstone Hill, on the side of which stands the church, rectory and greater part of Woolstone village.

Bredon Hill (960 ft.).—The broad-backed furthest outlier, situated four or five miles due north of Woolstone Hill.

Dixton Hill (537 ft.).—The lower outlying hill with bare and artificial-looking summit seen to right of Woolstone Hill, as viewed from Nottingham Hill or Cleeve Common.

Dumbleton Hill (674 ft.).—The outlier of considerable size to right or north-east, of Woolstone and Dixton Hills and due north of Langley Hill.

Alderton Hill and Washbourne Hill.—The two most prominent summits of Dumbleton Hill that face towards Nottingham Hill.

Postlip Warren (937 ft.).—The bare summit adjoining Cleeve Common on north-east side.

Sudeley Hill (977 ft. to highest part).—The hill whose road rises so steeply from near Sudeley Castle and Winchcomb. A portion of this road is visible from Cleeve Hill.

Salter's Hill (864 ft.).—The point of the hill line immediately behind Winchcomb, with wooded front.

Hailes Hill (953 ft. highest ground above wood).—The next prominent height in North Cotswold escarpment line beyond Salter's Hill.

Stanway Hill (843 ft. highest part of road) is beyond Hailes Hill.

Lidcomb Hill (900 ft.) rises to highest summit immediately beyond Stanway.

Shenberrow Hill (980 ft.) is beyond Lidcomb Hill and overlooks Snowshill village.

Stanton Hill (863 ft.) is beyond Shenberrow Hill.

Broadway Hill (1,024 ft. near the tower) beyond Stanton and distinguished by its tower.

Saintbury Hill (893 ft.) is the first-named eminence of the ridge of the Cotswolds which runs up north-east beyond Broadway to limit the Vale of Avon.

Ebrington Hill.—A large definite hill mass that stands behind the ridge running up north-east of Broadway. It has the small town of Chipping Campden two miles south-west of its base. It is seen from Broadway Tower and from the road between Broadway and Stow, etc.

Ilmington Hill is on the other side of Ebrington Hill, and finishes the ridge running north-east of Broadway, and practically ends the North Cotswolds in that direction.

Meon Hill (637 ft.) is the last outlier of the Cotswolds and can be seen from the Cleeve Hill locality jutting forth into Avon Vale from the end of the ridge beyond Broadway. It lies about six miles south-east of Stratford-on-Avon and near the large Gloucestershire village of Mickleton. It has extensive and well-marked trenches of an ancient camp around its summit, and affords good views.

Stow Hill (770 ft.) on which stands Stow-on-the-Wold.

Icomb Hill (799 ft.) is two miles south of Stow-on-the-Wold, and ends a ridge that passes above the three villages bearing the name of Rissington. It affords splendid views of the North Cotswolds, the valley of the Evenlode, the Warwickshire plain, etc.

Bourton Downs.—The highest part of the country that lies adjacent to the Stow and Broadway road above the village of Bourton-on-the-Hill.

Naunton Downs and Hawling Downs (850—900 ft.).—The highest country adjacent to the Stow-to-Cheltenham main-road, near the villages of the same names.

Hampen Hill (850 ft. at summit) is the long hill on the Stow main-road where it descends from the Hawling Downs towards Andoversford.

Roel Hill and Roel Gate (960 ft.).—The highest ground above the "outer park wall" of Sudeley Castle towards Hawling.

Hills in South Warwickshire beyond the Cotswolds.

Brailes Hill.—A massive outlier of the range that runs from the neighbourhood of Chipping Norton and the Evenlode Valley to Edge Hill, limiting the "Vale of Red Horse." Seen from Icomb Tower, Broadway Tower, etc.

Edge Hill, Warwickshire.—A level line of tree-clad hills running north-eastward beyond Brailes Hill towards the confines of the counties of Warwick, Oxford and Northampton. Well seen from Meon Hill, etc.

Hills seen from Cleeve Hill towards South-Western, Western, North-Western, and Northern points of the Compass.

Forest of Dean Hills.—A hilly country consisting of several ridges one beyond the other, the first as viewed from Cleeve Hill forming a long dark even line facing the River Severn on its further side, and passing away to the south-west beyond Gloucester. Within the district are the following heights: On the nearer ridge, Edge Hill, 900 ft.; Littledean Hill, 750 ft. In middle part: Ruardean Hill, 872 ft.; Speech House, 566 ft.; High Beeches, 745 ft. Above Coleford, 700 ft. Parts overlooking Wye: Staunton Meend (The Buckstone) 915 ft., St. Briavel's Common, 861 ft.; Tidenham Chase, 778 ft.

May Hill (969 ft.) is an oval-backed hill with a small fir copse on its summit situated as the last hill of the Forest of Dean Hills at their northern end.

The Blorenge (1,834 ft.)—A mountain mass with bold summit rising on the south side of the River Usk, two miles from the town of Abergavenny, Monmouthshire in whose neighbourhood it is a most prominent object. From Cleeve Common, and its vicinity, when the view point is high enough, the Blorenge is seen showing over the Forest of Dean Hills to the left or south of May Hill, its northern slope falling about in a line with Ruardean.

Mountains of Mid-Monmouthshire.—Some of these, situated in the neighbourhood of Pontypool also show over the further away portions of the Forest line of hills.

Skirrid Fawr (1,596 ft.).—A lone mountain mass of well defined shape, with a narrow hyena back and angular fall at right end,

FOSSILS FROM THE ROLLING BANK QUARRY ⅔RDS. NAT. SIZE.

1.—Terebratula Phillipsiana. 2.—T. Buckmaniana. 3.—T. Globosa. 4.—Avicula. 5.—Natica. 6.—Cardium. 7.—Limea duplicata. 8.—Lima gibbosa. 9.—Pleuromya. 10.—Gresslya. 11.—Rhynchonella quadriplicata.

FOSSILS FROM THE ROLLING-BANK QUARRY, $\frac{2}{3}$RDS NAT. SIZE.

1.—Bourgetia. 2.—Ptenostreon (cast). 3.—Gasteropod. 4.—Pholodomya. 5.—Trigonia (cast). 6.—Gryphœa Sublobata.

situated in Monmouthshire. It is seen from the Cleeve HIll locality as the first more distant mountain to the immediate right of May Hill, and seeming to begin that distant line commonly alluded to as the "Welsh Mountains." It lies four miles from Abergavenny on the east side of the Abergavenny-Hereford road from which it can be well viewed. It lies on the west side of the Abergavenny-Skenfreth road from which its other side can also be well viewed. It is about four miles nearer to Cleeve Hill than the "Sugar Loaf," next mentioned.

The Sugar Loaf Mountain (1,955 ft.).—It is situated next on the right, or north, of Skirrid Fawr, from which it is separated by an apparent notch allowing its angular form to be well appreciated. It lies on the north side of the Usk, very near the Brecknockshire border of Monmouthshire, distant from Abergavenny about five miles. It is well viewed from the Abergavenny-Hereford road, where its relations to Skirrid Fawr and the Blorenge are easily determined.

Graig Serrerthin, or "The Graig" (1,369 ft.).—This is a solitary mass of mountain of greater bulk than either of the last two mentioned, and as viewed from Cleeve Hill appears to continue the distant mountain line to the immediate right of the Sugar Loaf. In that occasional condition of the light which results in a detachment of the individual mountains, the fact of its being a separate hill is plainly evident even from this distance. In reality it lies in Monmouthshire about ten miles nearer Cleeve Hill than the Sugar Loaf. It is a dozen miles north-east of Abergavenny and about eight miles in the same direction from Skirrid Fawr.

The Black Mountains are constituted by the remainder of the line of distant mountains apparently extending to the right or north of the Graig, until the line ends by a sudden drop called Peny Beacon or Hay Bluff, named after the Herefordshire Border town of Hay that lies near it. The Black Mountains form the border land of Herefordshire and Brecknockshire. At several points they exceed 2,000 ft. in altitude, "Waun Fach" being 2,660 ft., Pen Alt Mawr 2,360 ft., Pen-y-Gader Fawr 2,624 ft.

The Brecon Beacons (2,906 ft.) are situated in Mid-Brecknockshire. A portion of these mountains can be seen in clear weather lying in fainter outline and forming a high filling to an apparent corner that lies beyond the Usk Valley between "The Graig" on the left and the beginning of the continuous line of the Black Mountains on the right, the latter appearing almost as high as the Beacons. The Brecon Beacons lie nearly twenty miles further back than the Sugar Loaf and are distant from Cleeve Common about sixty-five miles.

Garway Hill (1,203 ft.), Herefordshire.—It lies beyond the Wye, a short distance north of the Monow, where that river forms the border line of the counties of Hereford and Monmouth. It is seen from Cleeve Common as a rounded mass of hill lying at a nearer distance than the Black Mountain line, and in front of its southern end.

Orcop Hill (957 ft.) is a lower hill just north of Garway Hill, which is practically continued into it. It shows three summits.

Aconbury Hill, still higher up the country to the right than the last two, and in a line with them, forms a simple sharp obtuse angle lying nearly in front of Hay Bluff, as viewed from Cleeve Hill. It indicates the position of the city of Hereford, which lies 5 miles north-east of it behind Dinedor Hill, whose top is also visible.

Penyard Hill is the little hill whose top makes a dark, low, even line till it ends suddenly and squarely, and which juts forward from behind May Hill to overlap the position of "The Graig." From its end the town of Ross, Herefordshire, is within 2 miles.

The Malvern Hills, Worcestershire and Herefordshire.—These form a ridge stretching across the country in the north-west which is very conspicuous from Cleeve Hill in clear weather. The distance of these hills is from seventeen to twenty miles. The outline of the range is somewhat serrated, there being about a dozen points or protuberances along the extended summit. The two furthest northward of these, which overlook the town of Great Malvern that lies at some elevation on their slopes, are called respectively the North Hill (that is the end hill), and the Worcestershire Beacon (1,395 ft.), this being the highest point. Another chief prominence, situated about the middle of the range, is the Herefordshire Beacon, and this has upon it an ancient camp of very perfect formation. A large obelisk situated in Eastnor Park may be discovered on the hills towards the lower end of the range.

The Radnor Forest (2,166 ft.).—This mountain, distant from Cleeve Hill about fifty-five miles, is distinguished in clear weather as a bold mass ending in an abrupt drop at its northern end behind the lower part of the Malvern Hills as viewed from Cleeve Common.

Plinlimmon (2,468 ft.).—This mountain, distant ninety miles from Cleeve Hill, can be found when the atmosphere is at its clearest by following back the hills at the horizon from Radnor Forest, when standing on the highest ground of Cleeve Common, where a somewhat pointed mountain is discovered that, though most distant, gives the impression of being higher than the hills that lead up to it.

The Cambrian Mountains, which lie on the further sides of Radnorshire and Brecknockshire, and over the border of Cardiganshire, may at the clearest times be seen extending across the space behind, from the Radnor Forest and the end of the Malvern Hills to Hay Bluff. They rise to various altitudes between 1,000 and 2,000 ft., and appear dim and far away. Gorllwyn (2,009 ft.) behind the town of Builth, is prominent.

The Woolhope Hills (630 ft.).—In the middle distance of the scene which shows the Cambrian Mountains, beginning behind the tail of the Malvern Ridge, lie the lower Woolhope Hills, including Seagar Hill and Marcle Hill.

The *Clee Hills* consist of two oval-backed hills, the nearer being named "The Titterstone" (1,749 ft.), the further "The Brown Clee Hill" (1,780 ft.). These lie in South Shropshire at a distance of forty to fifty miles, and appear to the right of Malvern.

The Abberley Hills.—As viewed from Cleeve Hill these lie immediately to the right of the Clee Hills but at nearer distance, being in North Worcestershire. Their western end is in fact overlapped by the Brown Clee Hill behind. The Abberley Hills form a short hill-line stretching straight across the great vale, and exhibit a pair of nearly equal more elevated portions with a lower part between. The right-hand protuberance is Abberley Hill. The left-hand one Woodbury Hill (904 ft.). On the lower central portion is an elaborate "folly" tower, which can be plainly seen in clear weather by the unaided vision. It contains a clock and a large number of bells.

Berrow Hill is a low hill situated between Woodbury Hill and the Malverns.

The Wrekin.—This Shropshire mountain (1,335 ft.) shows on the ultimate northern horizon, well away to the right from the Abberley Hills as viewed from Cleeve Common. The apparent altitude as viewed from the higher parts of the Common is about half that of the Clee Hills, which is equivalent to saying that it lies very low on the horizon, where its appearance is like a shallow and regular segment of a circle.

Lower Hills in North Worcestershire, Shropshire and Staffordshire are visible northward in the great vale from Cleeve Hill and its vicinity, including those that form Wyre Forest, and others, to north and west of Kidderminster, and to north-west of Birmingham, etc.

The Lickey and Clent Hills, which lie to the west of Birmingham, can be seen in the neighbourhood, though from some points of view they are hidden by Bredon Hill.

The Ridgway, on the borders of Worcestershire and Warwickshire, is on the further side of the Avon and runs up to Redditch towards the Lickey Hills.

The Lench Hills are immediately on the other side of the Avon, beyond Evesham. The Ridgway begins from their northern end.

Charnwood Forest (912 ft. highest point) lies to the north-north-east over Coventry and Nuneaton, and must form the furthest horizon in that direction over Avon Vale. It is in Leicestershire.

Northamptonshire Hills, near Naseby (632 ft.), will similarly end the view straight up Avon Vale.